W9-DJI-287

FICTION, FILM, AND
F. SCOTT FITZGERALD

FICTION,
FILM, AND
F. SCOTT
FITZGERALD

GENE D. PHILLIPS, S.J.

A Campion Book

Loyola University Press
Chicago

Loyola University Press
3441 North Ashland Avenue
Chicago, Illinois 60657

Designed by J. L. Boden

Library of Congress Cataloging in Publication Data
ISBN 0-8294-0500-3

Phillips, Gene D.
    Fiction, film, and F. Scott Fitzgerald.

    (A Campion book)
    Bibliography: p. 197.
    Filmography: p. 203.
    Includes indexes.
    1. Fitzgerald, F. Scott (Francis Scott), 1896-1940—
Film adaptations.   2. Fitzgerald, F. Scott (Francis
Scott), 1896-1940—moving picture plays.   3. Moving-
pictures and literature.   I. Title.
PS3511.I9Z815 1986   791.43'75   85-24123
ISBN 0-8294-0500-3

TO JOHN SCHLESINGER

CONTENTS

Part One:
Fitzgerald As Screenwriter

Part Two:
The Films of Fitzgerald's Short Fiction

Part Three:
The Films of Fitzgerald's Novels

LIST OF PHOTOGRAPHS

ACKNOWLEDGMENTS

First of all, I am most grateful to Scottie Fitzgerald Smith, who corresponded with me about the film versions of her father's fiction and encouraged me in this project. Also, she has granted me her kind permission to reproduce the photograph of herself with her parents that appears elsewhere in this book.

I would also like to single out the following people from among those who have given me their assistance:

Film directors Henry King, Elia Kazan, and Richard Brooks, all of whom have been involved in Fitzgerald films, and who were willing to talk with me about the problems involved in the adaptation of literary works to the screen.

Film director George Cukor for his recollections of Fitzgerald and of producer Irving Thalberg; Irving Thalberg, Jr., the son of Thalberg and actress Norma Shearer, for sharing with me his memories of his father and mother—two people who figured in various ways in Fitzgerald's life and work; screenwriter Maurice Rapf, who knew Fitzgerald during his Hollywood years; Sidney G. Harper, who was acquainted with Fitzgerald's wife Zelda during her high school days in Montgomery, Alabama.

The research committee of Loyola University of Chicago for giving me a summer grant in order to pursue this project.

Jean F. Preston, manuscript curator of the Firestone Library of Princeton University, where Fitzgerald's papers are housed; Roger Lewis of George Mason University; Bernard Dick of Fairleigh Dickinson University; Adam Reilly of the Denver Center for the Performing Arts.

Those of my colleagues at Loyola University of Chicago who provided me with special materials include Agnes Donohue, a life-long Fitzgerald aficionado; Michael Grace, S.J., university archivist; John Reinke, S.J., an expert in the popular music of the Jazz Age; and John Connery, S.J., who was invaluable in dealing with the doctrinal issues associated with Fitzgerald's Catholic background.

Acknowledgment is made for the use of Budd Schulberg's essay on Hollywood and the screenwriter, which appears as the foreword to this book; it is reprinted with permission of the Dartmouth alumni magazine (November 1982 issue) and the author, Budd Schulberg, © 1982. Acknowledgment is also made for the use of Dewitt Bodeen's essay on the Fitzgerald films, which appears as the preface to this book; it is reprinted by permission of the National Board of Review of Motion Pictures, and is under copyright to *Films in Review.*

FOREWORD

HOLLYWOOD AND THE SCREENWRITER

> You wait to get inside the gate, you wait outside the great man's office, you wait for your agent to make the deal, you wait for the assignment, you wait for the instructions on how to write what they want you to write. . . .
>
> Eventually this waiting sawed you off at the base of your self-respect.
>
> —*The Disenchanted*, Budd Schulberg

I hope it won't sound pretentious to say that I was born a screenwriter, but it would be difficult to deny that I came by it naturally. My father, B. P. Schulberg, had been one of the early screenwriters, writing photoplays (as they were called then) for Edwin S. (*Great Train Robbery*) Porter before he was old enough to vote. By the time I started grammar school in Hollywood, B. P. was running his own, small independent film company, sharing the now-forgotten Mayer-Schulberg Studio with mogul-to-be L. B.

The year I entered Los Angeles High School, 1928, when my old man had been running Paramount Studios for several years, the first

Best Picture Academy Award went to his film *Wings*; and his foreign import, Emil Jannings, was voted Best Actor for *The Way of All Flesh*.

Through my high school years, story conferences in the library after dinner were part of our family routine. Father coped with the movie stars, but his heart was with the writers; and I was privileged to sit in on crash writing sessions with some of Hollywood's best—Herman Mankiewicz, Vincent Lawrence, young Joe Mankiewicz, Edwin Justus Mayer. Long into the night they hammered out story lines and debated characters' motivations. On weekends, if a screenwriter had fallen down badly, I would work on the delinquent script with my father, who could write a pretty fair scene to his dying day.

One of B. P.'s most gifted assistants was David   Selznick whose career would be crowned by *Gone with the Wind*. In the summer before I entered Dartmouth, David had left Paramount to become the thirty-year-old head of RKO. One Sunday afternoon at our Malibu beach house, I told David a story I was working on . . . .

He not only bought my little yarn for $1,500, but hired me to adapt it with an older collaborator, the mystery novel writer Stewart Palmer. When I arrived at Middle Fayerweather Residence Hall I somewhat ostentatiously displayed a framed photo of Selznick's check on the wall of my room in the dorm.

Graduating in 1936, when F.D.R. and the New Deal were still seeking new cures for unemployment, I was one of the lucky ones who had a nice job waiting for him in Hollywood, in Dave Selznick's story department, earning what seemed then a rather ample $50 a week. Six months later I graduated to junior writer at $75. Junior writer might be described as pinch hitter pulled in from the bench at opportune moments. . . .

That may sound exciting, but after a year or so of patchwork assignments, I asked David Selznick *not* to pick up my option for another year at $100 a week. He was annoyed with me, saying he had hoped to carry me as a writer long enough to prepare me to assist him in production as he had assisted my father. His sense of Hollywood hierarchy and "royal succession" was very deep. When I told David I didn't want to be "carried as a writer"—I wanted to *write*, he frowned and said his plan had been to keep me there long enough for my "producer's blood" to assert itself. In time, that anecdote would find its way into Scott Fitzgerald's Hollywood novel, *The Last Tycoon*.

Free of my seven-year contract, I went to work for Walter Wanger on the now legendary—if not notorious—*Winter Carnival*. When my script faltered, Walter brought in Scott Fitzgerald, a glorified but now somewhat tarnished pinch hitter. Scott and I made a near-fatal journey to the actual Dartmouth Winter Carnival that ten years later I would use as the spine of my novel *The Disenchanted*. After a bibulous two days in Hanover, Scott and I were both fired and virtually run out of town. In New York, Walter rehired me, replacing Scott with my boyhood friend Maurice Rapf, who labored on the picture with me to the end.

Written piecemeal, inevitably the picture was a mess, though somehow it seems to have improved with age. In 1982, it was shown in London at the National Film Theatre, where I lectured on the role of the film writer. It was the humiliating condition of the writer in Hollywood that in 1939-40 drew me back to Norwich and Hanover, where I wrote my first novel, *What Makes Sammy Run?*

The *succès scandale* of that novel helped to free me from economic and emotional dependence on Hollywood. The films I made with Elia Kazan in the fifties—*On the Waterfront* and *A Face in the Crowd*—were written and shot entirely in the East. Even though the writer is still the low man (or woman) on the Hollywood totem, I've never lost my enthusiasm for film writing, only for living in Hollywood. My years at Dartmouth as an undergraduate and afterwards literally changed my life. For the rest of my days, Hollywood would continue to fascinate me—but preferably from afar.

—*Budd Schulberg,* novelist and screenwriter

PREFACE

HOLLYWOOD AND THE FICTION WRITER

Youth is the keynote of every Fitzgerald tale—its careless ecstasy during one's twenties and the inevitable loss of it in one's thirties. Fitzgerald was not speaking lightly when he described Anson Hunter at the end of "The Rich Boy" as "an old man of twenty-wenty-nine." His characters are all sad young men whose flame of life has burnt down to a lambent glow by the time they've got out of their twenties. This has become the basic problem in translating to the screen the stories of F. Scott Fitzgerald: very few actors who have names are young enough to interpret them believably.

F. Scott Fitzgerald, just turned twenty-three, sold his first story to *The Saturday Evening Post* in 1919. It was called "Head and Shoulders" and was an unlikely romance between a chorus girl and a university sophomore. It was bought for films by Metro; and the picture made from it, *A Chorus Girl's Romance*, starring Viola Dana with Gareth Hughes, was frothy and light, with just enough headiness to make it appealing. It was released in 1920, and Miss Dana was then only twenty-one. No problem with age this time.

She starred in another film adaptation of a Fitzgerald short story, released the following year, in January of 1921, when she played an heiress, Ardita Farnam, kidnapped by her uncle and imprisoned on his yacht to save her from marrying a Russian fortune-hunter. Like the story, also published in the *Post,* it was called *The Off-Shore Pirate;* and it was a light, tongue-in-cheek romance, with Miss Dana once again giving an utterly enchanting performance as the much-desired heiress. In fact, Viola Dana may be said to be the quintessential Fitzgerald heroine—youthful, charming, reckless, fun-loving, but a flapper with a good head on her shoulders. It is the heroes, hopelessly romantic, as Fitzgerald himself was, who have to be led and loved.

Released in between these two Dana films was a performance by a blithe-hearted, blue-eyed blonde, Eileen Percy, who had been four times leading lady to Douglas Fairbanks in four of his best Artcraft features. Young and vivacious, Miss Percy had also been in the cast with, and remained a good friend to, Marion Davies from *Stop! Look! Listen!* on Broadway. In 1920 Fox was starring Miss Percy in a series of gay-hearted romances; and one of them was adapted from a Fitzgerald short story, "Myra Meets His Family." On release, it was re-titled *The Husband Hunter*, a title the author must have lamented he hadn't thought of himself, because it describes exactly what the engaging little flapper heroine is.

In December 1922, Warner Bros. released its version of Fitzgerald's second novel, *The Beautiful and Damned*, with Marie Prevost as Gloria and Kenneth Harlan as Anthony, two darlings of the Jazz Age who Charlestoned and cocktailed their way into an early decline long before they could inherit a fortune; by then Anthony was, at best, a semi-invalid in his thirties, and Gloria's enchanting beauty had begun to fade like a discarded orchid corsage. The picture was only a pedestrian commercial attempt to cash in on the Fitzgerald vogue, but Miss Prevost and Harlan (who soon married in real life) were just right as the two who were beautiful but damned.

So far, so good. The romancing couples dancing their way along a primrose path, heedless of a tomorrow that could only mean bankruptcy, ulcers, and crowsfeet, were played properly by young actors, some of whom would be, like Miss Prevost, all too soon the victims of their own personal extravagances. But in 1922, Marie Prevost was herself the darling of Hollywood fame.

From then on, every screen version of a Fitzgerald story has been flawed by miscasting and a direful misunderstanding of the story itself....

First to get the mistreating finger was the initial silent version of *The Great Gatsby*, released in 1926 by Paramount, directed with no understanding whatsoever by Herbert Brenon from an indifferent scenario adaptation, and distressingly miscast with Warner Baxter as Gatsby and Lois Wilson as Daisy. To date, *The Great Gatsby* has been filmed three times—1926, 1949, 1974. You would have thought they might have learned from the mistakes of the first version, but the fatal flaw was twice more perpetrated: no explanation in any version was given as to how Gatsby became the richest bootlegger on Long Island; three times he is embalmed as "a man of mystery." Yet, read the sixth chapter of the novel and you'll see how expertly and with what cleverness Fitzgerald in a flashback tells exactly how Gatsby became "great." Without the character of Dan Cody, and the knowledge of what Gatsby learned during those five years when he served Cody as steward, mate, skipper, secretary, and even jailer, you don't know the essential background for the tragedy of *The Great Gatsby*.

In 1947, when I thought RKO might not pick up my option as a contract writer, I let myself be wooed by Paramount, going into their library on Saturdays and perusing their story files for likely properties that had never been filmed or were ripe for remake. Heading a list of about ten such titles on my list was *The Great Gatsby*; for Paramount had the right actor for it then, I thought, in Alan Ladd. D. A. Doran, head of the story department, set up a screening of the 1926 film, and the print kept breaking so I'm not surprised that it's now listed as "lost." Paramount was interested, however, in remaking it, because they needed a strong Ladd property.

Shortly thereafter, I met Ladd and his wife, Sue Carol, at a party given by Louella Parsons. Mrs. Ladd knew about the revived interest in *Gatsby*; but, as her husband's agent, warned that Ladd might not re-sign with the studio unless certain financial adjustments were made in his contract then being arbitrated. Ladd had never read *Gatsby*, and I took it upon myself to send him a paperback copy. A few weeks later I received a warm and appreciative note from him in Palm Springs; he had read the book and was anxious to do it on the screen. By the time his contract was adjusted satisfactorily, however, my own option was taken up by RKO and I was back on *I Remember Mama*, with George Stevens now definitely set to direct and wanting a revised screenplay. So I never got a chance at *Gatsby*; but I was glad Paramount did it with Ladd, because he proved he understood the role, and Betty Field was certainly the best of all three screen Daisys. Unfortunately, the screenplay was confused and lacklustre. Elliott Nugent was having his own problems then, and the direction suffered. Also, once again, all Gatsby's background, so astutely recorded in the novel, was not in the final script. They had settled, as before, for Jay Gatsby, man of mystery.

In 1974, Paramount released a big, new, sumptuously produced version of *The Great Gatsby*, starring Robert Redford, with Mia Farrow as Daisy, directed by the estimable Jack Clayton. The remake had been scheduled to co-star Steve McQueen with Ali McGraw; but when Miss McGraw left her husband, Robert Evans, head of production at Paramount, for McQueen, it was hardly likely that Evans would continue the Fitzgerald project with the wife who had deserted him and her lover as the stars. In her limited way, Miss McGraw would have been as wrong for the part as Mia Farrow was in hers; but McQueen would have been an admirable choice for Gatsby, better than Redford by far. I heard Redford speak one Sunday afternoon at the National Film Theatre in London when he was abroad filming the Long Island backgrounds in England because Long Island has so drastically changed its shoreline; he said then that the character of Gatsby was the most difficult he had ever tried to give substance and flesh to.

Fitzgerald himself once admitted in a letter to John Peale Bishop: " . . . you are right about Gatsby being blurred and patchy. I never at any one time saw him clear myself—for he started as one man I knew and then changed into myself—the amalgam was never complete in my mind." It would have helped the production, nevertheless, had they incorporated the flashback Fitzgerald had put into his novel, and you would then have seen Gatsby, a young man named James Gatz working on the south shore of Lake Superior as a clam-digger, when Dan Cody's yacht drops anchor in Little Girl Bay, and the millionaire Cody looks down upon the young man, who smiles up at him with his wistful crooked smile, knowing that "people liked him when he smiled." And thereafter Cody took him on, showing him the ways of the world as only a very rich man could.

Thus, three times Paramount has boldly tried to do right by *The Great Gatsby*, but it remains unfilmed as Fitzgerald wrote it; and all three productions are hopelessly flawed. It remains, however, un-questionably the best piece of fiction Fitzgerald ever accomplished, an admirable short novel, concise, jewel-like, telling a bitterly ironic story of a man who lived and died cavalierly and the girl he loved and died for, who wasn't worthy of him and his sacrifice. . . .

Scott Fitzgerald loved film as a medium for audience entertain-ment. All his characters are moviegoers, and he frequently mentions films by title in his writings and also refers to screen personalities of the day by name. In Gatsby, when the principal characters motor to Manhattan on that hot afternoon for want of something better to do, they sit around in their Plaza suite, sip tall iced drinks and mention possibilities of action. "Those big movies around Fiftieth Street are cool," Jordan suggests; but they drive back to Long Island, and one of their autos becomes the ill-fated death car. . . .

—*DeWitt Bodeen,* screenwriter

Hollywood is a surreal place. The first time I saw a crane planting a full-grown tree in a garden, I realized that Hollywood is not organic; nothing grows or develops naturally there.

—*John Schlesinger to the author*

PROLOGUE

I am not averse to taking all the shekels I can
garner from the movies . . . because you can
always say, "Oh, but they put on the movie in
a different spirit from the way it was
written!"

—*F. Scott Fitzgerald*

The campus of Princeton University has been associated with
Scott Fitzgerald ever since he praised his alma mater for its lazy
beauty back in the twenties. The shady campus is dominated by
several cathedral-like structures, one of which, the Firestone Library,
houses Fitzgerald's private papers. The centerpiece of this invaluable
collection is Fitzgerald's *Ledger*, a diary which he started when he first
began to emerge as a promising young writer.

Fitzgerald's *Ledger*, which is so-called because he kept it in the sort
of large notebook normally used by accountants, constitutes the most
significant personal document in modern American literature. Ernest

Hemingway recalls in his autobiographical book *A Moveable Feast* that he was much impressed with the *Ledger* when Fitzgerald showed it to him. The records it contains, Hemingway commented, were as carefully kept as the log of a ship. Mrs. C. Grove ("Scottie") Smith, Fitzgerald's daughter, describes it in the following manner:

"It contains a summary of each year of his life to 1937, with memorable events of each month, and at the top of each page a capsule comment as to whether the year was fruitful, wasted, sad, happy, etc. It also contains a complete list of everything he wrote, where it was published (or not published), and what became of it: whether it was collected, made into a movie, 'stripped' (his word for taking sentences out of a story for a novel), or translated. It also has a list of his earnings year by year."

After examining the ups and downs of Fitzgerald's financial status as outlined in the *Ledger*, one can agree very easily with Scottie Smith's observation that money was one of "the two great adversaries that he battled all his life." (Alcohol, as we shall see, was the other.) Indeed, as his daughter suggests, Fitzgerald's *Ledger* presents us with the paradox of a man who was meticulous "about making and keeping personal records," and yet seemed "congenitally incapable of balancing a budget."[1]

Fitzgerald's *Notebooks,* which incorporates materials accumulated during the last eight years of his life, does not function as a diary in the same sense that the *Ledger* does. He rather intended the *Notebooks* to be primarily a storehouse of observations and memories, as well as of excerpts from his "stripped" stories which might be worked into his novels. The *Notebooks* do, however, include several recollections of an autobiographical nature, which are helpful to the present study —although the entries in the *Notebooks*, unlike those in the *Ledger*, are undated. The same can be said of the scrapbooks that Fitzgerald filled with memorabilia; such as, letters and reviews of his work. All of these materials are an enormous help to anyone interested in charting the life and work of F. Scott Fitzgerald.

The present book is meant as a companion volume to my study of the film versions of the fiction of Ernest Hemingway, since Hemingway and Fitzgerald, besides being personal friends, have a great deal in common. For one thing, both Hemingway and Fitzgerald were among the foremost American writers of their generation; for another, both men have had nearly all of their major works committed to celluloid. Moreover, both writers, like other literary talents of their age, thought movies relatively inferior to fiction as an art form, although Fitzgerald was in fact willing to serve time writing screenplays in order to subsidize his career as a serious fiction writer, while Hemingway was not so inclined.

Hemingway firmly believed that when a writer went to Hollywood he had to write as though he were "looking through a camera lens. All you think about is pictures, when you ought to be thinking about people."[2] As far as he was concerned, the best way for a writer to deal with the film industry was to arrange a rendezvous at the California border with the movie men who wanted to purchase a story: "You throw them your book, they throw you the money; then you jump into your car and drive like hell back the way you came."[3] Hence he steadfastly refused to cross the California state line to work as a Hollywood screenwriter in any capacity, even when he was asked to collaborate on the film adaptations of his own fiction.

By contrast, Fitzgerald spent a considerable amount of time in Hollywood, particularly in the last years of his life. Just before he died in 1940, he had poured his experiences as an indentured servant of the studios into his final, unfinished novel, *The Last Tycoon*, a dark fable about Hollywood as a land of unfulfilled ambitions and broken dreams. As Pauline Kael points out, fiction written by a screenwriter about Hollywood usually represents the author's revenge on the movie capital. In Hollywood the writer sees himself as "an underling whose work is trashed," she writes; "or at best he's a respected collaborator without final control over how his work is used." By writing an anti-Hollywood book, then, he gets his own back. "Typically, he himself is the disillusioned hero; and the studio bosses, the producers, the flunkies are his boob targets—all of those people who he feels have no right to make decisions about his work," but do so just the same.[4]

It is, consequently, deeply ironic that, despite the bitter complaints that Fitzgerald voiced about the way he was treated while working as part of the studio system, so much of his fiction, including *The Last Tycoon*, was brought to the screen by the same industry that he felt had used his talents as a screenwriter so badly. Indeed, one of his keenest disappointments was that no screen adaptation that he made of one of his own works ever found its way onto film. Hence, the primary purpose of my present study is to determine to what degree the films of Fitzgerald's fiction—all scripted by hands other than his own—are worthy renditions of the stories from which they were derived, especially since his own screen adaptations of these same works went unproduced.

That this topic deserves to be explored is evidenced by the fact that all of the books so far published on Fitzgerald's life and work treat his association with Hollywood by concentrating mainly on his employment as a screenwriter there, and ignore almost entirely the body of films mined from his fiction.

It is, of course, a truism that a movie can never be a replica of the literary source on which it is based; and Fitzgerald himself was well aware of the crucial differences between fiction and film as two separate media of artistic expression. "A writer's instinct is to think in words," he once wrote; the director, on the other hand, must "turn the writer's words into visual images for the camera."[5] And therein lies the precise problem of bringing Fitzgerald's fiction to the screen. For, as Fitzgerald scholar Matthew Bruccoli has noted, Fitzgerald was by nature a storyteller accustomed to constructing scenes on the printed page that could not be easily transferred to film. Like Hemingway, Fitzgerald sometimes created delicate monologues in which he detailed a character's subjective reflections on his past experiences in nuanced prose that simply cannot be visualized or verbalized on the screen with equal effectiveness. Hence, Bruccoli concludes, no screenwriter thus far has been completely successful in translating Fitzgerald's narrative voice into visual images.

As New York Times writer Michiko Kakutani points out, the change of medium demands, among other things, subtle alterations of language. "Dialogue that seems artless on the page may sound stilted and contrived when spoken by actors." Thus a beautifully written passage, filled with stylized wordplay, may not work as well on the screen as it did in the book because "the explicitness of film tends to turn metaphor and symbol into fact." For example, Gatsby's romantic pursuit of the American dream of success is summed up in Fitzgerald's novel The Great Gatsby by his longing to possess the girl of his dreams; this idyllic aspiration might be reduced on the screen, however, merely to "a rich man's fancy for a pretty girl."[6] A filmmaker must therefore try to rethink in cinematic terms the literary source he is bringing to the screen by seeking to find visual equivalents for what a fiction writer has expressed in literary language, rather than attempt to maintain a slavish fidelity to the printed text of the original work.

"I lost my inhibitions about filming literature long ago," says director Peter Brook, who has filmed Golding and Proust. "The only way to be faithful is to be unfaithful. . . . One must create a new work of art that stands on its own as a movie; otherwise all one has done is strung together a series of dead photographs that illustrate a text like nineteenth-century engravings."[7] The director's only constraint, Brook concludes, is to be true to the original author's personal vision; that is, the latter's fundamental conception of the human condition, as it is embedded in the work of his that is to be filmed.

Fitzgerald's personal vision, as we shall see in the third part of this study, was heavily influenced by his Catholic upbringing. In essence, he believed that one must conduct one's life by adhering to a fixed set of moral principles or pay the consequences in terms of bringing unhappiness to one's self and to others. There are some indications of this theme reflected in his own screen work, which is taken up in part one of this book, and in the short stories of his that were filmed, which are dealt with in part two. But Fitzgerald's moral vision will be most apparent in our examination of the novels of his that were adapted to the screen. These are analyzed in part three—which constitutes the heart of this book, toward which the earlier sections are ultimately geared.

The faithful film adaptation, then, is one in which any superficial alterations in dialogue, characterization, or plot are designed to capture on film the thematic meaning; that is to say, the essential spirit of the source story. Significantly, the quotation found at the beginning of this chapter indicates that, from the very beginning of his professional career, Fitzgerald realized the importance of preserving the spirit of a fictional work when it was filmed.[8]

It follows that a filmmaker must respect the spirit and theme of the material he is filming, even to the extent of consciously tailoring his personal directorial style to the demands and specifications of the tale he is translating to the screen. Furthermore, since it is the director who is ultimately responsible for the overall quality and artistic unity of a motion picture, Fitzgerald was himself convinced that writer and director should work in close collaboration; and that the latter, as the true creator of a film, should supervise every phase of the production process.

Indeed Fitzgerald looked forward to the day when it would be, not the exception, but the rule for a director to write the screenplays of the films he made: "One man in control from the inception of the film to the finish."[9] Although he once assured a friend that he had "no desire to be a movie director,"[10] he wrote his wife Zelda near the end of his life that, if he ever got the chance to direct as well as to write a film, he would have attained his real goal in going to Hollywood as a screenwriter in the first place.

In fact, Fitzgerald believed that the director was the heart and soul of a motion picture, to the extent that he predicted that the artistic level of motion pictures would rise only when better and more experienced directors were developed in the industry. Since major directors like Richard Brooks, Henry King, and Elia Kazan did not turn to making movies of Fitzgerald's fiction until long after his death, it will be interesting to see to what degree his prophecy about motion pictures improving as an art form actually came true by analyzing the screen adaptations of Fitzgerald's work done over a period of more than half a century.

Before doing so, however, let us first examine Fitzgerald's own work as a screenwriter, in order to ascertain how successful he was in composing screenplays from the writings of other authors. In this context it is appropriate to recall the words of Ivan Moffat, who was charged with writing the script for the movie of Fitzgerald's *Tender Is the Night*. After expressing doubts that his screenplay had genuinely captured the flavor of Fitzgerald's novel, he added in his own defense, "F. Scott found it extremely difficult adapting things to movies, himself."[11]

So he did.

PART ONE

FITZGERALD AS SCREENWRITER

ONE

CRAZY MONDAYS:

THE EARLY SCREENPLAYS

Screenwriters are the highest-paid secretaries
in the world.
—*Joseph L. Mankiewicz*

What's all this business of being a writer? It's
just putting one word after another.
—*Irving Thalberg*

W hen British director John Schlesinger, to whom this book is
dedicated, visited Hollywood for the first time, he had
already read *Day of the Locust*, a novel about the movie capital by
Nathaniel West, a novelist and screenwriter who was also a friend
of Fitzgerald's. (Coincidentally, Fitzgerald and West died a day apart
at the end of 1940.) Schlesinger, who later filmed West's novel, has
since told me that when he got his first look at Hollywood, he was
astounded to see the bizarre picture of the town which West had
depicted in his novel virtually coming to life as he drove through
the film colony.

The director's astonished eyes beheld moribund palm trees planted in concrete courtyards and shrouded in a mist of smog; clashing styles of architecture, typified by New England colonial mansions, Spanish bungalows, and Assyrian split-levels, all looking like leftover sets that had somehow been uprooted from a studio back lot and transplanted onto residential streets. All of this was topped off by sprinkling systems that were watering fake flowers and cement walks, spilling over into swimming pools, where they ended by watering water. Like Fitzgerald before him, Schlesinger was overwhelmed by what he called "the garish quality" of the city.

"Isn't Hollywood a dump—in the human sense of the word," Fitzgerald wrote to a friend toward the end of his last sojourn there as a screenwriter. "A hideous town, pointed up by the insulting gardens of its rich, full of the human spirit at a new low of debasement."[1] He would, no doubt, have agreed with the old adage that if one looked underneath the fake tinsel that covered the surface of Hollywood, one would find—the real tinsel.

Fitzgerald may have despised the movie industry, yet he loved movies all his life; his fiction is filled with references to them, as DeWitt Bodeen points out in his prefatory essay to this book. In his *Ledger* Fitzgerald recalls his delight at being given "a moving picture machine" when he was ten; and he records in the same entry that he regularly attended Wild West movies as a youngster.[2]

Although his love of movies played no small part in drawing him to Hollywood as a screenwriter, he also saw this occupation as a way of augmenting his earnings as a novelist. From his earliest days as a writer he looked to Hollywood as a potential source of income. As early as December 1919 he inquired of his literary agent, Harold Ober, if there was any money in writing for movies. By March 1920 he had already sent off three scenarios to a man named Rosenbaum, who marketed scenarios and had shown some interest in seeing samples of this aspiring young screenwriter's work. That same year D. W. Griffith invited Fitzgerald to tour his studios at Mamaroneck, New York, where the would-be screenwriter was awestruck in the presence of actors whose faces he recognized from the pioneer director's *Birth of a Nation*.

Fitzgerald tried unsuccessfully to convince Griffith that a romantic movie dealing with tinsel town would prove enormously popular. Four years later Fitzgerald was vindicated when *Merton of the Movies* swept the country.

In March 1922 producer David Selznick asked Fitzgerald to prepare a story outline for a proposed film titled *Transcontinental Kitty*, which was to be a vehicle for silent star Elaine Hammersmith. According to the *Ledger*, Fitzgerald visited the Selznick Studios in New York, presumably to discuss the venture. But this project was aborted when Selznick turned down the fifteen-hundred-word synopsis, which Fitzgerald submitted to him. Years later, in a letter to an associate dated January 28, 1951, Selznick recalled that the original material Fitzgerald had offered him was simply awful (but that did not stop Selznick from hiring Fitzgerald in 1939 to assist in revising the screenplay for the producer's epic film, *Gone with the Wind*).

Although nothing came of Fitzgerald's initial attempts to write for the screen, after he became a famous author he was invited to Hollywood on no less than three separate occasions to work on movie scripts. Because he was usually paid top dollars for his screen work, Fitzgerald began to look more and more to Hollywood as a potential source of income, especially in his later life, when his debts mounted to the point that the royalties from his fiction would no longer pay his bills. Yet, despite the handsome financial rewards which he gleaned from screenwriting, Fitzgerald came more and more to dread these trips to the film capital, primarily because he found composing film scripts much less congenial work than writing fiction.

As a matter of fact, Fitzgerald never became particularly proficient at writing screenplays. This was true for several reasons. First of all, most of the scripts on which he worked in Hollywood involved his having to adapt another writer's work to the screen. Fitzgerald found this a very unfulfilling task because, as a creative writer in his own right, he disliked dealing with characters and situations not of his own invention. Yet as a movie adaptor he was expected to compose a screenplay that would preserve the flavor of the material that he was adapting; and he had to avoid dramatizing any scenes in a manner that was not in keeping with the tone and style of the original source. If a scriptwriter finds this difficult to do, scriptwriter A. E. Hotchner once quipped, it is because adapting someone else's work to the screen is something like adopting a fully grown orphan. Scriptwriter Philip Dunne has used a different but equally vivid metaphor to make the same point. For him the adaptor must be a stylistic chameleon because he or she is expected to write in the same style as that of any source he or she happens to be working on. Needless to say, Fitzgerald much preferred creating his own original scenarios; but he rarely got the chance to do so.

But whether Fitzgerald was working on a screen adaptation of another writer's work or on an original screenplay of his own, he always had problems with plot construction—his scripts were invariably marred by overplotting. As he explained in a letter to his literary editor, Maxwell Perkins, he firmly believed that only "lowbrows went to the movies"[3] and that their attention span was considerably shorter than that of people who read books. Thus he stated in a lecture which he "ghost-wrote" for Hollywood columnist Sheilah Graham that in a good film "there can be no uninteresting parts, nor even any highly complicated parts. Everything has got to be simple, forthright, and compellingly interesting."[4] What his attitude meant in practice was that Fitzgerald would sometimes needlessly overload a screenplay with an endless succession of melodramatic plot complications in a frantic attempt to keep the audience's attention from flagging, instead of developing his characters more deeply for the sake of the viewer's understanding.

Veteran screenwriter (later director) Billy Wilder, to whom Fitzgerald turned for advice during his last trip to Hollywood in the late thirties, sensed that Fitzgerald had no real feeling for story construction. "He made me think of a great sculptor who is hired to do a plumbing job," Wilder recalled. "He did not know how to connect the pipes so that the water would flow."[5] In essence Fitzgerald simply fashioned more plot complications than he could handily "connect."

Another drawback from which Fitzgerald's scripts suffered was that they tended to depend more on dialogue than on action. It is true, as noted above, that Fitzgerald realized that in a good film the images should be allowed as much as possible to speak for themselves. Yet, deep down inside, he never fully accepted this primacy of the visual over the verbal, which should characterize a first-class motion picture; and this attitude was implicitly reflected in the wordy scripts he often turned out. In a 1936 essay he bemoaned the fact that the novel was becoming subordinated to what he saw as the more glittering, grosser art of the movies, which in his view was capable of depicting only the tritest thought and the most obvious emotion—precisely because film "was an art in which words were subordinate to images." After the advent of sound pictures, he continued, he had a hunch that eventually "the talkies would make even the best-selling novelist as archaic as silent pictures."[6]

Because the written word was Fitzgerald's stock-in-trade, he often forgot that screen dialogue must perforce be more spare and condensed than literary dialogue, if for no other reason than that long, convoluted sentences, which one might easily grasp in their written form, would prove difficult to grasp in the form of film dialogue. As a result, in a typical Fitzgerald script for a talking picture, the emphasis frequently fell on the word *talking*, rather than on the word *picture*.

Still Fitzgerald did conscientiously try, according to his lights, to turn out movie scripts to specification. "Scott was anxious to learn the trade," recalled fellow screenwriter Dwight Taylor. "I remember he was always worried about camera angles, but I pointed out that it was his dialogue and characterization that they were after; and if he could manage to get his story down he could be sure that they would photograph it."[7] Nevertheless, even though he worked hard in Hollywood, Fitzgerald never got over the nagging feeling that scriptwriting was fundamentally hackwork, which he endured only in order to earn enough money to go back to his more serious writing. Hence his remark in a letter to his daughter, which he wrote to her while he was working in Hollywood for the last time, that what he was doing there represented the efforts "of a man who once did something finer and better."[8]

One of the things, besides fiction, which Fitzgerald considered finer and better than movie work was writing for the theater. His juvenilia include several short plays, and while at Princeton he collaborated on the annual student musical revue. Moreover, his first two novels include some key scenes which are dramatized as playlets, rather than written in the customary narrative style which characterizes the rest of each book. It was not surprising, therefore, that he eventually tried his hand at a Broadway play.

Nevertheless, *The Vegetable* (1923) proved to be his only attempt to launch a full-scale original play on Broadway, for it closed out of town. A political satire that admittedly was the precursor of Gershwin's *Of Thee I Sing* a decade later, the play never rises above the level of the heavy-handed college humor of the shows that Fitzgerald had helped to write at Princeton. Perhaps one critic best summed up this witless comedy when he called it a sophomoric farce that was, besides, not very entertaining.

In addition to the short-lived theatrical production of *The*

Vegetable, Fitzgerald was personally involved with the production of two silent films in the course of the twenties. The first was a film adaptation of Edith Wharton's *Glimpses of the Moon* (1923), made by Famous Players (later Paramount), for which Fitzgerald wrote the dialogue titles. The film was directed by Allan Dwan, who was at the time a friend of the Fitzgeralds. The weakest of all of Ms. Wharton's novels, the book, as one literary critic put it, is reminiscent of those superficial Broadway comedies in which the curtain goes up on sporty juveniles bouncing through the French doors, carrying tennis rackets. Little wonder that, by all accounts, this inferior material yielded nothing more than a fairly forgettable movie.

Although James Mellow's hefty 1984 biography of the Fitzgeralds, *Invented Lives: F. Scott and Zelda Fitzgerald*, adds little that is new to our previous store of knowledge about them, he does note that Scott and Zelda Fitzgerald spent a day in January 1924, watching Dwan film *Glimpses of the Moon*. Zelda, for one, was not particularly impressed with the performers she observed on the set. She thought one of the stars of the picture, Nita Naldi, who specialized in playing vamps of the Theda Bara variety, looked as if her head were filled with ozone and her mouth were too chock-full of teeth.

The following year Fitzgerald received $2,000 from the Film Guild, one of whose bosses was Townsend Martin, an old college buddy of his, for providing the original screenplay for *Grit* (1924). Fitzgerald's scenario was turned into a full-scale script by screenwriter James Ashmore Creelman. *Film Daily* described the resulting film—of which no known copies survive—as a gangster melodrama in which the once cowardly "Kid" Hart (Glenn Hunter), son of a deceased mobster, helps to bring a gang of crooks to justice and wins the love of an underworld type named Orchid McGonigle (Clara Bow) in the bargain. The reviewer for *Film Daily*, an influential trade paper in the film industry, turned thumbs down on the movie, excoriating Fitzgerald for his weak plot line, which was "further injured by a rather amateurish production, and a cast incapable of putting any realism or conviction into the characters of the story."[9]

When Fitzgerald got around to seeing *Grit* himself, he indicated his own keen displeasure in a letter to John Peale Bishop, an old college friend, by asking whether or not the Film Guild, the production company that made the movie, had as yet gone bankrupt as the result of "their last two pictures—one from my story."[10]

Lipstick

It was Fitzgerald's fame as a fiction writer, then, and not his rather undistinguished stage and screen credits, which prompted Hollywood some four years later to issue a call to him to come out to the coast to compose an original scenario, this time for silent-film star Constance Talmadge, to be entitled *Lipstick* (not to be confused in any way with the 1976 film of the same name, which starred Ernest Hemingway's granddaughters Margaux and Mariel).

In his Hollywood novel, *The Disenchanted*, Budd Schulberg imagines a producer handing a pencil to a distinguished writer on the latter's first day at the studio with the command, "I want to see this worn down to here by quitting time."[11] While Schulberg is playfully exaggerating the imperious behavior of the typical Hollywood producer, there is no question that movie moguls expect a full day's work for a full day's pay. Honest man that he was, Fitzgerald was the first to admit that during his first stint as a writer in Hollywood in 1927 he had not given his bosses their money's worth. His "bosses" at the time were United Artists (and not First National Pictures, as Aaron Latham erroneously states—one of the several howlers that mar *Crazy Sundays*, his book on Fitzgerald's Hollywood career).

Writing to his daughter some ten years later, Fitzgerald sheepishly recalled that, because he was by 1927 generally acknowledged as a top American fiction writer, he was "confident to the point of conceit" that he could compose a worthy screenplay that would please United Artists. Consequently, he did not invest a sufficient amount of time or effort in the composition of *Lipstick*. "Total result: a great time and no work."[12] As it happened, he was to be paid only a small amount for his work if the studio decided not to make the picture, and that is precisely what happened. John Considine, the producer who had invited Fitzgerald to Hollywood to write the scenario for *Lipstick*, took one look at the results of Fitzgerald's meager efforts and promptly cancelled the entire project. In the end, Fitzgerald received only a scant $3,500 for his scenario, which did not begin to defray the living expenses which he and his wife incurred during their expensive stay in the movie capital, which meant that the trip wound up costing them money.

Fitzgerald told Harold Ober that the studio had turned down

his scenario primarily because of a row he had had with Constance Talmadge, in the course of which she had apparently accused him, for whatever reason, of "middle-class snobbishness";[13] and that shortly thereafter she bowed out of the production for good. Be that as it may, one needs only to read the treatment (extended synopsis) of *Lipstick*, which Fitzgerald submitted to United Artists, in order to see that the primary reason for the studio's rejection of *Lipstick* was the one which he gave to his daughter a decade later: that he had not taken the pains necessary to develop a scenario that was screenworthy.

The plot of *Lipstick* concerns Dolly Carrol, an ex-convict who inherits a magic tube of lipstick that makes every man she meets want to kiss her. The payoff comes when the young man whom she really wants to fall in love with her does so on his own initiative; that is, without any prompting from the magic lipstick. This flimsy story line might have conceivably served as the basis for a respectable silent comedy, were it not for the fact that in writing the treatment Fitzgerald developed the plot as if he were writing a short story to be read, not a movie to be seen. In fact, some of the most telling lines in his screen treatment for *Lipstick* are humorous authorial asides which could not be filmed. There is, for example, the description of the students on the campus of the college which the hero attends:

> The young men are dressed in knickerbockers that are not too big, flannels not too wide, or in 'business' suits that have no collegiate look about them; if they wore sweaters, which they don't, there would be no letter on them, no matter how legitimately won; for this is one of the oldest and most conservative of eastern universities, given over in large measure to the education of those who have had money for several generations. . . .[14]

There is absolutely no way to convey visually on film the nuances of this passage detailing as it does the subtle atmosphere of a conservative Eastern college campus—short of printing it verbatim on the screen. (How does one photograph the letterless sweaters the boys are not wearing?) And, as Latham correctly comments, Fitzgerald's treatment abounds in similar ideas and emotions which likewise could never be photographed. Matthew Bruccoli says that *Lipstick* proved unacceptable to the studio because, in concocting its frivolous story line, Fitzgerald had "written down to the movies" by once again underestimating the "lowbrows" who go regularly to the movies.[15] That may be; but for myself I feel it is more a case of Fitzgerald having in effect written a short story aimed at his reading public, without really considering a movie audience at all.

Red-Headed Woman

If Fitzgerald was willing to blame himself for the failure of his first excursion to Hollywood, he insisted that the equally unsuccessful outcome of his second trip there was not his fault at all. His second assault on movieland, which took place in 1931, a few years after the advent of sound, had its genesis in a conversation with Irving Thalberg, who was in charge of production at Metro-Goldwyn-Mayer during the course of Fitzgerald's first Hollywood stay. Four years later it was at the behest of Thalberg that Fitzgerald returned to Hollywood. As a matter of fact, both of Fitzgerald's remaining two trips west would be initiated by MGM, so that the lion's share of Fitzgerald's screen work would be done for that studio.

Fitzgerald found Thalberg's offer especially tempting because it involved a much more favorable financial arrangement than had marked his first trip to Hollywood. His assignment was to revise an earlier draft of a screenplay for *Red-Headed Woman*, a Jean Harlow vehicle, which had been done by two other writers. Fitzgerald had no particular objection to reworking someone else's material, but he was dismayed to discover that he had been saddled with a collaborator.

Although having writers work on a screenplay in teams was a common Hollywood practice, Fitzgerald, as a writer accustomed to working alone, found the very notion of collaborating with another writer well-nigh intolerable. To make matters worse, the co-writer to whom the studio had yoked him was an erratic, self-destructive has-been, Marcel de Sano. Budd Schulberg who, as already mentioned, grew up in Hollywood, remembers de Sano as a once-promising film director whose career had been in a non-stop nosedive for some time. Thalberg nonetheless kept him on the MGM payroll in the hope that he would eventually pull himself together and fulfill his early promise. With all due respect to the production chief's generosity to de Sano, it must be pointed out that it was Fitzgerald, not Thalberg, who was forced to work with him.

Fitzgerald could make no headway in revising the screenplay of *Red-Headed Woman* as long as it entailed his having to cope with his strange and unpredictable partner, whose curious, capricious behavior is encapsulated in a brief entry in Fitzgerald's *Notebooks* which reads, "De Sano tearing the chair" (#1128); presumably this incident occurred during one of their bitter quarrels over the screenplay. Fitzgerald soldiered on as best he could, however, determined to make the best of a bad situation.

In addition to the numerous emendations that he made in the original version of the screenplay, Fitzgerald also put together a four-page memo recommending additional changes in the script. Although the studio would have liked him to stay on to do further rewrites, the unpleasant circumstances under which he had been forced to work had made him jittery, with the result that, as he later admitted to his daughter, "I was beginning . . . to drink more than I ought to."[16]

Playwright-screenwriter Laurence Stallings, who was also on the MGM payroll at the time, later recalled that Thalberg was very disappointed with the emended version of *Red-Headed Woman* which Fitzgerald gave him, largely because the heroine came across as so unsympathetic that the mass audience would never have been able to identify with her or her problems. During a production meeting at which Stallings was present but Fitzgerald was not, Thalberg stated, "We have an unusable work in the Fitzgerald script. I do not think it would serve any purpose to tell him so. . . . I'd rather compliment him on the quality of his work and let him leave here with his head up."[17]

Given the fact that Fitzgerald's work on *Red-Headed Woman* had come to naught, it comes as no surprise that MGM did not beckon him to come back to the West Coast for some time—not for another six years, to be exact. By that time the self-destructive Marcel de Sano had made good his oft-repeated threat to do away with himself, and Thalberg had died an untimely death while still in his late thirties. Although Fitzgerald confided to Ober that, due to his previous two unpleasant experiences in Hollywood, he had come to "hate the place like poison,"[18] the waning popularity of his fiction in the thirties made it imperative that he bolster his sagging bank account by accepting screen work.

It was Edwin H. Knopf, a story editor at Metro and an old friend of Fitzgerald's from the twenties, who convinced his superiors at the studio that Fitzgerald was worthy of another chance. For his part, Fitzgerald was anxious to vindicate Knopf's trust in him, particularly because the latter had arranged a very handsome salary for him.

Writing to his daughter while he was en route to California in July 1937, Fitzgerald recalled his first two disastrous brushes with the film industry and insisted that things would be different this time. He planned to ingratiate himself with the studio's front office so that he would be allowed to work alone on a picture, because that was the way he worked best. Furthermore, since he was painfully aware that he had begun drinking to excess during his previous trip to Hollywood, he was determined to stay on the wagon, lest he should jeopardize his chances for long-term employment. And so he came back to the film colony, as he later put it, "with a feeling of new worlds to conquer."[19]

Because he wanted the companionship of other screenwriters, Fitzgerald moved into the old Garden of Allah, an apartment-hotel where humorist Robert Benchley and several other Hollywood writers were living. The studio assigned him an office in the Thalberg Building, named for the recently deceased head of production. Fitzgerald, who had fictionalized his previous Hollywood experiences in a short story called "Crazy Sunday," was to learn that laboring in the studio salt mines could provide just as many crazy weekdays.

A Yank at Oxford

Possibly because his first novel, *This Side of Paradise*, had dealt with college life, he spent his first three weeks at Metro polishing the screenplay for the Robert Taylor film *A Yank at Oxford*. It was during this period that British novelist Anthony Powell lunched with Fitzgerald in the MGM commissary. Powell remembers him as "smallish, neat, solidly built," a man who radiated a kind of unassuming dignity.[20] Fitzgerald engaged his British colleague in a lively discussion that afternoon about the dialogue he was writing for *A Yank at Oxford*, asking him, for example, if English undergraduates would say shiner or black eye. So it was evident that

Fitzgerald was taking seriously his task of writing authentic dialogue for the picture.[21]

Still, when he had finished his revisions of the script for *Yank*, the studio decided that his contribution to the final shooting script was not sufficient to warrant his name being included as one of the authors in the opening credits of the screenplay. Nonetheless Fitzgerald was determined to receive a screen credit for the next film to which he was assigned, a project which he was in on from the beginning.

Three Comrades

Since at least some of the material which Fitzgerald had incorporated into the screenplay for *Yank* eventually found its way to the screen, MGM judged that he was ready to try his hand at preparing on his own a screen adaptation of Erich Maria Remarque's novel *Three Comrades*. Fitzgerald accepted this challenge gladly, because he wanted to prove that he could turn out a finished screenplay without the assistance of a collaborator at any stage of the script's development.

At the beginning of the six months during which Fitzgerald worked on *Comrades*, his relationship with the film's producer, Joseph L. Mankiewicz, who had been a screenwriter before he became a producer, was fairly amicable. When Fitzgerald had completed the first draft of the screenplay, however, Mankiewicz assigned him a more experienced screenwriter to cooperate with him on revising the script. Fitzgerald's partner was none other than Ted Paramore who, like Edwin Knopf, happened to be a friend of Fitzgerald's since the twenties. As a matter of fact, Fitzgerald had playfully satirized Paramore in his novel *The Beautiful and Damned* back in 1922 as Fred Paramore, a rather silly college chum of the hero's. But their past relationship was beside the point as far as Fitzgerald was concerned, and his immediate response to having a collaborator thrust up on him was to declare war on both Mankiewicz and Paramore, in an effort to retain artistic control of the screenplay.

To be fair to Mankiewicz and Paramore, there were definite indications in Fitzgerald's first draft of *Comrades* that he was in need of a co-writer at this stage of the game, as film scholar Tom Dardis has said. At one point, for example, when Erich, the hero (Robert Taylor) places a phone call to Pat, the heroine (Margaret Sullavan), Fitzgerald indicates in his first draft of the script that a white-winged angel is to be seen sitting at a switchboard, saying to Erich, "One moment, please, I'll connect you with heaven."[22] When Fitzgerald described this shot to Stallings, the latter remembers that he later thought to himself, "Time was when Scott Fitzgerald could have brought that sort of thing off in a story with matchless grace; but it was an enchantment that a camera, with its prosaic eagle eye, could never understand."[23]

Putting the matter more frankly, the intrusion into the film of a fanciful celestial phone operator is totally out of keeping with the realistic tone of the rest of the movie, a tragic tale set in turbulent post-World War I Germany. Surely, then, Fitzgerald needed someone to keep his imagination on the right track at this point in his development as a screenwriter. Perhaps Fitzgerald eventually realized this; since, as time went on, he gradually became reconciled to working with Paramore. Together the team spent several weeks whipping into shape a revised draft of the script which even Fitzgerald was fairly satisfied with.

It was then that Mankiewicz administered what Fitzgerald saw as the *coup de grace* to his aspirations of having the final shooting script of *Comrades* remain essentially his work. Mankiewicz himself went after the revised script with his blue pencil and altered several things that Fitzgerald wanted to leave just as they were. Consequently the furious screenwriter fired off two blistering memos to Mankiewicz protesting the changes and reminding the producer that he was dealing with a novelist who knew how to handle dialogue.

"To say I'm disillusioned is putting it mildly," the outraged author says near the beginning of the second memo; and he continues with a bitter remark that appears in the carbon copy of this memo (preserved at Princeton), but not in its transcription in Turnbull's edition of Fitzgerald's letters: "I had an entirely different conception of you." Fitzgerald then goes on to make a desperate plea that the producer reconsider the changes he has made in the screenplay: "Oh, Joe, can't producers ever be wrong? I'm a good writer, honest. I thought you were going to play fair."[24]

Reminded of this episode by various interviewers over the years, Mankiewicz has countered testily that he has always resented being attacked as if he had spit on the American flag just because he had presumed to tamper with something written by F. Scott Fitzgerald. "Writing dialogue for a novel and writing dialogue for the stage or screen are two different crafts," he told film critic Andrew Sarris. According to Mankiewicz, Margaret Sullavan informed him that she would not be able to speak "most of Scott's lines, and I rewrote them. That's all. It happens all the time."[25] Fitzgerald may have written acceptable literary dialogue in his fiction, Mankiewicz went on; but the novelist's screen dialogue tended to be too cerebral, and therefore literally unspeakable.

Because of the conflicting views of Fitzgerald and Mankiewicz over the latter's alterations of the revised script which Fitzgerald and Paramore had submitted to the producer, it would be constructive to trace briefly the history of the various stages that the screenplay of *Three Comrades* went through. Fitzgerald's first draft was turned in on September 1, 1937. The revised version which he and Paramore worked on together was handed in on December 21. It was this version, which Fitzgerald considered definitive, that Mankiewicz reworked, thereby occasioning Fitzgerald's acrid memo of January 20, 1938.

Admittedly Fitzgerald's initial screenplay was overlong and the dialogue at times was too literary; but the point is that between September 1 and December 21 he had conscientiously tried to lick these problems with the assistance of the collaborator, whom Mankiewicz himself had assigned to him. Fitzgerald most likely felt, quite understandably, that by now the script had been worked over enough, and that Mankiewicz's additional changes, done in a single hasty week according to Fitzgerald, were therefore totally superfluous. This was not an unreasonable stand for a writer to take at this point in the proceedings; hence his response to Mankiewicz was perhaps not as temperamental as the producer has suggested.

Mankiewicz has stated that he has no recollection of ever receiving Fitzgerald's memo of January 20. But novelist-screenwriter Gore Vidal, who has studied the different versions of the *Comrades* script quite carefully, thinks that Mankiewicz not only received the memo but that he actually acted upon some of the suggestions pertaining to Mankiewicz's own revisions.

For example, in the scene where Pat is dying in Erich's arms, Fitzgerald objected to the dialogue that Mankiewicz had added, because the dialogue that Fitzgerald had used in this scene was directly from the novel; and he truly felt that it was perfect just as it was. Conversely, Fitzgerald called Mankiewicz's additional dialogue utter drivel straight out of *True Romances*, in which references to God, cool lips, and lightning were all lumped awkwardly together, to no worthwhile purpose.

Between Fitzgerald's memo of January 20, 1938, and February 2, the date of the final shooting script, Mankiewicz rewrote this passage, as well as some other bits of dialogue that he had introduced, precisely along the lines that Fitzgerald's letter suggested. For example, Mankiewicz shortened Pat's dying speech by excising portions of his own additional dialogue. Quoted below, a section of this particular speech is enclosed in brackets to indicate where Mankiewicz deleted some of his own insertions in accordance with Fitzgerald's comments:

> All these months I'd figured out what you would say and I would say—word for word. Do you want to hear? We'd be sitting here on the foot of this bed like this, hand in hand; and I'd ask, is that the road home. And you'd say, yes; it's five hundred miles. And I'd say, that doesn't matter now. And you'd say, that's right. [God's in this room with us, lightning's in this room and the sea and the sky and the mountains are in this room with us.] And you'd kiss me [on the forehead and I'd say, how cool your lips are, don't move away].[26]

Fitzgerald very likely experienced a modicum of satisfaction when he learned that Mankiewicz had, to some extent at least, heeded his advice about making adjustments in the film's final shooting script, especially since Mankiewicz had insisted all along that novelists did not understand the nature of screen dialogue. He could also take consolation in the fact that the bittersweet ending of the film, though somewhat modified, was left essentially intact, despite the anxiety expressed in some quarters at MGM that audiences might find the film too downbeat if the heroine died at the end as she did in the book.

Thus, at the fadeout Pat, now deceased, is pictured with the three comrades (her husband Erich, plus his two closest friends), marching hand-in-hand toward the horizon, symbolizing that the dead are still united with those whom they have left behind. Fortunately, attempts to do away with this moving denouement to the film were overruled. As Fitzgerald explained to one of the Metro executives with whom he argued the point, *Camille* had made a fortune, even though the heroine coughed away her life just as Pat did. For once Fitzgerald had not felt compelled to "write down" to the mass audience by replacing a sad ending with a happy one, which is what he did every time he adapted one of his own fictional works to the screen. Would that he had had the same confidence that the tragic conclusions of his own fiction would hold up on the screen.

Although he estimated that he could only lay claim to about one-third of the finished film as entirely his own work, the front office informed him that he would receive an official screen credit, along with Ted Paramore, as co-scriptor of the movie. (This is in fact the only screen credit as a scriptwriter that Fitzgerald ever received during the entire time he worked in Hollywood.) His contract with MGM, which initially had only been for six months, was accordingly extended for another year, with a commensurate raise in salary.

In justice to Mankiewicz, then, it must be conceded that Fitzgerald did not fare all that badly under that producer's aegis. Moreover, *Three Comrades* was not the flop that Fitzgerald ruefully predicted it would be as a result of what he considered to be Mankiewicz's eleventh hour meddling with the screenplay. The film became both a critical and box office success when it was released in the summer of 1938. In addition, it was named by *The New York Times* as one of the ten best pictures of the year, while Margaret Sullavan received an Oscar nomination for her performance, as well as a New York Critics' Award and a British Academy Award.

Even the co-authors of the screenplay came in for their share of kudos, since more than one reviewer noted that their adaptation of Remarque's novel had been remarkably faithful to their source. But best of all, as far as Fitzgerald was concerned, was the fact that his creative association with such a prestigious and popular film was instrumental in earning him the opportunity to write another screenplay without a collaborator. It was to be written especially for Joan Crawford who, upon meeting the author of the screenplay of her next picture, greeted him with the enthusiastic exclamation, "Write hard, Mr. Fitzgerald, write hard!"[27] And so he would.

TWO

REVISITING BABYLON:

FURTHER SCREENPLAYS

Hollywood is still held together by palm trees,
telephone wires, and hope.
> —*John Schlesinger*

This is no art. This is an industry.
> —*F. Scott Fitzgerald*

After he had finished with *Three Comrades* and moved on to *Infidelity*, the Crawford picture, Fitzgerald wrote to Ober that "a good deal of the glow of Hollywood has worn off for me" because of the struggles he had endured while writing *Comrades*; "but I would as soon be here as anywhere else. After forty, one's surroundings don't matter so much."[1] So he had decided to continue his "exile in Babylon" indefinitely; although he would get away occasionally for a breather, he would always come back.

Infidelity

Fitzgerald sometimes referred to *Infidelity* as an original screenplay because he was working on it alone, but it was actually based on a short story by Ursula Parrott. During the four months that he labored on the screenplay in the spring of 1938, he got on fairly well with his new boss, producer Hunt Stromberg, whom he described as a fine showman who kept him from making any amateur mistakes (such as, perhaps, the heavenly phone operator in his first draft of *Comrades*).

Unfortunately the project ran into trouble with the industry censor board presided over by Joseph Breen, who was best known around movieland for demanding that Walt Disney erase the udders from the cows in his animated cartoons. Since Breen and his confederates were known to be nervous about the treatment of adultery in Hollywood films, Stromberg deemed it wise to submit Fitzgerald's partially finished script to the censor in order to see if Breen thought that Fitzgerald's handling of the plot was in keeping with the tenets of the Motion Picture Code.

As Fitzgerald had envisioned the story line of the film, Althea Gilbert becomes estranged from her husband Nicholas when she discovers him in the arms of Iris, an old flame. In retaliation she temporarily toys with the affections of a former sweetheart of her own named Alex, but is ultimately reconciled with Nicholas. Because Fitzgerald's plot line for the proposed film ended with Althea and Nicholas being happily reunited, Breen decreed that the scenario was not in harmony with the Production Code, which clearly stipulated that adultery must always be punished. It seemed to Breen that Fitzgerald was rewarding the Gilberts for their moral transgressions by allowing them to live happily ever after.

"According to the provisions of the Code at the time," film director George Cukor once told me, a leading character could not commit adultery "without suffering some kind of dreadful punishment, like breaking a leg or falling down a well." Although Fitzgerald had not projected any such clear-cut physical punishment for his principal characters, he felt that the mutual reconciliation of the repentant Gilberts would provide an exceptionally uplifting finale for the film. In outlining his analysis of the theme of the projected movie as he saw it, Fitzgerald commented that it is the Gilberts' ultimate faithfulness to the ideal of marital fidelity, and not their temporary infidelity, "which is finally rewarded."[2]

Elsewhere he added that it was his fond hope that if the chief censor could only be made to see the story in the light in which he was trying to present it, "a Catholic like Breen would, I think, accept the morals of this situation completely."[3] It is clear from his negotiations with the Breen office over the screenplay that the theme of the movie would have been very much in harmony with his usual thematic preoccupations with people who must suffer for their moral transgressions before they can achieve happiness in life; for the hero and heroine of the screenplay experience a great deal of anguish during the period in which they are estranged from one another because of their indiscretions. But nothing Fitzgerald could do or say could make Breen look upon the project in a more favorable light—not even the scenarist's last-ditch offer to change the name of the film from *Infidelity* to *Fidelity*! Regretfully the production was abandoned.

Fitzgerald's uncompleted screenplay for *Infidelity* is of an uneven quality, though this may be because, once it became abundantly clear that the film was not going to be made, he did not have the chance to revise what he had written, much less to finish it, but had to move on to other work. Still the script as it stands contains some wise and witty lines, among the best of which is in a dialogue between Althea and Alex. When Alex, who would like to win Althea away from Gilbert for good, suggests that her marrying Nicholas was merely an accident, she replies very touchingly, "I don't think so. I think I'd have found Nick—or spent the rest of my life vaguely looking for him."[4]

The Women

Fitzgerald next turned his attention to the film version of *The Women*, Clare Boothe Luce's sophisticated Broadway comedy about high society, on which he labored through the summer and early fall of 1938. At first he worked alone, but later on he joined forces with an old friend of his youth, the distinguished screenwriter Donald Ogden Stewart. "In our month together," Stewart later recalled, "our old friendship came back."[5] Unfortunately their mutual efforts never seemed to please Hunt Stromberg.

In Fitzgerald's case, it seems that he was once more succumbing to his old habit of overplotting. Stromberg rejected out-of-hand Fitzgerald's attempt to insert an elaborate opening that would have provided a kind of prologue to the action by tracing the life of the heroine from childhood to the first episode of the original play. This excessively long introduction to the action of *The Women* would of course have extended the total running time of the finished film well beyond the customary length of a standard feature.

Stromberg's negative reaction to Fitzgerald's attempt to fill in the details of the heroine's past life before beginning to tell the story of *The Women* may well be reflected in a passage from *The Last Tycoon*, which appears in the manuscript of the novel but not in the published version. The hero, film producer Monroe Stahr, says, "When you extend a play with a prelude, you're asking for it; you're including a lot of situations the playwright has already rejected."[6] Applying this observation to *The Women*, once again Fitzgerald had spun out more plot material than any single movie would need or could accommodate.

In any case, because of their various disagreements about the script of *The Women*, Fitzgerald later remarked that "Hunt and I reached a dead end on *The Women*. We wore each other out."[7] Hence Fitzgerald made little or no fuss when Stromberg passed him on to still another producer. When Fitzgerald failed to come up with a viable screenplay on this latest project, he feared that it might be his last assignment at Metro. It was. MGM's executives decided that, since Fitzgerald had not made a significant contribution to a Metro film for some time, he was just not giving them their money's worth. And so, when it came time to renew his contract, the studio declined to do so.

Gone with the Wind

While sitting out the remaining few weeks of his MGM contract, which would run until January 27, 1939, he was loaned on January 6 to independent producer David Selznick to do some last-minute retouching of the screenplay for *Gone with the Wind*, which was slated to go into production on January 26. "Do you know, in that *Gone with the Wind* job," he later wrote to Maxwell Perkins, "I was absolutely forbidden to use any words except those of Margaret Mitchell; that is, when new phrases had to be invented, one had to thumb through as if it were Scripture and check out phrases of her's which would cover the situation!"[8]

Interestingly enough, Fitzgerald's main contribution to the screenplay of *Gone with the Wind* was not so much what he put into the script, but what he took out of it. As film scholar Alan Margolies has pointed out, although Fitzgerald usually needed to have his own natural tendency toward writing long-winded dialogue curbed, he never failed to summon the objectivity required to spy out superfluous verbiage in the work of other screenwriters, as in his criticism of Mankiewicz's additional dialogue for *Comrades*. Likewise he perceptively deleted more than one poor passage of dialogue from the script of *Gone with the Wind*, about each of which he noted in the margin of his copy of the screenplay that it was false or dull, stagey or trite.

Hence Selznick's remark some time afterward that Fitzgerald had contributed nothing to the script of *Gone with the Wind* is at best inaccurate and at worst unfair. For there is no doubt that the script of *Gone with the Wind* was all the better for Fitzgerald's revisions of it.

George Cukor, who directed some of *Gone with the Wind* and all of *The Women*, both of which Fitzgerald worked on, retained an admiration for the writer that dated back to his directing the stage version of Fitzgerald's novel *The Great Gatsby* on Broadway in 1926. Cukor accordingly invited Fitzgerald to lunch one day around this time, just for old time's sake. "Yet it seemed we had nothing to talk about," Cukor recalled. "Fitzgerald looked grim and ate in silence. I told him that the only people I had ever known to eat as fast as he did had both died young." A year or so later, so would Fitzgerald.

Cukor's sad, silent luncheon guest was certainly not the same good-humored Scott Fitzgerald with whom Anthony Powell remembered lunching shortly after Fitzgerald had arrived in Hollywood in the summer of 1937. But then, once Fitzgerald had been let go by MGM, he had little to be cheerful about. At the time he left Metro, he told his literary agent, "I hope I may never see the Metro factory again."[9] But once he began freelancing, he soon discovered that the lot of the freelance writer in Hollywood was no happier than that of one attached to a major studio like MGM.

Biographer Henry Dan Piper summed up Fitzgerald's situation as a freelancer very vividly when he wrote that Fitzgerald "had to be ready to go to work with little advance notice"; and the jobs lasted only a short time, because they usually involved merely "tinkering with someone else's script," as in the case of *Gone with the Wind*.[10]

Because he preferred to work on material of his own invention, from time to time he circulated proposals for original screenplays to the studios around town, but there were no takers. One such projected screenplay was *The Feather Fan*, a fantasy in the manner of *Lipstick*, but with a tragic ending. A college girl finds a magic feather fan which, like Aladdin's lamp, grants her every wish. She discovers that the fan is less a blessing than a curse, however, because the power of the fan is such that, in the words of Fitzgerald's synopsis, "all things touched by it will be tainted."[11] And so the heroine dies rich but unhappy. It is not hard to see why this uneasy mixture of fantasy and realism failed to attract a prospective producer.

Winter Carnival

The first freelance job that Fitzgerald undertook after completing his work on *Gone with the Wind* was to work on a scenario for a film entitled *Winter Carnival* for producer Walter Wanger. Budd Schulberg makes reference in the foreword of this book to his short-lived collaboration with Fitzgerald on the film in February 1939. The *Winter Carnival* episode marks one of the few times that Fitzgerald fell off the wagon while working in Hollywood, and he was abruptly fired by Wanger for doing so.

Concerning this particular fall from grace, Fitzgerald explained to Ober afterward that "the sudden outburst of drink was a result of an attempt to keep up my strength for an effort of which I was not capable."[12] At the time he accepted the assignment, which promised to be a lucrative one, he was still worn out and depressed by the months that he had spent working at Metro on one script after another, usually with the result that his contributions, for one reason or another, were not incorporated into the final shooting script. In retrospect, it was very unwise of him to attempt the journey to

Hanover, New Hampshire, for the Dartmouth Winter Carnival, on which the plot of the screenplay would turn. But Wanger, who had himself attended Dartmouth, insisted that Fitzgerald spend a few days there with Schulberg and members of the film's production crew, in order to soak up the atmosphere necessary to write a screenplay that would give an authentic picture of college life at Dartmouth. Unfortunately, Fitzgerald soaked up great quantities of alcohol during the junket to Hanover, and was for all practical purposes in no condition to work the entire time the film unit was there.

Although Schulberg joined in some of the revelry, he could not help being disenchanted by Fitzgerald's sophomoric behavior, much more so because he had initially been so thrilled to learn that a writer he had idolized ever since college was to be his partner on the screenplay. The day that Wanger had broken the news to him back in Hollywood, Schulberg remembers blurting out in excited disbelief, "My God, I thought Scott Fitzgerald was dead!" To which Wanger responded, "Not unless your treatment bored him to death. He's in the next room reading it now."[13]

Even though Schulberg was saddened and bewildered by Fitzgerald's subsequent spree at Dartmouth, Fitzgerald biographer Andrew Turnbull is wrong in suggesting that Schulberg felt "a little superior to this derelict 'genius,' who was not only making a fool of himself but compromising Schulberg's first big assignment."[14] On the contrary, the neophyte writer remained permanent friends with Fitzgerald after the fateful Dartmouth fiasco. This is made evident in the graciously contrite message that Fitzgerald himself inscribed in a copy of one of his novels a year or so later for Schulberg's small daughter Vicky: "In memory of a three-day mountain-climbing trip with her illustrious father—who pulled me out of crevices into which I sank, and away from avalanches."[15]

In any case, Schulberg was allowed to continue working on *Winter Carnival*, while Fitzgerald was replaced by screenwriter Maurice Rapf, who, like Schulberg, was a Dartmouth alumnus, and happened to be attending the Winter Carnival while the film unit was there. "At the time I came on board," Rapf has told me, "Budd and Scott still had not worked out a story line. That means that they had to guess which parts of the campus the camera crew should photograph for use in the picture as location backgrounds." Under the circumstances they had usually guessed wrong; "and so we weren't able to work most of these authentic background shots into the movie when it came to shooting the film in the studio back in Hollywood; so the picture wound up having a phony, cheesy look."

Fortunately Fitzgerald's peremptory dismissal from *Winter Carnival* did not ruin his chances to obtain further offers for free-lance writing when he returned to Hollywood. Next came *Air Raid*, on which he worked at Paramount (not MGM, as Piper states). After a month of rewriting an earlier draft of the script, he was informed that the picture had been cancelled. Fitzgerald later mentioned in a letter to his Hollywood agent, Leland Hayward, who was handling his picture deals, that at one point he had been teamed on *Air Raid* with Griffith. Alan Margolies, in his study of Fitzgerald, assumes that this reference is to D. W. Griffith, for whom Fitzgerald had years before been interested in preparing an original scenario. The notion that these two distinguished artists, D. W. Griffith and F. Scott Fitzgerald, were collaborating on a movie in the twilight years of both of their Hollywood careers is a fascinating one, but Margolies's assumption, the stuff of which Hollywood legends are made, is unfortunately a mistaken one. The filmmaker in question must have been Edward H. Griffith, who was to have directed *Air Raid*.

Raffles

Fitzgerald's free-lance film work, increasingly sporadic, included a week in September 1939 of revising the script of *Raffles* for independent producer Sam Goldwyn. David Niven, who had the title role in the movie, that of a debonair, gentleman-burglar, recalls in his memoirs of Hollywood, *Bring on the Empty Horses*, that Goldwyn told him he was unhappy with the screenplay and was bringing in Fitzgerald to tone it up a bit. Although Goldwyn (and the rest of Hollywood) had heard about the Dartmouth fracas, the producer hired Fitzgerald with the encouragement of the story editor at the Goldwyn studios, who was formerly an editor at the *Saturday Evening Post* and admired the short fiction of Fitzgerald's that had appeared in the *Post*.

Niven remembered that Fitzgerald often sat in a remote corner of the sound stage, filling up the pages of the large yellow writing pad in his lap, while he apparently was going over the screenplay. Nearby there was an ever-present six-pack of Coca Cola, his substitute for stronger beverages. Whenever the director asked him to alter a line in the script, he would dutifully look up from his pad and do so immediately, supplying just what was needed. Otherwise, said Niven, "he just melted into the background, scribbling away on his big writing pads."

Niven did not find Fitzgerald any more talkative at lunchtime than had George Cukor. Fitzgerald would break his long silences by recounting his bad luck at not being able to earn any more screen credits for his script work. "But his was a genuine frustration," Niven continued, "because he really had studied filmmaking, and was fascinated by the medium."

Just when Niven was beginning to like Fitzgerald, Goldwyn fired him for having contributed relatively little to the screenplay of *Raffles*. "It always happens," Fitzgerald said laconically as he packed up his gear to leave the studio. Niven concludes this account of his brief encounter with Fitzgerald in movieland by adding that Fitzgerald said he took his dismissal calmly because, thanks to Goldwyn, he could now afford to work full-time on a novel he had started—"and upon which," Niven notes wryly, "he had presumably been using up his yellow pads at a great rate," as he sat in the shadows of the sound stage.[16]

A year later, in August 1940, he was asked by Twentieth Century-Fox to adapt for the screen *The Light of Heart*, a play by Emlyn Williams about a has-been actor who is a lush. But Fitzgerald's screenplay was rejected as being too glum, and the project for the time being was shelved, not to go before the cameras for another two years when it emerged under the title, *Life Begins at 8:30*. Hence Fitzgerald's career as a screenwriter ended as ingloriously as it had begun more than a decade earlier—with rejection.

Since Fitzgerald's scriptwriting was largely concerned with adapting other writers' work for the screen, there was not much room for him to reflect his own personal vision in his screen work. This was possible only when he was working on an original scenario of his own, notably *Infidelity*. But when working on a scenario based on material not of his own invention, Fitzgerald endeavored to be true to the thematic intent of his literary source. For example, he fought successfully to retain the stark ending of his screenplay for *Three Comrades*, in which the dead and the living are shown facing the future together at the fade-out, because it was true to Remarque's book.

The only Fitzgerald screen work yet to be considered are the scenarios that he derived from his own fiction, all of which the movie moguls turned down. These will be analyzed in tandem with the films actually made of these same fictional works of Fitzgerald's from screenplays composed by other film writers. In turning to these film adaptations, we shall endeavor to see to what extent movie and TV writers—and the other artists involved in transferring one of his works to either the big screen or the little screen—have created films worthy of Fitzgerald's fiction.

PART TWO

THE FILMS
OF FITZGERALD'S
SHORT FICTION

THREE

ECHOES OF
THE JAZZ AGE:
THE EARLY FLAPPER FILMS

I used to try scenarios in the old days. Invariably
they came back. Now, however, I am being adapted to the screen. I suspect it must be difficult to
mold my stuff into the conventional movie form,
with its creaky mid-Victorian sugar.

—*F. Scott Fitzgerald*

Lincoln Center for the Performing Arts, with its gushing fountains, lush shrubbery, and impressive architecture, has long been the annual site of the prestigious New York Film Festival. In 1976 a film based on one of Fitzgerald's early short stories, "Bernice Bobs Her Hair," was screened at the festival. No doubt Fitzgerald would have been pleased that a film version of one of his stories was being shown at a major international film festival more than half a century after he had written it.

The movie of "Bernice" represents one of the more recent examples of a film adaptation of Fitzgerald's short fiction. However, other Fitzgerald short stories were first filmed back in the silent era, starting in 1920 with "Head and Shoulders," which was retitled *The Chorus Girl's Romance* for Metro's movie version. "Sold first movie," his *Ledger* jubilantly declares in February 1920. He received $2,500 for the screen rights to the tale, which had appeared in *The Saturday Evening Post* the year before, the first of many Fitzgerald short stories that this mass circulation magazine was to publish.

Fitzgerald, who considered himself a novelist first and foremost, developed the habit over the years of denigrating his short fiction, which he maintained was written, like his screenwriting, solely to pay the rent, so that he could get on with the more serious business of writing novels. Nonetheless I am inclined to agree with Bruccoli when he says that Fitzgerald's more than 160 stories constitute a significant part of his creative output. Hence it simply will not do to write them off as hackwork, as Fitzgerald himself tended to do; for as Bruccoli observes, "they were published by the top magazines and required Fitzgerald's best professional efforts. They were not dashed off between drinks; Fitzgerald sweated over them."[1]

The Early Flapper Films

Certainly his short stories were not overlooked or dismissed by Hollywood, which filmed three of them in two years in the early twenties. Besides *The Chorus Girl's Romance*, there was *The Husband Hunter* (1920), based on "Myra Meets His Family," and *The Off-Shore Pirate* (1921), based on the story of the same name. Unfortunately, no copies of these films have survived. The reason that these and some of the other Fitzgerald silent films have been declared lost is that motion pictures in those days were printed on perishable film stock. These films had disintegrated before copies could be transferred to permanent film stock, which later came into general use in the film industry. Thus the print of one of the Fitzgerald silents that DeWitt Bodeen screened at Paramount had already badly deteriorated by the time he saw it.

One might ask why Hollywood produced three films based on Fitzgerald's short stories in such quick succession; the answer is not far to seek. His early short stories about the carefree flappers of the Roaring Twenties captured the imagination of readers of popular fiction all over America. Consequently, producers thought it safe to assume that these same tales of the Jazz Age would likewise appeal to moviegoers. This observation is borne out in Fitzgerald's renowned essay on the era, which he himself christened the Jazz Age (so named because the frenetic beat of jazz music typified the restless twenties). In it he writes that Hollywood followed the lead of the slick commercial magazines in celebrating the "wildest of all generations,"[2] which was of course epitomized by the flapper.

Journalist Margaret Reid, in an interview with Fitzgerald published around this time, defined the flapper, as popularized by Fitzgerald's fiction and the films made from it, as an audacious young lady of college age "who rolled her stockings, chain-smoked, . . . mixed a mean highball, and radiated 'It'"(sex appeal).[3] That description fits each of the heroines of the Fitzgerald films made in the early twenties.

The Chorus Girl's Romance

In *The Chorus Girl's Romance*, for example, the heroine, Marcia, is a glamorous showgirl and a typical flapper—until she falls in love with Horace, a scholarly academic. Once married, in fact, the pair virtually exchange roles: Horace becomes a professional entertainer and Marcia becomes a successful author. The studio's advertising copy for the film made the movie sound very appealing indeed to filmgoers of the period: "She shook a wicked shoulder and she owned a wicked wink"; but after she was married, "she proved to have a wise little head on those naughty little shoulders."[4]

The movie got a fairly positive reception from the critics, partly because, as Bodeen points out, the leading lady was Viola Dana, a young actress who excelled at portraying a flapper with a good head on her shoulders. Still, at least one of the industry's trade papers thought that Fitzgerald's name deserved to be displayed prominently in ads for the film, because he was a young writer with fresh ideas.

The Husband Hunter

Possibly with this accolade from the trade press in mind, Fitzgerald sought to interest Metro in another of his stories, "Myra Meets His

Family." Although the studio did want to film another Fitzgerald story, Metro was not interested in that particular tale. So Fitzgerald took it to a Ms. Webster, whom he identified for Ober as "a movie agent of no particular standing."[5] Yet she managed to peddle the screen rights of "Myra" to Fox for $1,000, which was surely a sum not to be sneezed at; and the movie was produced under the title of *The Husband Hunter*.

Myra (Eileen Percy) sets her sights on marrying Knowleton Whitney, a wealthy bachelor who fears that she may be nothing more than a golddigger. He consequently decides to test the sincerity of her love for him by having her meet a strange assortment of eccentrics whom he introduces as the members of his immediate family. Actually Whitney has engaged a group of actors to stand in for his real relatives, just to see if Myra would put up with them sheerly out of devotion to him. When Myra learns the truth, she walks out on her snobbish fiancé, but not until she has retaliated by staging a little ruse of her own at Knowleton's expense.

When the film version of "Myra" was released, it was not as well received by the critics as *The Chorus Girl's Romance* had been, since its plot was too far-fetched even for a farce. Hence Metro was evidently wise to pass up this story in favor of "The Off-Shore Pirate."

The Off-Shore Pirate

This story also involves a deceptive masquerade. Ardita Farnam is apparently kidnapped by a romantic river pirate. In reality it is Toby Moreland, a rich young suitor who seeks to sweep her off her feet by this highly imaginative way of wooing her, since she had earlier refused even to meet him. Toby succeeds in his elaborate charade where Knowleton Whitney totally failed in his, because Ardita is completely captivated by this dashing display of Toby's venturesome spirit.

Among the positive reviews that the film drew from the critics, none was more favorable than that of Robert Garland, who found Viola Dana once again thoroughly charming as another Fitzgerald flapper. But Garland reserved most of his praise for Fitzgerald, whose original story had provided the basis of a film that was in his view even more amusing than *The Chorus Girl's Romance*. In short, he said that there were two good reasons for going to see *The Off-Shore Pirate*: "One is F. Scott Fitzgerald. The other is Viola Dana."[6]

The Pusher-in-the-Face

The first talking picture derived from Fitzgerald's fiction was *The-Pusher-in-the-Face* (1929), a two-reel comedy short, directed at Paramount by Robert Florey, who co-directed the Marx Brothers' first film the same year. The plot of "Pusher" tells of a timid soul who suddenly turns tough when he is finally driven too far by the overbearing people who surround him, most notably his flapper girlfriend. He decides that it is time that he begin to push other people around for a change, and becomes very aggressive indeed, with the result that he gets into one hilarious scrape after another.

Because the author of the screenplay for this short movie is not listed in any of the documentation available on the film, some film historians have hazarded the guess that Fitzgerald adapted his short story to the screen himself. But there is no evidence in the *Ledger*, in which he customarily kept careful account of his screen work, to substantiate this conjecture. One must therefore assume that Fitzgerald did not figure in the preparation of the screenplay for the movie, beyond creating a short story that was easily adaptable to the screen. For, as Bruccoli has written, "The Pusher-in-the-Face" reads in its original fictional form very much "like a movie scenario": it is fundamentally an action-filled slapstick comedy almost ready-made for filming.[7]

Bernice Bobs Her Hair

The most distinguished film made from Fitzgerald's early fiction is, of course, *Bernice Bobs Her Hair*, which, as mentioned, was showcased at the 1976 New York Film Festival. Writer-director Joan Micklin Silver opted to make a mini-feature from the story, so that she could develop Fitzgerald's compact short tale to its full dramatic potential on the screen, without having to manufacture the additional plot material which would have been required to turn the story into a feature-length film.

Bernice is another young flapper cut from the same cloth as the heroines of the earlier Fitzgerald flapper films. When first published in the *Post* in the spring of 1920, "Bernice" caused a minor sensation, because it depicted how a lonely small-town girl visiting her cousin in the big city finally comes into her own by summoning the audacity to have her hair cut short like a boy's. Both author and editor were swamped with letters from outraged parents protesting Bernice's unladylike hairdo. Nevertheless, the new hairstyle soon caught on; and, as Piper points out, by November of that same year the *Post* cover girl was sporting boyishly bobbed hair just like Bernice's.

Because "Bernice" is so wedded to the period in which it is set, Ms. Silver said in an interview about the making of the movie that she never seriously considered trying to update the setting of the story to the present. Instead she opted for bringing the story to life on the screen pretty much as Fitzgerald himself had conceived it more than a half-century before. In order to get a feel for the post-World War I setting of the tale, she carefully researched Fitzgerald's life and times, looking all the while for realistic period details which might enhance her screenplay.[8]

For example, one passage of dialogue between Bernice and Marjorie, her condescending cousin, grew out of a letter which Fitzgerald, while a student at Princeton, wrote to his younger sister Annabel about how to go about gaining popularity with the male population. Fitzgerald, who later said that this letter was the genesis of "Bernice," told his sister that "a pathetic, appealing look is one every girl ought to have." This is accomplished, he went on, "by opening the eyes wide and drooping the mouth a little," gazing straight into the eyes of the young man who is being addressed, and then confessing shyly and sadly that one is unpopular.[9] The purpose of this ploy, Fitzgerald explained, was to touch the young man's affections, so that he would feel gently protective towards her.

In her screenplay Joan Silver smoothly integrates this concept of "the pathetic look" derived from Fitzgerald's letter into a conversation between Bernice and Marjorie which is already in the original short story, thereby adding a telling detail to Marjorie's "lecture" to Bernice on how to be more attractive to the opposite sex. "You've got to perfect a pathetic look," Marjorie tells Bernice; and this is done by first opening the eyes wide. "Now droop your mouth a little," she continues. "Now look right in the man's eyes and say, 'I hardly have any beaux at all.'"[10] Even though Fitzgerald's sister Annabel reminisced years later that "Scott and I were so different that I guess he did not accomplish much in the line of making me a belle,"[11] this advice certainly works for Bernice.

Ms. Silver's fidelity to the tone and spirit of Fitzgerald's story is further evidenced by the fact that she incorporated a significant amount of Fitzgerald's dialogue from the story into the screenplay. But because film is primarily a visual medium, she did so by judiciously condensing his original dialogue for the screen. In the following speech of Marjorie's, taken from the story that Ms. Silver edited for use in the screenplay, the brackets show how the screenwriter neatly trimmed Fitzgerald's literary dialogue for screen purposes. Marjorie is discussing "sad birds" (lonely boys):

> No girl can afford to neglect them. They're the big part of any crowd. [Young boys too shy to talk are the very best conversational practice. Clumsy boys are the best dancing practice. . . .] If you go to a dance and really amuse, say three sad birds that dance with you; [if you talk so well to them that they forget they're stuck with you, you've done something.] [t]hey'll come back next time, and [gradually so many sad birds will dance with you that] the attractive boys will see there's no danger of being stuck—then they'll dance with you.[12]

The climax of both the story and the film is brought about when Marjorie prods Bernice into believing that bobbing her hair is the most spectacular way to attract the attention of eligible young males. Because bobbed hair has not yet become the fad it soon will be, however, the reaction of the passel of the young men who watch Bernice's shearing is more one of embarrassment than enthusiasm. Bernice gradually realizes that Marjorie counted on the fact that her convention-shattering haircut would backfire. What's more, Marjorie had slyly engineered the whole thing in order to discredit Bernice with Warren, a lad whom Marjorie jealously sets her sights on capturing for herself.

To get even, Bernice stealthily sneaks into Marjorie's room late at night, just before leaving for home, and amputates both of Marjorie's beautiful blond pigtails as she sleeps. On the way to the train station, Bernice spies Warren's car parked in front of his house. On an impulse, she dumps the severed tresses on the front seat of Warren's auto and then marches triumphantly down the middle of the street toward the depot.

The dénouement of the short story, which encompasses Bernice's revenge on Marjorie, is particularly noteworthy: its emphasis, both as written by Fitzgerald and filmed by Joan Silver, is on visual storytelling, since it is totally free of dialogue. The way in which Fitzgerald favors the visual over the verbal in this key scene of his story demonstrates the cinematic potential of the tale, and would have been reason enough to prompt a perceptive filmmaker like Joan Micklin Silver to see in it the source of a compelling motion picture.

Scottie Fitzgerald Smith has told me that she thought the film of "Bernice Bobs Her Hair" was delightful, although she had reservations about the manner in which Shelley Duvall, who played the title role, seemed to be "trying too hard to be young and innocent"—very likely because Ms. Duvall was twenty-seven years old when she played the teenage Bernice, and was doing her best to seem believable while playing a character several years her junior.

For her part, however, Scottie Smith still feels that the film version of Fitzgerald's story "The Last of the Belles" is "among the best dramatizations of my father's writing I have ever seen."[13] Unlike "Bernice," the screen adaptation of "The Last of the Belles" was extended to feature-length. But, as we shall see in the coming chapter, the expansion of the storyline of "Belles" was accomplished in an unconventional manner.

FOUR

PARADISE LOST:

"THE LAST OF THE BELLES" AND

THE LAST TIME I SAW PARIS

A man digs his own grave and should, presumably,
lie in it.

—*F. Scott Fitzgerald*

For me the past is forever.

—*F. Scott Fitzgerald*

In the spring of 1927, Fitzgerald took a two-year lease on a secluded nineteenth-century mansion called Ellerslie, which was situated on the Delaware River. "The squareness of the rooms and the sweep of the columns," wrote Zelda Fitzgerald of the huge old place, "were to bring us a judicious tranquility."[1] It was at Ellerslie that Fitzgerald wrote several stories for the slicks, as commercial magazines were called, because he could not bring himself at the time to settle down and make steady progress on a novel. It was here too that his wife started to take ballet lessons, in the hope that it was not too late for a young woman nearing thirty, who had briefly studied the dance as a girl, to take up the study of ballet once more, in order to become a full-fledged ballerina at long last.

Sidney Harper, who was a couple of years ahead of Zelda in high school in Montgomery, Alabama, has told me that she was "an extremely talented dancer as a girl; definitely a devotee of the dance. My sister Amelia had a dance studio in Montgomery, and Zelda used to practice there." Harper remembers Zelda as "a vivacious, very pretty young lady," with more than her share of male admirers. Hence it was not surprising that the popular Ms. Zelda Sayre was invited to several college dances while she was still a senior in high school. One of these balls was held at the Alabama Polytechnical Institute at Auburn, where Sidney Harper fondly recalls that he "had the pleasure of several dances with her." The following summer Zelda Sayre met Lt. Scott Fitzgerald at still another dance; and the rest, as they say, is history.

F. Scott Fitzgerald and "The Last of the Belles"

The two-hour teleplay entitled *F. Scott Fitzgerald and "The Last of the Belles,"* first broadcast on ABC-TV on January 6, 1974, centers on Fitzgerald's writing of "The Last of the Belles" at Ellerslie. It begins in the fall of 1928 with the Fitzgeralds returning to Ellerslie after a summer in Europe, where they both sensed a growing estrangement developing between them. The TV play then goes on to dramatize the interplay between Fitzgerald's personal and professional lives at the time, concentrating on the manner in which the inspiration for this particular short story grew out of his effort to come to terms with his conflicting feelings towards his wife.

The autobiographical circumstances in which "The Last of the Belles" was created thus provide the narrative frame which surrounds the dramatization of the story. The TV adaptation of the short story is accordingly stretched out to fill a two-hour time slot by employing the author's life to lend an added dimension to the dramatic presentation of his tale. This rather unusual format for the television version of a short story, which was the brain child of producer Herbert Brodkin, might have become unwieldy, "mingling fact and fiction as it does," critic Hollis Alpert wrote in *The Saturday Review* prior to the premier telecast. But an advance screening of the teleplay had convinced him otherwise.[2]

During the opening credits of the TV play we see Scott and Zelda Fitzgerald (Richard Chamberlain and Blythe Danner) in the ballroom of the luxury liner "Carmania," returning home from their European trip. "There's that writer," someone says to a companion at another table, "and his wife who was the original flapper." As the credits end, the Fitzgeralds are seen driving to Ellerslie with Scott's old roommate from college. "As soon as we settle down here," Scott confides to his friend, "I will have to write a story to pay for our trip; and I haven't even got an idea."

Nor are any ideas for a story forthcoming as he sits silently, drinking alone, while his wife practices her ballet routines elsewhere in the house. Referring to their increasing estrangement, he mutters, "We used to dance together. . . ." Later, when they quarrel about her belated aspirations to be a professional ballerina, Scott accuses her of pursuing her own career as a way of having a professional life to rival his. Zelda counters that, in effect, she wants to carve out a separate self-identity for herself, so that she can be something other than simply Mrs. F. Scott Fitzgerald. "I was someone once," she exclaims, "the prettiest girl in Montgomery, Alabama."

With this remark still ringing in his ears, Fitzgerald walks around the grounds of Ellerslie. As he gazes at the old mansion, the house momentarily dissolves into the home of Ailie Calhoun (Susan Sarandon), the heroine of the story he is on the brink of composing. Later, when he is getting a haircut, his own image dissolves for a moment into that of Andy (David Huffman), the hero of the story, sitting in the barber chair in Fitzgerald's place, wearing a World War I uniform, Fitzgerald goes home to his study, takes out a fresh sheet of paper and writes across the top: "The Last of the Belles." Then he begins his story: "A day came when I went into Tarleton for a haircut and ran into a nice fellow named Bill Knowles. . . ."[3]

In this subtly visual manner scriptwriter James Costigan brilliantly introduces the bittersweet story which Fitzgerald has conjured up in his imagination, derived from Fitzgerald's memories of meeting Zelda while he was stationed at an army camp near her home in Montgomery during World War I. The teleplay then proceeds to dramatize the first segment of the short story, in which Bill introduces Andy to Ailie on the porch of the house which Fitzgerald had imagined earlier, when the plot of the tale first began to seep into his creative imagination.

In order to indicate the extent to which Fitzgerald identifies with his hero, Costigan more than once has Andy begin to comment on the action, voice-over on the sound track, and then has Fitzgerald's voice replace that of Andy's. Simultaneously the scene dissolves from Andy to the author at his desk writing down the lines we hear him speaking, which are in each case taken verbatim from the short story.

Thus, when Andy observes how carelessly Ailie is trifling with the affections of several service men, himself among them, he reflects on the sound track, "Of course I should have made one of those fine moral decisions that people make in books, and despised her." Then Fitzgerald's voice continues, "On the contrary, I don't doubt that she could still have had me by raising her hand."[4] With that, we are once more back with Fitzgerald in his study as he paces the room, mulling over where the plot should go from there, as Zelda's practice record blares in the background.

The story reaches its climax with Andy returning to Tarleton six years after the Armistice and proposing to Ailie, who politely declines his offer. No longer the ageless debutante, she explains that she is at long last going to settle down; she will be married in another month. Andy's proposal is significant, since it reflects his undiminished loyalty and devotion to Ailie; for he is still prepared to marry her after all these years, in spite of the fact that she is no longer the haunting young beauty that he had enshrined in his memory. Although she makes it clear to him that they will never see each other again, he invites her, just for old time's sake, to accompany him on a nostalgic tour of the old army camp where he had been billeted in the days when he and his buddies courted her; she obliges.

Andy wanders about the empty field that had once been the company streets of the camp, futilely searching among the rusty tin cans in the underbrush for his vanished youth. As he regretfully turns his back upon the scene, he begins to reflect sadly that he and Ailie have both been forced to reconcile themselves to the fact that the romantic interlude they once shared now belongs to an irretrievable past. On the sound track we hear Andy say, "All I could be sure of was this place that had once been so full of life and effort was gone, as if it had never existed"; and the author's voice goes on to conclude that, furthermore, "in another month Ailie would be gone, and the South would be empty for me forever."[5]

As we cut for the last time from Andy's words to his creator's, the site of the deserted army camp gives way to Ellerslie, where we see Fitzgerald writing down the last lines of the story we have just heard him speak. Having worked through the night, Fitzgerald goes out to the porch to greet the morning. His wife, attired in a tutu, joins him for a moment before beginning another day at her practice bar. She seems to sense that his newly completed story is about the days when she was the belle of the ball. "I know this house is supposed to be haunted," she says, "but I never thought I'd be the ghost." What she is implying is that Fitzgerald sees her as the ghost of her former self; that is, as the younger version of herself on whom he has just finished modeling the heroine of his story. She continues, "That's the wonderful thing about being a writer. If you don't like the way things turned out, you just make them be the way they should have been." This is perhaps her way of saying that she and her husband would both be better off if they resisted the temptation to live in the past and made a fresh attempt to accept themselves and each other as they are in the present—which is what the viewer knows the principals in "The Last of the Belles" were forced to do in the end. Fitzgerald looks at his wife wistfully, and on this note of tentative reconciliation the teleplay ends.

All in all, one can easily agree with Alpert that director George Schaefer brought off the wedding of fact and fiction which characterizes *F. Scott Fitzgerald and "The Last of the Belles"* superbly well, forging a telefilm "replete with charm and nostalgia" in the scenes devoted to the dramatization of the short story, which in turn serve as a counterpoint to the "bitter flavor" of the scenes set at Ellerslie."[6]

One must also praise the performances which Schaefer drew from all four of the principals in the production. The casting of newcomers like Susan Sarandon and David Huffman was particularly felicitous. It was very wise indeed not to have actors with familiar faces enacting the roles of Ailie and Andy, but to choose instead fresh, young talents who would not be identified in the viewer's mind with a number of previous parts they had played. Susan Sarandon and David Huffman filled the bill nicely, for both gave immaculate performances.

Scottie Fitzgerald Smith was particularly pleased with Ms. Sarandon, whom she felt was just giddy enough, but canny too, to be believable as the belle. So often, she went on to explain, the actresses who play her father's Southern heroines "are trying too hard to be Southern, which is hard for a non-Southerner (Mia Farrow [in the 1974 *Great Gatsby*], for instance)." But Susan Sarandon "seemed at ease in the part." As for the actors who played her parents, Scottie Smith thought that "Richard Chamberlain seemed a convincing FSF, though there is little physical resemblance. Blythe Danner had just the right wispy-though-intense quality" to be Zelda Fitzgerald.

Scottie Smith was also happy with the location photography, which was shot in Savannah, Georgia, for the fictional part of the telefilm. In fact, it was the dramatization of the short story which caused her to rank *The Last of the Belles* among the very best adaptations of her father's work, as opposed to the biographical sections of the teleplay centered on her parents, which she found "full of cliches and exaggerations."[7]

It is true that Costigan's script simplified to a considerable degree the sources of tension between the Fitzgeralds at this point in their married lives, basically boiling down their disagreements to the question of whether or not Zelda should have a career of her own. Admittedly their marital problems were more complicated than that, as we shall see later. Still, given the format of the telefilm, which was committed to dramatizing a short story as well as to depicting the Fitzgeralds' personal lives, Costigan perhaps delineated their emotional conflicts as fully as could be expected under the circumstances.

Although some reviewers shared Scottie Smith's reservations about the biographical segments of the TV play, several critics who saw an advance screening of the telefilm were so favorably disposed to *F. Scott Fitzgerald and "The Last of the Belles"* that they suggested that it be released as a theatrical feature. Ed Vane, national program director for ABC-TV, replied that, since the drama was designed for TV, that was where it belonged. "Wouldn't it seem as though we were diminishing our own medium if we set out to do quality work, achieve it, and then say in effect that it's too good for the medium" for which it was made.[8]

"Babylon Revisited": The Short Story

The last time that a Fitzgerald short story was made into a full-length movie for theatrical release, rather than dramatized for television, was in 1954 when MGM produced the movie version of "Babylon Revisited," which was entitled *The Last Time I Saw Paris*. Even though this film was produced long before the teleplay of "The Last of the Belles" with which it is paired in this chapter, the short story on which

The Last Time I Saw Paris is based takes place during the depression rather than during the earlier Jazz Age, the setting of most of the Fitzgerald stories that have been adapted to either the big screen or the little screen.

In contrast to the telefilm of "The Last of the Belles," the plot of "Babylon Revisited" was expanded to make a feature-length film by the more conventional method of creating additional episodes for the movie version which were not in the original short story. But *The Last Time I Saw Paris* was not the first attempt to fashion a screenplay from "Babylon." Fitzgerald himself had tried his hand at composing a screen adaptation of "Babylon" toward the end of his life; and we shall of course first consider his scenario for the film, before going on to analyze the movie that was actually made of the story from a different script.

As for the short story itself, its origin is even more intimately associated with Fitzgerald's private life than was "The Last of the Belles." In fact it grew out of a serious crisis in Fitzgerald's life. By 1930 Zelda Fitzgerald was hospitalized in the wake of the first of a series of mental breakdowns, and Fitzgerald's continuing drinking problem was becoming more acute. Under the circumstances, he feared that his sister-in-law, Rosalind Sayre Smith, might take steps to have him declared unfit to be in charge of his daughter Scottie. After a quarrel with Rosalind Smith, in which she strongly suggested that perhaps Scottie would be better off living with her and her husband than remaining under the care of her father, Fitzgerald was moved to write "Babylon Revisited," which appeared in the *Post* in early 1931.

In the story Charlie Wales forfeits the custody of his nine-year-old daughter Honoria to his mean-spirited sister-in-law Marion Peters, whereas in real life Fitzgerald never at any time lost legal guardianship of his daughter. In the short story, then, he depicted the intolerable anguish that this turn of events would have caused him, had it ever come about.

Judging by Fitzgerald's on-going correspondence with his sister-in-law, one can see that Rosalind Smith's opinion of him was no better than Marion Peters's estimation of Charlie Wales. Three years after the publication of the short story, Fitzgerald was still accusing Rosalind Smith, with some justification, of being "irreparably prejudiced" against him.[9] At one point she intimated in a letter to Fitzgerald that the unstable lives which he and Zelda had lived in the first decade of their marriage had been one of the principal causes of her sister's emotional collapse. Rosalind even went so far as to state in one angry letter that she wished that Zelda might die in a mental institution, rather than return to the mad world that she and Scott had created for themselves.

Although I shall subsequently have more to say about the root causes of Zelda Fitzgerald's mental illness, suffice it to say at this juncture that it is true that during the course of the Roaring Twenties the Fitzgeralds did live an unsettled existence. They were constantly on the move, restlessly traipsing around Europe as well as the United States. As a matter of fact, there were times when Zelda had felt lonely and depressed, as they found themselves temporarily sojourning in yet one more foreign capital—and her husband thoughtlessly left her alone while he went on the town without her. Yet, when Fitzgerald honestly expressed his regrets about his behavior toward his wife to Dr. Paul Bleuler, one of the psychiatrists who was treating her, the latter was reassuring. Had Fitzgerald been more sensitive and solicitous towards his wife in the past, the doctor said, he might have slowed down the progress of his wife's emotional decline; but in any case he could not have prevented her breakdown. Nonetheless, one senses in his correspondence during this period that, in the light of Zelda's present plight, he believed that he should have been more caring and dependable in his relationship with his wife; and that sense of remorse permeates "Babylon Revisited."

Fitzgerald was nothing if not aware of his shortcomings; so he did not really need Rosalind Smith or anyone else to tell him that he and Zelda, along with a lot of other people, had lived too high, wide, and handsome during the boom days of the twenties. Moreover, the dissipation in the decade of the twenties looked even more reprehensible from the vantage point of the Great Depression in the bleak, austere decade of the thirties. "Somebody had blundered and the most expensive orgy in history was over," he wrote in an essay published shortly after "Babylon Revisited." "Now once more the belt is tight, and we summon the proper expression of horror as we look back at our wasted youth."[10]

If he had heralded the birth of his young illusions in his fiction of the early twenties when the nation was embarking on the Jazz Age, he once told a *Post* editor, then "Babylon Revisited" announced the death of those same illusions. In Charlie Wales, then, Fitzgerald compellingly expressed that disillusionment with himself and the frivolous era he had just lived through.

When Charlie returns in 1930 to Paris, where he (like Fitzgerald) had spent some time in the twenties, he finds the city still recovering from the dissolute Babylonian bacchanal that boatloads of American tourists had helped to create in the City of Lights throughout the previous decade. Charlie's own irresponsible conduct is epitomized by the mad moment the year before, when he climaxed a liquor-fueled quarrel with his wife Helen by locking her out in the snow, thereby accelerating her death from heart disease.

It never occurred to him that she would suffer serious harm as a result of his impulsive action, Charlie wails poignantly. In those days a man thought he could cavalierly toss someone out in the snow with impunity, "because the snow of twenty-nine wasn't real snow. If you didn't want it to be real snow, you just paid some money."[11] In other words, Charlie made the mistake of thinking that one could always buy off misfortune, even when one had brought it on one's self and others. Charlie's insight into his earlier reprehensible behavior has come too late to avert his personal tragedy, but his willingness to own up to what he has done makes his story a heartbreaking tale, one of Fitzgerald's best.

"Babylon Revisited": Fitzgerald's Scenario

During the last year of Fitzgerald's life, while he was freelancing in Hollywood, independent producer Lester Cowan (*My Little Chickadee*) purchased the screen rights to "Babylon Revisited" for $1,000. In addition, he offered Fitzgerald a weekly salary of $500 to cover his living expenses while he composed a movie scenario based on his story, all with a view to the film being eventually made for Columbia Pictures.

Fitzgerald wrote to Scottie that he was delighted to be able personally to adapt what he rightly termed this "magnificent story" to the screen[12] and later wrote to his Hollywood agent that he was really sweating over the scenario. But because he was adapting one of his own fictional works for filming, it was "pleasant sweat, so to speak, and rather more fun than I've ever had in pictures."[13]

Fitzgerald worked on his screenplay, which he called *Cosmopolitan*, throughout the spring and summer of 1940, even after Cowan stopped his salary in June. In mid-August Fitzgerald wrote to Maxwell Perkins, "I finished the job, ... working the last weeks without pay on a gamble."[14] He had continued laboring over the *Cosmopolitan* script without remuneration because he was betting that some producer, if not Cowan, would be willing to finance the picture, once they had read his completed script; in which case, as he explained later to his wife, he might finally gain some real status in Hollywood, "as a movie man, and not a novelist."[15] No such luck.

Why had Cowan lost interest in a project which he himself had initiated? First of all, Cowan had originally counted on securing Shirley Temple for the key role of Charlie Wales's daughter (called Victoria, not Honoria, in the screenplay); but he failed to obtain the services of the young superstar for the part. Because Fitzgerald realized the importance of having a box office favorite like Ms. Temple appear in the picture, he spent an entire afternoon with the young actress and her mother vainly trying to charm them into accepting Cowan's offer to do the picture.

"I remember Fitzgerald as a kindly, thin and pale man," the actress said many years afterward. Like David Niven, who also met Fitzgerald during this period, Shirley Temple was impressed that Fitzgerald could consume an entire six-pack of Coca Cola in just a couple of hours. "As a young girl, I thought this to be a stunning accomplishment. In fact, I still do!"[16] Beyond that, nothing came of the visit.

The second reason why *Cosmopolitan* never reached the screen was that, despite some reports to the contrary, the script was not nearly as good as Fitzgerald thought—or hoped—it would be. One story goes that several years after Fitzgerald's death Cowan called in another scriptwriter to revise the screenplay; but the latter returned it untouched, with the accompanying comment that *Cosmopolitan* was the most perfect movie script he had ever read. "You're absolutely right," Cowan is supposed to have replied. "I'll pay you $2,000 a week to stay out of here and keep me from changing a word of it."[17]

This patently apocryphal anecdote has been naively recounted as Gospel by Fitzgerald's biographer Arthur Mizener, despite the fact that the same frugal producer who only paid Fitzgerald $500 a week to write the screenplay in the first place would hardly have capriciously offered someone else four times that much to leave it alone. Whatever truth there is to be found in this little tale probably derives from an actual encounter between Cowan and Budd Schulberg, whom the producer wished to rewrite Fitzgerald's script for *Cosmopolitan*. After examining the screenplay, Schulberg told Cowan that his late friend's script was "astonishingly good just as it was."[18]

In contrast, the frank assessment of *Cosmopolitan* by another Fitzgerald scholar, Henry Piper, is that Fitzgerald's adaptation of "Babylon Revisited" is just not very good; and I am inclined to agree with him, for the reasons he puts forth. According to Piper, the fundamental problem with the screenplay is that, in trying to stretch the plot of one of his best short stories into a feature-length film, Fitzgerald cheapened his original story by padding out the plot of his fragile tale of love and loss with the sort of glossy melodramatic material that he all too often assumed was necessary to hold what he considered to be the limited attention span of the mass audience.

"To the story of Charles Wales's touching effort to regain custody of his small daughter," Piper writes, "he added a sentimental love story between Wales and a hospital nurse, as well as a gangster subplot," in which Charlie's crooked business partner Dwight Schuyler seeks to have him murdered in order to cash in the insurance policy their firm holds on Charlie.[19] In the process, Piper concludes, the portrayal of the tender relationship between father and daughter is well-nigh obliterated. As film scholar Robert Gessner suggests, in essence Fitzgerald tried so hard to make his screen adaptation of "Babylon Revisited" a saleable commodity in the Hollywood marketplace, that he wound up altering his short masterpiece almost beyond recognition.[20]

Just about all that is left of "Babylon Revisited" in the screenplay for *Cosmopolitan* is the confrontation between Charlie and his sister-in-law over the guardianship of his little daughter. In fact, this scene contains one of the few bits of dialogue brought over from the original story, as Marion tells Charlie, "My duty is entirely to Helen. . . . I try to think what she would have wanted me to do."[21] Otherwise, as film scholar Lawrence Stewart states in his exhaustive study of *Cosmopolitan* in the *Fitzgerald/Hemingway Annual* for 1971, Fitzgerald's script has little in common with what he himself had called his magnificent short story. Indeed, Fitzgerald even cancels the tragic finale of the short story by allowing Charlie to be reunited with his daughter in *Cosmopolitan*. In consequence, Latham's claim that this particular screenplay represents the culmination of Fitzgerald's years of screenwork is simply wishful thinking and is not borne out by a close analysis of the work at hand.

But the question remains, would the shooting script of the 1954 motion picture version of "Babylon Revisited" be any better than

Fitzgerald's earlier screenplay? There was reason to believe that it would be.

The Last Time I Saw Paris: The Film

After Schulberg refused to rewrite Fitzgerald's script, Cowan shelved the project for some time, until he finally decided to engage two other screenwriters to start afresh on a new adaptation of "Babylon Revisited." This new screenplay, which Cowan eventually sold to Fitzgerald's former employer, MGM, for $40,000, was the work of Julius and Philip Epstein, a crack writing team of identical twins, who had both already earned Oscars for the script of *Casablanca* (1943), before turning their talents to adapting "Babylon Revisited" to the screen.

In addition to a script that was the handiwork of two distinguished screenwriters, MGM also had the services of the prominent filmmaker Richard Brooks to direct the picture. Brooks, who would become noted for his screen versions of such literary classics as Conrad's *Lord Jim*, was the first director of consequence to film a screen adaptation of one of Fitzgerald's stories, short or long. So it might have been hoped that a creditable film version of "Babylon Revisited" would at last be forthcoming from Hollywood, despite the fact that the studio brass made a couple of decisions regarding the production of the picture that were less than felicitous.

Replacing the title of the short story with the name of a sentimental love song by Jerome Kern, "The Last Time I Saw Paris," was relatively harmless. But then the front office went on to make the ill-advised decision to update the setting of the story from post-World War I Paris to post-World War II Paris, on the assumption that contemporary audiences could relate more readily to a film set in the recent past than to one set in the more distant past. Brooks, who discussed with me his adaptations of literature to the screen, did not agree with this decision, which was made before he was assigned to direct the picture; he firmly believed that since Fitzgerald's story was to some extent a requiem for the Roaring Twenties, the period setting was indigenous to the story as Fitzgerald had conceived it. But he was overruled.[22]

As for the ways in which the Epsteins overhauled the plot of

Fitzgerald's short story in order to make it fit the dimensions of a theatrical feature, the new material which the brothers invented for this purpose by and large fit into the fabric of their literary source. Fellow screenwriter Fay Kanin has since singled out Julius Epstein in particular as being adept at creating solid plot lines for films. "His stories always have good bones."[23]

The key element in the expansion of the story line to feature-length proportions was changing Charlie's occupation from that of a businessman to that of his creator, a professional writer. Most of the additional plot material which was invented for the film was spun out of this one fundamental modification in the characterization of Charlie Wills, as he is called in the movie. It was, for example, made the basis of the growing estrangement between Charlie (Van Johnson) and Helen (Elizabeth Taylor) in the film.

Since the reasons for the gradual breakdown of their marriage could only be lightly sketched within the narrow confines of a short story, the Epsteins opted to explain it in the film by showing how the deterioration of Charlie's career as a writer causes him increasingly to take refuge in the bottle, which in turn puts a strain on his marriage. Because Fitzgerald's own drinking became more of a serious problem when his literary career went into eclipse in the thirties, film scholar Foster Hirsch is correct in stating that in the movie "Van Johnson is clearly playing a variant on the fabled author himself."[24] I, for one, have no quarrel with this fact.

Granted, there are definite analogies between Scott Fitzgerald and Charlie Wills in the movie; but the essential parallel between them, namely, the effort which each must make to hold on to the love of a beloved daughter, was firmly embedded in "Babylon Revisited" long before it was turned into *The Last Time I Saw Paris*. It seems, therefore, dramatically and artistically right that the scriptwriters should follow Fitzgerald's lead in utilizing further details from the author's life, over and above those which he had himself already put into his story, in order to flesh out their screenplay. Unfortunately, although they did not introduce into the plot the kind of lurid melodramatics that Fitzgerald had laid on with a trowel in his script, the screenwriters did take other liberties with Fitzgerald's story, which cannot be so easily justified.

The crucial crisis of both short story and film is, once again, the bitter confrontation between Charlie and the small-minded Marion

(Donna Reed), who turns a deaf ear to Charlie's heartfelt petition that he be allowed to have his daughter Vickie back, so that he can make up for his previous wanton behavior by being both father and mother to the girl. At this point it looks as if the film will follow the short story by dramatizing its compelling conclusion, wherein Charlie and his daughter are once more separated, this time possibly for good.

Not a bit of it. Encouraged by her husband, who has all along been sympathetic to Charlie's cause, Marion experiences a last-minute change of heart. She catches up with Charlie, whom only moments before she had driven from her home, and turns Victoria over to him. So, instead of the film closing as the story does, with Charlie musing disconsolately that he is "absolutely sure Helen wouldn't have wanted him to be so alone,"[25] Charlie's sentiments are transferred in the film to Marion, who says to him, "I don't think Helen would have wanted you to be alone."

This far-too-facile attempt in the movie's final moments to retool Marion into a much more forgiving and generous character was dictated by the myth in the film industry, still subscribed to in those days by many producers, that films with upbeat endings usually attracted a larger audience than films with downbeat endings. Such producers saw popular "tearjerkers" like *Camille* and *Three Comrades* merely as the occasional exceptions that prove the rule. In the last reel of *Paris* the attempt to realign Marion's character in a way that would justify a happy conclusion rings false, precisely because the screenplay has been fairly faithful to the short story up to this point by presenting Marion as a calculating and selfish woman. Her abrupt about-face in the closing moments of the movie is inconsistent with her character as already established in the film and is, therefore, hardly credible.

The compromised ending of *Paris* was symptomatic of the fact that, as Richard Brooks states, many studio executives at the time had a predilection for sentimental endings of this sort. When he tried to tone down the sentimentality that tinged movies like *Paris* while he was making them, he was resisted by the front office. Studio boss Louis B. Mayer told him, "You seem like a nice fellow, but if you could only make our kind of movies it would be much better."[26] "I can't blame them" for their attitude, says Brooks; but he concedes, "I should just not have gone along with it," when it came to sending the audience away with a smile rather than a tear at the end of a picture like *Paris*.[27]

Still *The Last Time I Saw Paris*, when all is said and done, turned out to be a better picture than *Cosmopolitan* could ever have been. The MGM movie of "Babylon" may have departed from its source in some ways, as with Marion's eleventh hour change of heart; but Fitzgerald's screenplay, which he hoked up with the introduction of a new love interest for Charlie, not to mention a contract killer threatening Charlie's life, nearly lost sight of his original short story altogether.

On the other hand, since *The Last Time I Saw Paris* was deprived of the rich ambience of Paris after World War I, which permeated the short story, and since the movie was likewise deprived of the hard-edged conclusion of Fitzgerald's original story, it was written off by many reviewers as a classy contemporary soap opera. "The soft soap is smeared so smoothly, and that old Jerome Kern tune is played so insistently," smirked Bosley Crowther in *The New York Times*, that the movie "may turn the public's heart to toothpaste."[28] *Paris* was better than Crowther opined, but not as good as it could have been.

In sum, Fitzgerald's short fiction has not fared well on film, although *Bernice Bobs Her Hair* and *The Last of the Belles* do stand out as superior to the general run of adaptations of his short fiction. Nonetheless, all of the films discussed in this section of our study that are still extant are well worth watching. For all of them can boast some sequences that retain the flavor of Fitzgerald's narrative genius and that serve to rescue each film from foundering on the shores of mediocrity.

For example, *The Last Time I Saw Paris* comes to life when, following the short story, it dramatizes in a most touching manner a frantic father's efforts to win his cherished daughter away from a calloused in-law by sincerely pleading that he has by now surely expiated his past sins. Moreover, despite the fact that the film version of "Babylon Revisited" departs from the original ending of Fitzgerald's story, the film still reflects Fitzgerald's abiding theme that one can only transcend one's moral transgressions by accepting responsibility for the suffering that they have caused.

Most of the other Fitzgerald short stories that have been adapted to the screen, such as the early flapper tales, are lightweight yarns that do not profess to make a serious thematic point of this kind. There are, however, deeper thematic implications in Fitzgerald's novels and the films made from them.

Fitzgerald successfully fought to retain the stark ending of his screenplay for the anti-war film Three Comrades *in which the dead and the living are shown facing the future together.* Metro-Goldwyn-Mayer, 1938.

Fitzgerald worked on the scenario for The Women *which starred Norma Shearer (second from right) who, along with her husband, producer Irving Thalberg, inspired Fitzgerald's best fiction about Hollywood.*

Metro-Goldwyn-Mayer, 1939.

Vivian Leigh and Clark Gable are coached by George Cukor in one of the scenes he directed for Gone with the Wind, *the screenplay of which Fitzgerald was asked to revise just before the film went into production.*
Selznick International, 1939.

Shelley Duvall in the title role of Bernice Bobs
Her Hair, *the screen adaptation of one of
Fitzgerald's short stories.*
Learning in Focus, Incorporated, 1976.

Van Johnson, Sandra Descher, and Elizabeth Taylor as Charlie, Vicki, and Helen Wills in The Last Time I Saw Paris, *based on Fitzgerald's story* "Babylon Revisted."
Metro-Goldwyn-Mayer, 1954.

This photo of Marie Prevost and Kenneth Harlan playing Gloria and Anthony Patch in the film version of Fitzgerald's novel The Beautiful and Damned *is virtually all that remains of this lost film.*
Warner Brothers, 1922.

Daisy (Lois Wilson) renews her relationship with
Jay Gatsby (Warren Baxter) in the silent version
of The Great Gatsby, *now lost.*
Paramount, 1926.

The wartime courtship of Jay Gatsby (Alan Ladd) and Daisy (Betty Field) in the first sound remake of The Great Gatsby.
Paramount, 1949.

*The wartime courtship of Daisy (Mia Farrow) and
Jay Gatsby (Robert Redford) in the color remake of*
The Great Gatsby.
Paramount, 1974.

Jennifer Jones as Nicole Diver in Tender Is the
Night.
Twentieth Century-Fox, 1962.

Dick Diver (Jason Robards, Jr.) discusses his wife Nicole with her sister Baby Warren (Joan Fontaine) in Tender Is the Night.
Twentieth Century-Fox, 1962.

Producer Irving Thalberg (left), for whom Fitzgerald worked at MGM in the early thirties, was the model for the hero of his last novel, The Last Tycoon.

*Robert DeNiro (center, foreground) as Monroe
Stahr, the character based on Irving Thalberg, in
the film version of* The Last Tycoon.
Paramount, 1976.

Scott and Zelda Fitzgerald, pictured here with their daughter Scottie, have been impersonated by actors both in motion pictures and on television.

*Helen Vinson and Gary Cooper play Dora and
Tony Barrett, the screen counterparts of Zelda and
Scott Fitzgerald in* The Wedding Night.
Goldwyn Productions, 1935.

Scott Fitzgerald (Gregory Peck) and Sheilah Graham (Deborah Kerr) are told by a bookseller that Fitzgerald's books are no longer in stock. Twentieth Century-Fox, 1959.

PART THREE

THE FILMS
OF FITZGERALD'S
NOVELS

FIVE

THE LOST GENERATION:

THIS SIDE OF PARADISE AND

THE BEAUTIFUL AND DAMNED

> Here was a new generation ... dedicated more than the last to the fear of poverty and the worship of success.
>
> —*F. Scott Fitzgerald*

> You are all a lost generation. ... You have no respect for anything. You drink yourselves to death.
>
> —*Gertrude Stein*

The huge, florid Pulitzer fountain, in which Scott Fitzgerald splashed about one fabled night long ago, still stands in front of New York's Plaza Hotel, though it has long since gone dry. Fitzgerald once explained to his old friend from college, writer Edmund Wilson, that his reason for jumping into the fountain was to express his sheer joy at being once again in New York City, a town which he loved and often visited throughout his life.

It is not surprising that a Midwesterner like Fitzgerald, born and bred in St. Paul, Minnesota, would never cease to be dazzled by the glamor of New York, nor that, as a consequence, the heroes of most of his novels would spend a good deal of time there, starting with Amory Blaine, the central figure in his very first novel, *This Side of Paradise* (1920). *This Side of Paradise* is perhaps the most autobiographical of all of his novels, heavily drawing as it does on his memories of his Roman Catholic youth. Hence, I shall preface the analysis of the novel and the scenario that Fitzgerald derived from it with an examination of Fitzgerald's early years.

Portrait of the Artist As a Young Man

Francis Scott Key Fitzgerald was born in St. Paul at 3:30 P.M. on Sunday, September 24, 1896, to Edward and Mary McQuillan Fitzgerald. His best-known forebear—a second cousin three times removed on his mother's side—was, of course, the composer of the national anthem after whom he was named. The Fitzgeralds were staunch Irish Catholics; and Scott was duly baptized on October 6 by Father John T. Harrison, pastor of St. Joseph's Church.

Because his father's job as a business representative of Procter and Gamble required that the family move often during these years, in 1903 the Fitzgeralds settled for a time in Buffalo, New York. There Scott attended Holy Angels Academy and, so the *Ledger* tells us on page 158, "fell under the spell of a Catholic preacher," Father Michael Fallon, of Holy Angels Church. In September 1905 Scott passed on to Ms. Narden's, another Catholic parochial school, where the future professional writer composed what he called a "celebrated essay" comparing George Washington to St. Ignatius Loyola (*Ledger*, p.161), and where he began to take satisfaction in improving his budding writing ability.

The Fitzgeralds returned to St. Paul in 1908 and the family moved into a section of the city that was predominantly populated by well-to-do Catholic families, though the Fitzgeralds were less affluent than most of their Catholic neighbors, as Fitzgerald confessed in a letter to a friend which he headed "First Epistle of St. Scott."[1] Then, in the fall of 1908, Fitzgerald entered St. Paul's Academy, which was a nonsectarian school. Nevertheless his religious training continued, as evidenced by his noting in his *Ledger* that by 1910 he was not only praying quite a bit, but was becoming "desperately holy," and that he received Holy Communion for the first time in May of that same year.

In her book on Fitzgerald, Joan Allen writes that Fitzgerald must have been confused about the date of his initial reception of the Sacrament of Communion, since he was thirteen in 1910, several years older than it is now customary for youngsters to receive the sacrament for the first time. But it is Ms. Allen, not Fitzgerald, who is confused. When Fitzgerald received Holy Communion, Pope Pius X had not yet issued the proclamation that urged that children be allowed to receive Holy Communion soon after they reach the age of reason. Until that proclamation, young people regularly did not receive communion until they were in their early teens. I emphasize this point to underscore the fact that Fitzgerald was consistently careful and accurate in the way that he made entries in his *Ledger*; he did not do so carelessly, as Ms. Allen seems to imply that he did in the present instance.

Fitzgerald at no time in his academic career took his formal studies seriously, and his years at St. Paul's Academy were no exception. Instead of expending his energies on routine school assignments, he preferred reading the books of his choice and further developing his talent as a writer by turning out a considerable amount of juvenilia. Hence, in September 1911, the family packed him off to Newman School, a Catholic boarding school in Hackensack, New Jersey. At Newman, they hoped, young Scott would undergo a more disciplined and closely supervised training than he had had up to then while living at home. Although no one at Newman was able to inspire Fitzgerald to improve his scholastic record, he did respond positively to the influence of Father (later Monsignor) Sigourney Fay, on whom he would later model the character of Monsignor Darcy in his first novel. He also dedicated the book to Fay; and characteristically the young author, who was a wretched speller to the end of his days, misspelled Fay's given name in the dedication by leaving out the u in the dedicatee's first name. (Hemingway would be miffed in later years because Fitzgerald usually doubled the *m* in his last name.)

Fitzgerald took an immediate liking to Fay the first time he met him at Newman School because Fay fulfilled Fitzgerald's concept of the ideal priest: he was a gracious, urbane intellectual who, as Fitzgerald later wrote, represented the Roman Catholic Church to him as a "dazzling golden thing," with a ritual that possessed the "romantic glamour of an adolescent dream."[2] This new image of the

Church was important to the young Fitzgerald because, as he recalled in his *Notebooks*, back home in St. Paul, the non-Catholic boys his own age "still thought that Catholics drilled in the cellar every night," as part of their secret plot to make the pope "autocrat of the republic" (#1708). Hence, until meeting Fay, young Scott had always been somewhat on the defensive about being a Roman Catholic.

Besides giving Fitzgerald a more positive attitude toward his Irish Catholic heritage, Fay also won the lad's gratitude for being the first person of any consequence to take seriously his literary ambitions. In essence, Fitzgerald came to look upon Fay as a surrogate father, the more so because his own father, a self-effacing, mild-mannered, mediocre businessman, at no time ever made as profound an impression on his son as did this imposing cleric. Scott's attachment to Fay was such that for a time he even entertained the notion of following him into the priesthood, so that he could become a priest-novelist like the British fiction writer Monsignor Robert Hugh Benson. Fitzgerald's idea of entering the priesthood was further reinforced by his admiration for his own cousin, Thomas Delihant, a Jesuit, after whom he modeled the hero of his short story "Benediction."

Though Fitzgerald's aspirations to take sacred orders probably never amounted to much more than an acute case of hero worship, he did express his wish to become a priest one last time, when Fay died of influenza on January 10, 1919. In a letter to a mutual friend the devastated young man wrote that what impressed him most about his late mentor was that he was "so damned human"; and yet his faith always shone through "all the versatility and intellect."[3] Regardless of whether or not Fitzgerald at any time seriously entertained the notion of entering the seminary, this eulogy for Monsignor Fay is an index of his deep and lasting regard for the man who was a father-figure for him in every sense of the term.

It goes without saying that Fitzgerald never found anyone at Princeton to whom he looked up the way he did to Fay. During his college years, which lasted from the fall of 1913 to the spring of 1917, Fitzgerald maintained the same consistently poor scholastic record which he had established in his pre-college days. He devoted himself mostly to extracurriculars that helped him improve his writing skill, like contributing to the school newspaper and the literary magazine; he also served as one of the principal writers of the annual musical revue, mentioned before. Predictably, although Fitzgerald spent the better part of four years at Princeton, he never amassed enough credits to earn a diploma. Yet he remained loyal to his alma mater to the end of his life. Significantly, some two decades later, when he was stricken with the fatal heart attack, which killed him almost instantly, he was reading *The Princeton Alumni Magazine.* Scottie Smith put it best when she said, "My father belonged all his life to Princeton."[4]

During his undergraduate days Fitzgerald nurtured a college-boy crush on lovely Ginevra King, whose name first appears in the *Ledger* in July 1911, and thereafter recurs off and on until July 1918, when he met Zelda Sayre. Because Ms. King was attending finishing school in Connecticut, Fitzgerald was compelled to carry on his romance with her largely by mail, though they did see each other occasionally, as when she invited him to visit her at her family's wealthy home in Lake Forest, a fashionable suburb of Chicago, in August 1916. "Once I thought Lake Forest was the most glamorous place in the world," he reminisced in 1940 to his daughter; "maybe it was."[5]

It certainly must have seemed so to the young man from Minnesota, whose own family was clearly a rung or two below the Kings on the social ladder. As part of his *Ledger* entry about this visit, Fitzgerald set down a quotation, "Poor boys shouldn't think of marrying rich girls" (p. 170). It is not clear who made this observation in Fitzgerald's presence while he was staying in the Kings' posh home; but Richard Lehan contends in his book on Fitzgerald that it was probably Ginevra's regal father, stockbroker Charles King, who did so, because he wished to make it quite clear to Fitzgerald that he was definitely outclassed by the rich young men who were competing with him for Ginevra's favor. Lehan's reason is that Ginevra's sister Marjorie informed him many years later that there were abrasive feelings between her father and their house guest. In *This Side of Paradise* it is the mother of Rosalind Connage, the character modeled to a large extent on Ginevra King, who directs these words of warning to the novel's hero, Amory Blaine. But Fitzgerald may well have transferred the offending remark from father to mother in the novel in order not to have fiction parallel fact too closely.

Be that as it may, in the months that followed Fitzgerald's visit to Lake Forest, he and Ginevra drifted apart. Fitzgerald stoically records the end of their romance in his *Ledger* with the words, "Final break with Ginevra," in January 1917, and then goes on to mention in July 1918, "Ginevra married" (pp. 171-72). He placed the wedding invitation which she mailed him in a scrapbook with the notation, "The end of a once-poignant story."[6]

In some ways Fitzgerald never got over the loss of the first great love of his life. In point of fact, he replayed his rejection by Ginevra King more than once in his fiction, not only in *This Side of Paradise*, but also in *The Great Gatsby*, where Jay Gatsby also learns that poor boys should not aspire to wed rich girls. Commenting years later on Fitzgerald's use of his "grand passion" for her in his fiction, Ginevra King Pirie could only say that Fitzgerald was simply more serious about her than she was about him, and that she was "too thoughtless in those days" to realize how much she meant to him.[7] Twenty years after their romance, she lunched with him for old time's sake while she was passing through Hollywood; she was surprised to discover that he still cared for her. Indeed, he wrote his daughter that Ginevra was "still a charming woman," and that he regretted that he "didn't see more of her" while she was in town.[8]

Fitzgerald's student days at Princeton ended only a few months after he and Ginevra King broke off their relationship, when he applied for and got a commission in the infantry. During his stint in the service during World War I, he composed his first novel, so that he could leave something behind that would testify to his talent as a writer in the event that he did not come back from the war. (As a matter of fact, the war ended before he ever got overseas.)

Fitzgerald finished the first draft of the novel, initially entitled *The Romantic Egotist*, in March 1918. The manuscript was rejected by Scribner's, with the promise that the editors would be willing to reconsider the novel if it were extensively revised. He accordingly began revising the manuscript while he was still in the service. After he had been demobilized, he spent the summer of 1919 reworking the manuscript still more, while living in his parents' home at 599 Summit Avenue in St. Paul—which has since been designated a National Historic Landmark. He resubmitted to Scribner's his thoroughly revised novel, which he now called *This Side of Paradise*, with the result that this time it was accepted for publication.

The neophyte novelist was so euphoric about the acceptance of his novel for publication that he rushed down the street, stopping cars along the way, to share the good news with his friends. Well he might, for the book, which appeared on March 26, 1920, heralded his becoming at twenty-three the toast of the Jazz Age, the era just beginning that he himself was to name. The uncertainties of the war years were past, and America was embarking on what he termed "the greatest, gaudiest spree in history." There would be "plenty to tell about it" in his work.[9] And tell about it he would.

This Side of Paradise: The Novel

The title of Fitzgerald's first novel is derived from a poem of Rupert Brooke, which says that on this side of paradise there is little comfort to be found in the words of the wise. The younger generation coming of age at the dawn of the Roaring Twenties believed that there was little of worth to be learned from the earthly wisdom of their elders, representatives of the old order whose blundering had led the world into the global conflict that had just ended. In the novel Amory Blaine characterizes his contemporaries, who were just coming of age at the beginning of the hedonistic, devil-may-care era of the twenties, as a generation "dedicated more than the last to the fear of poverty and the worship of success; grown up to find all gods dead, all wars fought, all faiths in man shaken."[10]

In Amory we have a young man infatuated with wealth, whose personal ideal of success is summed up in his golden girl, a rich debutante named Rosalind Connage (coinage?), who is, for the most part, a caricature of Ginevra King. This mercenary young lady baldly refers to herself as Rosalind Unlimited: "Fifty-one shares, name, good-will, and everything goes at $25,000 a year" (p. 174). After Amory inevitably loses Rosalind to the highest bidder, he muses that he no longer wanted "her youth, the fresh radiance of her body and mind, the stuff she was selling now once and for all. So far as he was concerned, young Rosalind was dead" (p. 253).

By the end of the book Amory is convinced that he has grown substantially in self-knowledge and even attained a deeper understanding of life itself as a result of the loss of Rosalind and of the other disappointments and setbacks he has suffered in the course of the novel. Yet, like the love-sick adolescent he is, Amory continues to pine for Rosalind even after his golden girl has proven herself to be nothing more than dross. Hence, by suggesting that Amory has by no means shaken off the romantic illusions which he has crystallized in Rosalind, Fitzgerald undercuts Amory's smug conviction that he has reached maturity. It seems that the young novelist did not attempt to depict in Amory a maturity which he himself had not yet attained. To that extent, then, as Mizener puts it, "the book is hardly wiser than its hero."[11]

There is certainly no question that the author in many ways identifies with his hero. For example, Amory's religious doubts, which remain unresolved at the end of the book, are to some degree a reflection of Fitzgerald's own questionings about the teachings of the faith in which he had been schooled since childhood. At precisely the time that Fitzgerald was writing the first draft of the novel, he noted in his *Ledger* that 1918 was his "last year as a Catholic," during which he had experienced his "last Catholic revival" (p. 172). Literary critic Kenneth Eble takes Amory's speculations in the last pages of the novel as to whether or not he can get along without the faith of his fathers, coupled with the *Ledger* items just cited, to mean that *This Side of Paradise* represents Fitzgerald's own "definite and permanent" rejection of the Church.[12]

It may be true that Fitzgerald ceased to attend Catholic services as he grew older, but he never ceased to be a sincere believer all his life. Therefore it is safe to infer that his designation of 1918 as his last year as a Catholic referred to his drifting away from regularly attending services, rather than to his wholesale abandonment of the Catholic faith. After all, during the same period in which he made the *Ledger* entries just mentioned, he was busy immortalizing Monsignor Fay as Monsignor Darcy in his novel, and in the bargain making him the most sympathetic character in the book, thereby giving testimony for all time to his spiritual sonship of a man who stood for the very beliefs the author had espoused as a Catholic.

Moreover, as Mizener notes, those very beliefs are the basis of the "ingrained moral sense" by which the author evaluates the behavior of the characters in the book.[13] As indicated above, it was from his Catholic upbringing that Fitzgerald drew the moral vision of which Mizener speaks, and which one finds embedded in his fiction. This vision, we remember, implies that one must adhere to a specific set of moral values, and pay the price which one's departures from that code of behavior bring with it.

That Fitzgerald may have given up the external practice of Roman Catholicism but not his attachment to the tenets of its creed, is clear from a letter which he sent to Edmund Wilson while he was revising the manuscript of *This Side of Paradise*. "I am ashamed to say that my Catholicism is scarcely more than a memory," he wrote; but then he immediately corrected himself by adding, "No, that's wrong; it's more than that; at any rate I go not to the church."[14] That his Catholicism was undoubtedly more than a mere memory is further evidenced by a remark he made on another occasion to a friend just after they had left a speakeasy. Partying of that sort was, he said, "a form of suicide," and he added, "the old Catholic in me secretly disapproves."[15]

It is true that another acquaintance heard Fitzgerald muttering to himself as they drove past a Catholic Church one evening, "God damn the Catholic Church; . . . God damn God!"[16] Instead of proving that Fitzgerald had rejected his faith outright, however, these remarks can just as easily be taken as an expression, in one of his fits of black depression, of his feeling that God and the Church might have given up on him, rather than the other way round. Besides, in an interview which he gave in 1928, nearly a decade after the writing of *This Side of Paradise*, he still listed the Roman Catholic Church as among the chief influences on his life that stemmed from his youth."[17]

Then too, even Eble is prepared to concede that "the moral concern and the sense of evil to be found in all his serious work may be important consequences of his youthful religious interest."[18] Indeed they are, for, as Bruccoli has written, "the element of the supernatural found . . . continuing expression in his fiction," even after he had wandered from official church membership.[19] In the mid-twenties journalist Ernest Boyd perceptively summed up Fitzgerald's Catholic sensibility by saying that "there are still venial and mortal sins in his calendar, and . . . his Catholic heaven" is not so distant that he might be misled into thinking that the shabby dreams of the present era are "a substitute for paradise." Fitzgerald's religious vision, Boyd continued, is "permeated with the conviction of sin, which is much happier than the conviction that the way to Utopia is paved with adultery."[20] Given the novel's success, it was almost inevitable that Fitzgerald would receive offers for the film rights; for, as he rightly observed to Wilson, no one else had written so searching a novel about the youth of their generation. The first nibble came from an agent named Jay Packard two months after the publication of *This Side of Paradise*, but this deal failed to materialize.

Two years later Fitzgerald accepted an offer from William G. Kahlert and Einar A. Berg of Outlook Photoplays, who had already made a movie of Sinclair Lewis's novel *Free Air*. There was some talk of Scott and Zelda Fitzgerald co-starring in the film; but Maxwell Perkins was against the idea, insisting with some justification that acting in the picture would spell the end of Fitzgerald's reputation as a serious novelist. In any event, nothing came of this attempt to bring Fitzgerald's novel to the screen either; and so three months later he sold the screen rights to Paramount for $10,000, with the understanding that he would devise a screen treatment of the book.

This Side of Paradise: Fitzgerald's Scenario

Fitzgerald told interviewer B. F. Wilson in an article published in the November 1923 issue of *Metropolitan Magazine* that he had recently finished a ten-thousand-word condensation of his novel for Paramount, and described the treatment as including some variations on his original story that would make it more suitable for filming. Since the screen treatment of *Paradise* mentioned to the interviewer is much longer than the existing eleven-page typed scenario on file at Princeton, the latter is most probably a digest of the original treatment, presumably designed to give the studio executives an overview of the longer scenario. Nevertheless, the available synopsis of the screen story of *Paradise* is detailed enough to give anyone who peruses it a sufficient grasp of what Fitzgerald intended the film adaptation of his novel to be like.

In his screen treatment of *Paradise,* Fitzgerald turned his thought-provoking story into a piece of sentimental melodrama, the same kind of treatment he was to give his film adaptation of "Babylon Revisited," already treated. In the case of *Paradise,* he had to go to a great deal of trouble to engineer a happy ending, since it is not to be found in the original novel.

According to Fitzgerald's treatment, when Rosalind jilts Amory in favor of a wealthy rival, her new husband is killed in an auto accident immediately after the wedding. Amory, who had gone after the pair in the hope of persuading Rosalind at the last moment to return to him, comes upon the scene of the crash. Rosalind then tells Amory that the accident occurred *before* the marriage ceremony rather than *after* it; in doing so she magnanimously renounces any claim she might have had to her deceased husband's fortune, in favor of reassuring her impecunious suitor that she would never have gone through with the wedding anyhow, simply because she has never really loved anyone but him.

Having made over the crass, mercenary Rosalind of the novel into a generous, saintly heroine in the film treatment, Fitzgerald then goes on to transform Amory into nothing short of a Christ-figure. After Rosalind reassures Amory of her lasting love for him, he tenderly lifts the body of the dead man from the ground; and, as Amory stands peering compassionately into his face, Fitzgerald says that "a look that is Christlike comes over him."[21] In the wake of this "Christ vision," which Fitzgerald envisioned as the high point of the picture, the happy ending is at hand, in which Amory is to radiate confidence that he and Rosalind will work out their destinies in unison.

In summary, Amory and Rosalind turn out to be not only nicer people than they were in the novel but downright edifying and, hence, quite deserving of the reconciliation that the scenarist has finagled for them by conveniently dispatching Rosalind's first husband to kingdom come. It is all too good to be true; and Latham is fully justified in commenting that the novelist managed in his film treatment to reduce his true-to-life novel about the arrogance of modern youth to a gaslight melodrama "which would have been more at home back in the 1890s."[22] It goes without saying that the studio was not buying it.

The failure of Fitzgerald's first novel to reach the screen, however, did not keep Warner Brothers from snapping up the film rights to Fitzgerald's second novel, *The Beautiful and Damned* for $2,500; but this time Fitzgerald was to have no part in preparing the scenario for filming. Warners wasted no time in getting the film into production, and the studio released the final product in December 1922, only nine months after the book had been published.

The Beautiful and Damned: The Novel

Anthony Patch, the hero of *The Beautiful and Damned* (not *The Beautiful and the Damned*, as it is often erroneously called), is just Amory Blaine by another name, a little older but certainly no wiser. Richard Caramel, the novelist who appears in *The Beautiful and Damned*, refers to the earlier book with disdain: "Everywhere I go some silly girl asks me if I've read *This Side of Paradise*. . . . If it's true to life, which I don't believe," young people are "going to the dogs."[23] If the characters in the later novel are any indication, the younger generation is well on its way to the dogs. For the novel depicts, in Fitzgerald's own words, how Anthony and his beautiful young wife Gloria "are wrecked on the shoals of dissipation."[24]

Looking back at the Jazz Age from the vantage point of the Great Depression, Fitzgerald remembered that, almost from the beginning of the Roaring Twenties, he had harbored misgivings about the frantic optimism that postwar prosperity had bred in the nation. He had a hunch that living was not "the reckless, careless business" that a lot of people seemed to think it was; and his doubts were reflected in his fiction. All of the stories which came into his mind "had a touch of disaster in them," he wrote. "The lovely young creatures in my novels went to ruin, . . . my millionaires were as beautiful and damned as Thomas Hardy's peasants."[25]

The Beautiful and Damned, then, was a cautionary tale subtly aimed at his contemporaries; he and they were all eventually going to have to pay the piper for pursuing the madcap, roistering life of wealth and pleasure that seemed to be the order of the day. Specifically, *The Beautiful and Damned* examines a Jazz Age marriage. Needless to say, Fitzgerald fictionalized his own personal experience, drawing on it for purposes of plotting his novel. As he explained to his daughter during the last months of his life, he used "many circumstantial events" from the first years of his married life in composing *Beautiful*, but "the emphases were entirely different." For example, "Gloria was a much more trivial and vulgar person than your mother," he said; and on the whole during the first years of their marriage he and his wife "had a much better time than Anthony and Gloria did."[26]

In spite of the fact that Fitzgerald joked in a 1923 interview that he and his wife were married on April Fool's Day, Scott Fitzgerald and

Zelda Sayre actually exchanged vows on April 3, 1920, with Father William B. Martin presiding. The ceremony took place in the rectory of New York's St. Patrick's Cathedral, and not in the sanctuary of the church proper, because ecclesiastical law at the time dictated that the marriage of a Catholic to a non-Catholic could not be held within the precincts of the church itself; Zelda Sayre was Episcopalian.

The bride's Southern, Protestant family was not particularly opposed to her marrying a Northerner who was a Roman Catholic. As a matter of fact, before the wedding Zelda's mother wrote to Fitzgerald, "A good Catholic is as good as any other good man, and that is good enough. It will take more than the pope to make Zelda good; you will have to call on God Almighty direct."[27] Father Martin's advice to the newlyweds after the ceremony was a bit more optimistic. "You be a good Episcopalian, Zelda; and, Scott, you be a good Catholic, and you'll get along fine."[28] Fitzgerald later commented that these words returned to his mind more than once in the years that followed.

After honeymooning at a New York hotel, the Fitzgeralds stayed on in the city throughout the spring, but spent the summer of 1920 in a secluded country house in Westport, Connecticut, so that Fitzgerald could concentrate on the composition of his second novel in earnest, free of the distractions of the big town. But even there the partying, which had marked the couple's first weeks in New York, continued on weekends and was stepped up again when they returned to the city to take an apartment there in the fall.

As a result of this heady social whirl, the Fitzgeralds were gradually establishing an extravagant, erratic lifestyle which was not calculated to establish either their marriage or his professional career on a firm footing. That his work was suffering because of the continued round of parties was made painfully clear to him when he was forced to admit to himself that he had fallen woefully behind schedule in his efforts to complete his second novel.

Bruccoli remarks that Fitzgerald methodically prepared similar schedules for the accomplishment of his professional work all his life, and adds wryly: "that he rarely kept to these plans did not discourage him from making them."[29] Nonetheless Fitzgerald always castigated himself whenever he fell behind in his work. In August 1921, he told Perkins how depressed he was because he had been loafing instead of getting down to doing the final revisions of his second novel. He was so gloomy that he felt like sitting down with half a dozen companions and drinking himself to death once and for all, because he was "sick alike of life, liquor, and literature."[30]

These melancholy sentiments sound very much like Anthony Patch, the hero of *Beautiful*, as he contemplates his dissolute life. After some half-hearted endeavors to obtain gainful employment, he decides that his sole hope of realizing his goal of becoming "immensely rich as quickly as possible" is by inheriting his grandfather's fortune (p. 43). But Adam "Cross" Patch, who disapproves of Anthony's lack of initiative and pronounced propensity for consistently living above his means, finally disinherits him.

Anthony spends his last cent contesting his grandfather's will, always looking ahead to the good life, which he and Gloria hope to have "when we get our money" (p. 277). But by the time he eventually wins his court case, he and Gloria have so ruined their lives in dissipation that they cannot derive any genuine satisfaction from their newly acquired riches. Too late Anthony realizes that whenever one desperately yearns for some prize in life, it inevitably turns to dust in one's hands once it is acquired. "Because desire cheats you," he muses in a rare moment of insight; it is like a sunbeam skipping about a room which "stops and gilds some inconsequential object; and we poor fools try to grasp it—but when we do the sunbeam moves on to something else, and you've got the inconsequential part; but the glitter that made you want it is gone" (p. 341). Anthony's reflections are perfectly epitomized in his remark to Richard Caramel that all too often the victor winds up belonging to the spoils; and that is certainly Anthony's fate at the close of *The Beautiful and Damned*. The strain of the long legal battle involved in breaking his grandfather's will has in turn broken his own spirit and left him a spiritual and physical wreck, in keeping with Fitzgerald's constant theme that one must responsibly govern one's life by a set of valid principles if one is to merit genuine happiness.

Many critics found Fitzgerald's dark tale of wasted lives to be a more mature work than *This Side of Paradise*. Because it was more cohesively structured than its rather episodic predecessor, reviewers were surprised to find one notable flaw in the novel's narrative structure. At one point Gloria advises Anthony that she is with child, and there is some question about whether or not she will go ahead and have the baby. Just when the reader begins to wonder what will come of this potentially dramatic turn of events, Gloria casually announces a few pages later that she is not in a family way after all, and the matter is dropped. Hence one wonders why Fitzgerald did not elaborate on the incident, portraying as it does the Patches' unwillingness to face the responsibilities of parenthood.

Fitzgerald ultimately decided against dramatizing the episode as fully as he had originally intended to do because the question of abortion had already arisen between the Fitzgeralds before it came up for discussion between the Patches; and the author's better judgment dictated that he keep his treatment of the topic of abortion in the novel to a minimum, lest the passage in question hit too close to home.

As a matter of fact, a few weeks before the Fitzgeralds were wed, Zelda mistakenly thought she was pregnant; but she absolutely refused to take the pills which her fiancé had somehow obtained for her with a view to halting the progress of the pregnancy. She informed him that she had thrown away "those awful pills" because "they just seem to place everything on the wrong basis."[31]

When Zelda learned two months after the birth of her daughter in October 1922, that she was pregnant again, however, the Fitzgeralds apparently decided against having the child. The *Ledger* records the words "Zelda and her abortionist" as part of an entry covering their trip to New York in March 1922 (p. 176). In addition, there is a cryptic reference in the *Notebooks* to another abortion, in which Fitzgerald states that "my son" was aborted in "the XXXX hotel after Dr. X—pills" (#1564). Beyond those two laconic remarks, Fitzgerald makes little or no reference to these abortions in his private papers; so one can only guess at his private feelings in the matter.

In her book on the Fitzgeralds, Sara Mayfield, a friend of Zelda's from childhood onward, comments that, in the light of what she terms "Scott's Catholic prejudices against birth control," it is surprising that he encouraged his wife to have these abortions. Moreover, since she feels that Zelda was reluctant to have them, Ms. Mayfield adds that in her opinion the abortions "drove another wedge into their marriage."[32] To make matters worse, when the Fitzgeralds decided in the fall of 1924 to have another child, Zelda had to undergo an operation to restore her fertility; but, as she recalled in a letter to Scott, the surgical procedure failed, and much to their mutual regret the Fitzgeralds were never to have another child.[33]

Years later, after Zelda's mental collapse, her sister Rosalind inquired of Fitzgerald, "Do you think Zelda's abortions could have had anything to do with her illness?"[34] Whatever Fitzgerald's answer on that occasion—if in fact he offered any—when one considers the anguish that Zelda expressed on the subject in her letters (only one of which has been quoted here), and couples that with Sara Mayfield's first-hand observations, it seems that one must respond to Rosalind Smith's question in the affirmative.

Concerning the use that her husband made in *Beautiful* of the touchy marital problems characteristic of their own marriage, Zelda Fitzgerald commented with remarkably good humor in her review of the novel in the April 2, 1922, edition of the *New York Tribune* that passages from some of her letters and also from an old diary had surfaced in the book; and though these excerpts were "considerably edited," they still sounded more than a little familiar to her. Apparently, she concluded, Mr. Fitzgerald "seems to believe that plagiarism begins at home."[35]

All in all, *The Beautiful and Damned* marked a step forward in Fitzgerald's progress as a serious novelist, for the book was an uncompromising look at the tragic tensions which can beset a marriage. The question remains, to what degree would the dark undertones of the novel be carried over into the film version which, as mentioned, Warners released at the end of 1922.

The Beautiful and Damned: The Film

Fitzgerald for his part was deeply disappointed with the movie version of *Beautiful*, and he wrote to Harold Ober that the studio had "mutilated the picture."[36] Expressing himself more bluntly still in a letter to his friend Oscar Kalman, a St. Paul banker, the novelist expanded on his observation to Ober by saying that the picture was "*by far* the worst movie I've ever seen in my life—cheap, vulgar, ill-constructed snd shoddy."[37] By all accounts, there is something to be said for the author's acrid reaction to the film, which, like the other silent films of Fitzgerald's fiction, is now lost.

The review in the *New York Times* began by saying that "whether F. Scott Fitzgerald is responsible, or whether those who made *The Beautiful and Damned* into a picture should be held to account, is a question one unacquainted with the novel is not qualified to answer"; but certainly someone was to blame for a motion picture that failed either to amuse or to deliver a message.[38]

In the words of *Photoplay*, the picture starts out by depicting the life of the younger set "as a series of petting parties, cocktails, mad dancing, and liquor on the hip."[39] Then the movie temporarily turns serious when Anthony and Gloria (Kenneth Harlan and Marie Prevost) lose the Patch millions, and Anthony takes to drink in a most self-destructive fashion. But when at last the lucky pair do get their hands on the inheritance, Anthony abruptly snaps out of his prolonged stupor. Together he and Gloria hop aboard a luxury liner bound for Europe, and Anthony promises his wife that from now on he will try to be worthy of both her and their good fortune. At the fade-out, therefore, the implication of the movie is that, though the Patches were for a time damned to destitution, they can now be numbered among the beautiful people who have all the money they need to bring them perfect happiness. This contrasts sharply with Fitzgerald's novel, which is about some not-so-beautiful people who in the end are damned by wealth, not by poverty.

The import of the film's finale, then, is that his newly found wealth will enable Anthony to pick up the pieces of his splintered marriage and start life afresh with Gloria. The movie therefore deliberately negates thematic implications of the novel's ironic outcome, which clearly portrays Anthony as a wretched, withdrawn, emotionally bankrupt creature who is totally incapable either of enjoying the riches he fought so hard to acquire or of revivifying his arid, sterile marriage. Fitzgerald's sardonic study of a feckless young married couple who never knew when they were well off is thus fricasseed in the film version into a lighthearted, lightweight fairy tale, all flappers and bathtub gin, about a couple whose marriage is saved by their having found a pot of gold at the end of the rainbow.

It may be objected that, in providing the picture with an upbeat ending which the book did not have, the makers of the film version of *Beautiful* were doing no more than Fitzgerald himself did later in his own rejected scenario for the movie adaptation of *This Side of Paradise*; and there is some truth in this allegation. Indeed, it is a pity that Fitzgerald did not take more to heart his own severe criticism of the film adaptation of *The Beautiful and Damned* when he composed his own bowdlerized screen treatment of *This Side of Paradise* a few months later. But then, he always seemed to have a much keener eye when it came to spotting artistic flaws in other scriptwiters' work than he ever did in spying out the faults in his own.

Still Fitzgerald's negative reaction to the film version of *Beautiful* seems to be justified; and film critics who were familiar with the novel knew that the book was better than the movie. The novel contains some scenes of great power, such as the incident in which the destitute Anthony makes a long trek up Sixth Avenue, visiting one pawnship after another, as he tries to collect enough money to buy some liquor. Piper points out that this episode was the source of a strong scene in both Charles Jackson's 1944 novel about alcoholism, *The Lost Weekend*, and in the subsequent film version of Jackson's novel.

In retrospect, one suspects that Warners bought the screen rights to *Beautiful* on the strength of its serialization in *Metropolitan Magazine*, in which about one-quarter of the novel was excised in order to keep the serialization from running beyond the magazine's customary number of installments. In the course of these deletions, much of the in-depth psychological analysis of the characters Anthony and Gloria was shorn away. Hence, during an interview with Fitzgerald after *Beautiful* was published in book form, Thomas Boyd, the literary editor of the *St. Paul Daily News*, remarked that the *Metropolitan* serial, because it lacked so much material that gave depth and meaning to the book, turned out to be "nothing but cheap sensationalism."[40] And that seems to be a fair assessment of the film version as well. It appears that the movie adaptation of *Beautiful*, like the serial version, offered Fitzgerald's story without the thought-provoking psychological study of the deterioration of the Patches's marriage.

Without realizing it, Fitzgerald had forecast in the novel itself the kind of simplistic screenplay that would be derived from his lengthy, complex book. In the course of a conversation about "the influence of literature on the moving picture," movie mogul Joseph Bloeckman tells Dick Caramel that "many novels are full of . . . psychology," and that "it's impossible to make much of that interesting on the screen" (p. 103; p. 96). Apparently *Beautiful* was "full of psychology" that had to be systematically cut away in order to produce a routine Hollywood movie.

An interesting footnote to the novel is that Joseph Bloeckman's production company, Films Par Excellence, would turn up again in *Tender Is the Night* as the studio that employs actress Rosemary Hoyt, one of the principal figures in that novel. More importantly, Bloeckman, who is the first movie tycoon to be given a detailed portrait in Fitzgerald's fiction, presages film producer Monroe Stahr, the hero of Fitzgerald's final novel, *The Last Tycoon*.

One wishes that Hollywood had produced a more worthy adaptation of Fitzgerald's Jazz Age novel than it did. British novelist and screenwriter Christopher Isherwood composed, in collaboration with screenwriter Don Bachardy, a fresh screenplay of *The Beautiful and Damned*, but was unable to find a producer for it. One need not suppose, however, that the novel is so tied to the twenties that a remake of it would not be relevant to contemporary audiences; for Fitzgerald's fiction consistently transcended the period in which it was written or that it was written about.

Speaking of the perennial appeal of Fitzgerald's fiction in *The Lost Weekend*, Charles Jackson has one of his characters say, "Don't be fooled by what the Sunday reviewers say about his Jazz Age . . . popularity. People will be going back to Fitzgerald one day. . . . His writing is the finest, the purest, the most entertaining and most readable that we have in America today."[41] There is no better example among Fitzgerald's writings of what Jackson says than *The Great Gatsby*.

SIX

KNIGHT WITHOUT ARMOR:

THE THREE FILMS OF

THE GREAT GATSBY

I love Scott's . . . heroines. I love the ones that
are like me.
—*Zelda Fitzgerald*

I married the heroine of my stories.
—*F. Scott Fitzgerald*

The statue of Christopher Columbus standing atop its pedestal at Columbus Circle in downtown Manhattan portrays the discoverer of America as looking westward. His stance suggests that he is contemplating the limitless resources of the New World that stretch beyond his gaze all the way to the West Coast. Fitzgerald used this representation of Columbus at the end of his short story "May Day," which was published in 1920.

He later created a complimentary image at the close of his novel *The Great Gatsby* in which he pictures a group of Dutch mariners catching their first glimpse of the New Land, and coming for once, therefore, face to face with something commensurate with man's capacity for wonder. Once again the image evoked is that of man being confronted with a vision of the incalculable potential of a still unspoiled continent. This sense of wonder that overwhelmed Columbus and the explorers who followed him is shared in *The Great Gatsby* by the title character, who holds firmly to his conviction throughout the novel that there is no limit to what an individual can accomplish in such a land of opportunity, once he sets his mind to it.

In the spring of 1922 Fitzgerald laid out his plan for a new novel. He informed Perkins that it was going to take place just before the turn of the century and have a "Catholic element."[1] He began by writing a prologue about the book's hero which was designed "to be a picture of his early life." Fitzgerald eventually decided, however, that this prologue gave away too much information about the central character's background too early in the novel. He preferred instead to maintain a "sense of mystery" about his protagonist by gradually revealing the hero's past throughout the book.[2]

Never one to discard any material in which he had invested time and energy, in 1924 Fitzgerald published the rejected prologue of his novel as a separate short story under the title "Absolution." The story was inspired by some childhood experiences of the author which are documented in the *Ledger*. In his entry for September 1907, Fitzgerald recounts that he went to church to receive forgiveness for his sins in the Sacrament of Confession, and in the course of his interchange with the priest hearing his confession, the latter inquired about his honesty. He replied in a shocked voice, "Oh *no*, I never tell a lie"—which was, of course, itself a lie (p. 162). Another notation in the *Ledger*, dated the following month, recalls that during Sunday Mass a young girl made him feel very embarrassed because he did not have even a penny to drop into the collection basket.

Around these two boyhood memories Fitzgerald fashioned a tale of a boy named Rudolph Miller who is ashamed of his family's low social status, and longs to be a person of quality. Hence, he is ashamed when he thinks that the girl behind him in church may notice that he has nothing to put in the collection plate. Moreover, he often takes refuge in prevarications about his having come from a much more genteel background than is actually the case, and it is these lies that he is loath to admit to his confessor. This young man who nurtures delusions of grandeur about himself has much in common with the title character of *The Great Gatsby*, whom he clearly prefigures. For in the novel, young James Gatz likewise seeks to deny his humble origins by changing his name to the more cavalier Jay Gatsby and in other ways trying to pass himself off as a well-bred gentleman.

If there is something of Fitzgerald in Rudolph Miller, as the *Ledger* indicates, there is also something of Fitzgerald in Jay Gatsby; for the *Ledger* also tells us that the scenes in the novel in which Jay courts Daisy, the heroine of the book, during World War I, have as their source the wartime courtship of Scott Fitzgerald and Zelda Sayre.

While recovering from his rejection by Ginevra King, Fitzgerald, by this time a Yankee army officer, met Zelda Sayre, a popular Southern belle, at a country club dance in her hometown of Montgomery, Alabama, in July 1918. Fitzgerald was billeted at a nearby army camp; and so for the time being they were able to see quite a bit of each other. By September Fitzgerald was moved to record in the *Ledger* that he had definitely fallen in love with Zelda (p. 172), and their engagement became official when Fitzgerald gave Zelda his mother's own engagement ring.

After his discharge from the service, however, Fitzgerald failed to make any significant progress in his chosen profession as a writer; and so Zelda reluctantly broke their engagement in June 1919. "Zelda was cagey about throwing in her lot before I was a moneymaker," Fitzgerald recalled years later in his *Notebooks*, because a "worker in the arts" simply did not appear to possess the potential to be a good provider to the same degree as someone with a more steady income (#552). Although Zelda insisted in an undated letter written to Fitzgerald around this time that "all material things are nothing," she nevertheless put it to him that she would just "hate to live a sordid, colorless existence,"[3] because in such circumstances they might grow to love each other less and less.

Fitzgerald decided that getting his first novel accepted for publication was the most effective way of allaying Zelda's well-founded doubts about the possibility of his becoming a commercially successful author, fully capable of supporting a wife. As mentioned, *This Side of Paradise* was accepted by Scribner's in

September 1919; and shortly thereafter Scott and Zelda were once again engaged to be married.

Literary scholar Charles Shain has commented, "Fitzgerald did not hold Zelda Sayre morally responsible" for the seemingly mercenary view which she took toward their engagement. "They both felt poor, and they both were eager to participate in the moneyed society around them. In the United States of 1919, they agreed, the purpose of money was to realize the promises of life."[4] Although Zelda Sayre could not be blamed for hesitating to marry a man who she had reason to suspect might not prove a responsible breadwinner, Fitzgerald never got over the fact that he might have lost her to someone more successful than himself. The young writer, who ultimately married his girl a year after their betrothal had been broken off, would, as Fitzgerald later wrote, "always cherish an abiding distrust, an animosity toward the leisure class." This is because at one point in his life their privileged status might have entitled one of them to take away from him the girl of his choice.[5]

What's more, the thought that he had had somehow to "earn" the right to marry his intended wife left on Fitzgerald's impressionable young mind an acute awareness of the relationship between material success and success in the marriage market—in his view they constituted the twin goals of the American Dream. He was henceforth to chronicle in his fiction how the pursuit of the American success myth led more often than not to disenchantment and disillusionment. Thus the Patches make a mad scramble to gain the inheritance, which they insist is essential to render their married life a happy one but which, in the end, poisons their marriage altogether. And Jay Gatsby becomes so totally obsessed by the American Dream that he dedicates himself completely to achieving the financial and social status he believes necessary to be worthy of possessing the girl of his dreams, Daisy Buchanan, who has forsaken him for a more affluent rival. Indeed, the single-minded Gatsby perceives the winning of Daisy as tantamount to the knightly quest for the Holy Grail.

The Great Gatsby: The Novel

At the time that The Great Gatsby was taking shape in Fitzgerald's imagination, he and his wife moved to Great Neck, Long Island, which was to be called West Egg in the novel. The house that they leased from the fall of 1922 to the spring of 1924 on Gateway Drive was surrounded by the homes of an assortment of show business people, journalists, and even some of the more well-to-do bootleggers. Across the bay, on the opposite shore from the Fitzgeralds and the other nouveau riche residents of Great Neck, there lived such socially prominent and long-established wealthy families as the Pulitzers and the Astors. This exclusive section of the coastline Fitzgerald would christen East Egg in his novel.

In the book Gatsby makes enough money after leaving the army to move into an imitation French villa in unfashionable West Egg, so near and yet so far from exclusive East Egg, where Daisy and her husband, stockbroker Tom Buchanan, live in an opulent mansion. Gatsby gives a series of swanky parties at his place, hoping that Daisy will one evening be finally lured across the bay to attend one of them. (Gatsby's elaborate bashes are modeled on the much less pretentious soirees which the Fitzgeralds gave at their home in Great Neck, where, as Fitzgerald later reminisced, "it became a habit with many world-weary New Yorkers to pass their weekends."[6])

When Daisy does not take the bait, Gatsby persuades his neighbor, Nick Carraway, the novel's narrator, who happens to be a relative of Daisy's, to invite her for tea at his modest home, which adjoins Gatsby's estate, so that the erstwhile lovers can renew their relationship. With that, Jay and Daisy temporarily resume their doomed love affair, while Tom Buchanan continues to carry on his own extramarital romance with Myrtle Wilson, the wife of a gas station proprietor. It is Gatsby's naive hope that he and Daisy can relive the happiness they shared together in the past. Nick wisely warns Gatsby that he may be asking too much of Daisy if he expects her to be able to repeat her past relationship with him in the present. But Gatsby blindly reaffirms his conviction that he and Daisy can pick up their old lives just where they left off five years before, and go on together.

What Daisy does not know about Jay, but her husband makes it his business to find out, is that most of Gatsby's wealth is derived from a number of unsavory business operations, of which bootlegging is only a part. Fitzgerald biographer André Le Vot notes that Gatsby's shady activities as a racketeer were modeled on the criminal activities of one of the Fitzgeralds' neighbors in Great

Neck, a crooked entrepreneur named Edward M. Fuller, whose devious business deals were exposed in the press a few months after the Fitzgeralds moved to town.[7]

A second real-life source for Gatsby was Max Gerlach, who also lived near the Fitzgeralds in Great Neck. Zelda remembered him as being "in trouble over bootlegging." But the closest link between Gerlach and Gatsby is a note which Gerlach sent to Fitzgerald on July 20, 1923, which reads, "How are you and the family, old sport?"[8] The last two words comprise Gatsby's characteristic way of greeting his friends, which mirrors the studied nonchalance of a self-conscious individual trying too hard to make a good impression on others.

One of Gatsby's disreputable associates, Meyer Wolfsheim, was also drawn from life. He was based on Arnold Rothstein, a vice lord and bootlegger whom Fitzgerald once met. He was notorious for having fixed the 1919 World Series, an infamous exploit which Fitzgerald of course attributes to Rothstein's fictional counterpart in the novel. When Gatsby introduces Nick Carraway to Wolfsheim, Nick is astonished to learn that the latter engineered all by himself what came to be known as the Black Sox scandal. It had never occurred to Nick that one man could tamper with the faith of millions of people "with the single-mindedness of a burglar blowing a safe."[9] In this passage, then, Fitzgerald lets the reader know the kind of company that Gatsby keeps, even before Tom Buchanan reveals Gatsby's underworld connections to Daisy.

Gatsby has thus cheapened himself in his efforts to get rich quick, all for the sake of wooing back to him a spoiled, ungrateful young woman who in the end will abandon him. But to the misguided Gatsby, Daisy is the golden girl who embodies the American Dream for him, since she represents the fulfillment of his twin desires of combining love and wealth to create the perfect marriage. "Her voice is full of money," Jay remarks to Nick, as he futilely gropes for words to express in some minimal manner why she enthralls him so. Fitzgerald later explained the phrase by saying that Daisy's voice radiated "a certain deep confidence that money gave in those days."[10] Or to put it another way, Gatsby's way, Daisy symbolizes for him all the glamor of wealth and romance.

But the starry-eyed Gatsby will never win Daisy away from

Tom because—although Jay is not aware of it—there is a strong bond between them which Gatsby will never be able to sever. No matter how much wealth Gatsby is able to amass by fair means or foul, he will never be more than a gate-crasher in the upper-class society of inherited wealth in which the Buchanans move, where one must be to the "manor" born in order to be accepted. Daisy is willing to carry on a furtive affair with Jay, but at no time would she seriously consider leaving her husband for a social-climbing bootlegger whose gaudy pink suits and garish gold ties are the emblems of his perpetual status as an outsider in the private, privileged world which she inhabits with her husband.

In a real sense Daisy and Tom quite literally deserve each other, because these two selfish, spoiled individuals are really two of a kind. Nick, in fact, goes so far as to say that they have formed their own secret society in order to protect and preserve their mutual possessions. "They were careless people," he explains. "They smashed up things and creatures and then retreated back into their money or their vast carelessness, or whatever it was that kept them together," and left it to other people to clean up the mess they made (pp. 180-81).

One such mess is made when Daisy, while driving back to Long Island from New York City, accidentally runs over Tom's mistress, Myrtle Wilson, right in front of Wilson's gas station. Both Tom and Daisy allow Gatsby to "clean up the mess" by personally assuming the blame for the hit-and-run killing of Myrtle because he wants to exonerate his beloved Daisy.

The coincidence which seems inherent in Tom's wife being behind the wheel of the car that runs down his mistress has often been criticized by literary critics as too facile and contrived. On the contrary, Fitzgerald makes it quite clear in the novel that Myrtle dashes out onto the highway in order to try and stop the car that is speeding past her husband's gas station because she assumes that it is Tom, and not Daisy, who is driving the auto. She attempts to flag down the speeding vehicle because she wants Tom to protect her from the wrath of her husband George, who has just discovered that she is having an affair with Buchanan. Consequently, Fitzgerald has orchestrated this catastrophe with far more plausibility than he is usually given credit for.

As a result of his taking the rap for Myrtle's death, Gatsby is shot to death by Myrtle's revenge-crazed husband, George Wilson. One of the few mourners who shows up in the rain for Gatsby's funeral tearfully pronounces a heart-felt benediction over the grave of his friend, which, under the circumstances, could not be more appropriate. Wiping his glasses, the grief-stricken individual says, "The poor son-of-a-bitch" (p. 176). Being left in the end with nothing but his empty dreams about his lost love, Jay Gatsby was poor indeed. As far as Nick Carraway is concerned, his judgment about Gatsby is that, when compared to the ruthlessly self-centered Buchanans and their "rotten crowd," Jay is "worth the whole damn bunch put together" (p. 154).

Literary critic Marius Bewley says that the theme of *The Great Gatsby* is "the withering of the American Dream."[11] And rightly so, since Jay Gatsby recklessly squandered his life and his energies tenaciously trying to win the fickle favor of the counterfeit goddess who for him embodied the American Dream. As Mizener implies, Jay Gatsby might have been truly great had he but focused his qualities of devotion and loyalty on a more worthy object than Daisy Buchanan.[12]

Despite the fact that the novel did not immediately become a hearty best-seller when it appeared on April 10, 1925, it garnered some of the best reviews of Fitzgerald's entire career. Never before had Fitzgerald seemed so completely in control of his material. Without wasting a word, he tells this tragic tale of the corruption of the American Dream into Gatsby's own personal nightmare in such a compelling fashion that he demonstrated he had graduated from the ranks of promising young fiction writers and had become a full-fledged, mature novelist. In addition, the novel's continued acclaim over the years has warranted its translation into virtually every medium of artistic expression: it has been adapted for the stage, the screen, and television.

The Great Gatsby: The Play

First came the play, adapted by Pulitzer Prize winner Owen Davis and directed, as said before, by George Cukor. After a respectable run at the Ambassador Theater in New York, where it opened on February 2, 1926, the production was equally successful on tour the following season. Because the Fitzgeralds were in Europe all the time that the play was on the boards, they never saw it.

Fitzgerald's own specific comment on the artistic merits of the dramatization was that the script "read pretty badly";[13] but on second thought he added that he could hardly complain about the money that the production had brought him without a stroke of effort on his part. Max Perkins wrote Fitzgerald that in his judgment the novel's plot had been adhered to as closely as one could expect, given the physical limitations of the stage; and drama critics like Alexander Woollcott in *The New York Times* pretty much agreed with him.[14]

There is no doubt that the success of the Davis play sparked special interest in *Gatsby* as a promising film property; and Paramount bought the screen rights of the novel from Fitzgerald for $16,000, the most he ever earned from a movie sale. But then at least one reviewer of the novel thought that Fitzgerald had "one eye cocked on the movie lots" all the time he was writing the book: "The movie type of wild Bacchanalian revel, with the drunken ladies in the swimming pool and garden fetes that just drip expensiveness, are done to perfection," wrote book critic John Kenny at the time of the novel's publication; "and who knows but that they will offer some soulful Hollywood director a chance to display his art?"[15] In point of fact, since *Gatsby* was filmed not once but three times, it offered no less than three different filmmakers that chance; and all three in varying degrees did what they could to make the most of it.

In what must have been the most adulatory letter Ernest Hemingway ever wrote to his friend and colleague Scott Fitzgerald, he warmly congratulated the latter on selling the film rights of *Gatsby* while Gatsby was still appearing "in person at the Ambassador." Hemingway continued that, with the money that Fitzgerald had earned from both the stage and screen rights of the book, he should have the leisure to write "a pretty good novel. . . . Maybe some day you'll get the Nobel Prize."[16] (Ironically, Fitzgerald did not live to win the Nobel Prize, but Hemingway himself did.)

The Great Gatsby: The First Film

The director chosen by Paramount to make the silent version of *Gatsby*, now lost, was Herbert Brenon (*Peter Pan*), a competent but uninspired filmmaker. *The New York Times*, in fact, led off its review of the movie by lamenting that the picture did not have the benefit of a more imaginative director at the helm; and the majority of the critical fraternity echoed this judgment. In short, Brenon too often relied on words rather than pictures to get his story told, thereby allowing the visual flow of the action to be slowed down with an endless procession of exceptionally wordy subtitles.

As in the case of the film version of *The Beautiful and Damned*, the last printed title to appear on the screen is among the worst in the entire picture. After Gatsby has met his death at the hands of George Wilson, an inscription appears on the screen lugubriously explaining at some length that some people (namely Gatsby) live and die for the sake of bringing happiness to others. "The picture illustrating this subtitle shows Daisy and her husband Tom and their tot draped beautifully on the porch of their happy home," wrote one film critic. This title, he concluded, "fitted perfectly the generally bad English, inappropriate wording," and overall wordiness contained in the rest of the subtitles.[17]

On the credit side, the picture boasted an impressive group of actors, from whom, it must be conceded, Brenon drew uniformly good performances. It was generally agreed that Warner Baxter, best remembered now for his role as the Broadway director in the depression musical *Forty-Second Street* (1933), played the title role with conviction. The "childish pride" which he exhibits in showing off his overwhelming house and his dozens of monogrammed shirts, for example, serve to illustrate, said one critic, that the Gatsby whom Baxter brought to life on the screen is the same tragic figure who stands out from the pages of Fitzgerald's book.[18]

Other estimable members of the cast were William Powell (later to win renown in the *Thin Man* movies) as George Wilson, and Lois Wilson (Valentino's co-star in *Monsieur Beaucaire*) as Daisy. Ms. Wilson was voted in a nationwide poll one of the top box office draws of 1926, and no doubt the great popularity of *Gatsby*, released that same year, helped her to win that accolade. Ms. Wilson recently recalled encountering Fitzgerald at the time the movie was made and having him autograph a copy of *Gatsby* for her. She remembers him as "a gentleman, a charming, most attractive man . . . As far as I know, he approved of the film when it was released."[19]

Ms. Wilson was probably correct in her assumption that Fitzgerald liked the picture. For, as far as one can ascertain from the reviews of the film which he pasted in one of his scrapbooks, the silent version of *The Great Gatsby* stuck fairly close to the novel's story line, which, as we have seen, is more than can be said for the movie made from *The Beautiful and Damned.*

In discussing the production of the film so many years later, it is understandable that Ms. Wilson might assume that Fitzgerald autographed her copy of Gatsby on the set during the filming period, but that is not possible because the Fitzgeralds were in Europe from the spring of 1926 right through to the end of that year; and *Gatsby* was released a month before they got back to America. But, as noted already, Fitzgerald did go to Hollywood in January 1927, shortly after the movie opened; and it is very likely that Lois Wilson met Fitzgerald and received an autographed copy of the novel from him at that time.

Perhaps the strongest praise accorded the silent film of *Gatsby* came from Fitzgerald's friend and fellow novelist John O'Hara, who had a certain predilection for the picture. Writing many years after he first saw it, O'Hara said, "Even now I can remember my exultation at the end of the picture when I saw that Paramount had done an honest job, true to the book, true to what Fitzgerald had intended."[20] Some time after the advent of sound, O'Hara even tried to buy the screen rights of *Gatsby*, so that he could write the screenplay for a sound remake of the silent film. He was encouraged to do so by Clark Gable, who wanted to play the title role, and who had also discussed his interest in the project with Fitzgerald.

But no plan to make a sound version of *Gatsby* came to fruition during Fitzgerald's lifetime. It was not until 1949 that Paramount finally decided to produce a remake of *Gatsby* as a vehicle for its top star at the time, Alan Ladd, who had, as we know from Bodeen's remarks in the preface above, coveted the part of Gatsby for some time.

The Great Gatsby: The Second Film

Some felicitous bits of the novel's original dialogue found their way into the screenplay of the new sound version of *Gatsby*, as when

Daisy (Betty Field) introduces her little girl to Nick (Macdonald Carey) and recalls what she said when the child was born: "I'm glad it's a girl. And I hope she'll be a fool," because that's the best thing that a girl could be in this world, "a beautiful little fool" (p. 17). According to a *Ledger* entry for October 1921, this is virtually what Zelda Fitzgerald said as she was awakening from the anesthetic after Scottie was born. In the context of the story it implies Daisy's wish for herself, as well as for her daughter, to escape the unpleasant side of life by simply ignoring it.

Some of the symbolic nuances of the novel, such as the green light that burns every night at the end of the pier fronting the Buchanan mansion, were also incorporated into the film's script. Nick Carraway first notices the green light glowing on Daisy's dock when he spies Gatsby gazing at it as he stands on his own front lawn, stretching his arms toward the expanse of dark water that separates West Egg from East Egg, and thus separates him from Daisy. The color green, because of its association with the renewal of nature in the springtime, has always been symbolic of hope. Specifically, the green light implies Gatsby's hope that he will eventually be able to traverse the distance that divides Daisy's world from his, and possess her once more as his own. James Miller, in his book on Fitzgerald, adds that the green light is likewise linked with the green traffic signal, which summons the traveller to continue on his way—an appropriate symbol for Gatsby, a "man in hurried pursuit of a beckoning but ever-elusive dream."[21]

Another effective visual image brought over to the film from the book is that of the Valley of Ashes which lies between New York and Long Island. Sara Mayfield notes that, whenever Fitzgerald travelled on a commuter train from Great Neck to the city, he noticed "the wastelands along the tracks."[22] He decided that this desolate area, marred by mounds of ashes and refuse, would be the proper place to locate Wilson's garage and the shabby flat he shares with Myrtle. At one point he even contemplated calling the novel *Among Ash-Heaps and Millionaires* to point up still more the contrast between the dismal environment in which the Wilsons live and the lush landscape surrounding the estates of the Buchanans and their aristocratic coterie.

Near Wilson's garage in the Valley of Ashes, in the film as in the book, there is a billboard advertising an oculist by the name of

Dr. T. J. Eckleburg, which portrays a pair of enormous eyes rimmed in spectacles, surveying the depressing dumping ground that stretches in front of the sign. The image of Dr. Eckleburg's eyes originally came to Fitzgerald after he first saw a preliminary sketch of the novel's cover design. Gazing out at the author from the book's dust jacket were two gigantic eyes floating in the night sky above the blazing lights of Manhattan. The hint of mascara encircling the eyes implies that the artist who designed the jacket supposedly intended the eyes to be those of Gatsby's goddess, Daisy Buchanan; but for Fitzgerald they had a much more far-reaching significance. These "great, unblinking eyes, expressionless, looking down upon the human scene," as Perkins later described them, symbolized for Fitzgerald nothing less than the eyes of God Himself.[23]

This symbolic meaning of the eyes on the poster, which would be carried over from the novel to the film, is emphasized in the scene in which Wilson, while charging his wife with adultery, points to the eyes staring at her from the signboard across the way and solemnly reminds her that God sees everything: "You may fool me, but you can't fool God" (p. 160). Le Vot comments that Wilson's words to Myrtle illustrate how strongly Fitzgerald himself was still influenced by his Catholic upbringing; for as Le Vot attests, Fitzgerald "found it difficult to detach himself from the religion he had learned as a child,"[24] a point I made in treating *This Side of Paradise*. Putting it another way, literary critic Edwin Fussell writes that passages such as the one just described indicate that Fitzgerald's "Catholic apostacy was about half-genuine and half-imagined."[25]

The religious implications of the oculist's billboard are underscored in the 1949 *Gatsby* when Gatsby stops at Wilson's garage with a sidekick from his army days, Klipspringer (Elisha Cook, Jr.), en route to his home in West Egg. Spotting the oculist's poster, Klipspringer says with a touch of awe in his voice, "Those eyes getcha—like God bought himself a pair of eyeglasses, so He could watch us better."

Klipspringer's remark is visualized on the screen several times in the course of the movie. The eyes on the billboard are visible as they seemingly "watch" Tom (Barry Sullivan) surreptitiously picking up Myrtle (Shelley Winters) down the road a bit from the gas station for one of their trysts, as well as in the sequence in which

Wilson confronts his wife about her infidelity. And the eyes are watching once more as Tom who, as we know, was not with Daisy when she ran down Myrtle, stops his car at the scene of the accident and finds Myrtle's battered body lying dead, ironically enough, only a short distance from where they were accustomed to rendezvous for their assignations.

The Eckleburg signboard, which is the last image to appear on the screen at the film's final fadeout is used so effectively throughout the film to remind the viewer of Klipspringer's thought-provoking remark, that cinema critic Manny Farber must have been only half-joking when he quipped in his review of the movie that "the oculist's billboard, with the enormous spectacled eyes, steals the movie."[26]

Bodeen is correct when he says that some explanation of Gatsby's past, particularly his youthful association with his mentor, Dan Cody, is important to an understanding of Gatsby's character; but he is incorrect when he suggests that the second film of the novel ignores the Cody material in the same way that the other screen versions do. As a matter of fact, the second film, the 1949 version, remains most faithful to its source in its attempt gradually to sketch Gatsby's background for the viewer, with the aid of flashbacks.

In one flashback Gatsby recounts for Nick how a self-made millionaire named Dan Cody (Henry Hull) took him under his wing when he was still a youngster serving as a mate on the old man's yacht. It was under Cody's tutelage that this teenage lad confirmed his resolution to discard his former identity as James Gatz in order to forge a new personality for himself as Jay Gatsby.

Dan Cody, a rambunctious old sourdough whom Fitzgerald named after Daniel Boone and "Buffalo Bill" Cody, made his fortune in the Wild West. Hence the advice that this tough old buzzard passes on to his foster son has a ruthless, materialistic ring to it, based as it is on the assumption that one's personal happiness is determined almost exclusively by the size of his bankroll. So in the film, when ex-serviceman Jay Gatsby learns that he has lost Daisy to millionaire Tom Buchanan, the camera zooms in on a photograph of Cody on his bureau as he mutters, "The old gentleman was right; you can't compete without money."

As mentioned earlier, it is more difficult to imply in a movie than it is in a novel that a given account of past events is being presented from the subjective point of view of one of the characters, as here when Gatsby recalls the influence of Dan Cody on him. This is because the audience is always conscious that it is watching what is being dramatized in flashback on the screen, not through the eyes of the character who is narrating the event in question but through the eye of the camera. The screenplay may try to retain the subjective dimension of these memories by having the voice of the character who is recalling the event in question surface on the soundtrack occasionally to comment on the flashback as it unfolds on the screen, as is the case in the present film, but the viewer still does not have the sense that he is seeing the flashback from the point of view of the character who is retelling it, for the reason given.

Therefore the movie is robbed of some of the emotional intensity which one feels when one reads *Gatsby*, simply because in the book Nick frequently communicates to the reader his subjective reactions to the episodes from the past which he is narrating, whereas Nick rarely verbalizes his feelings in the film. For example, the viewer never grasps the extent to which Nick is profoundly touched by Gatsby's tragedy, since many of the sage reflections about Gatsby's life and death which Nick makes in the book are not in the film.

By the same token, Tom Buchanan does not come across in the film as nearly so corrupt and conniving as he appears to be in the novel because, once again, Nick's many observations about him are missing in the movie. Still even in the movie Tom Buchanan proves that he can be as brutal as any of the nefarious mobsters with whom Gatsby's name has been linked when the grief-maddened George Wilson (Howard da Silva) comes to his house gunning for the person who killed his wife; and Tom obligingly steers him back across the bay to Gatsby's.

Gatsby's criminal connections are stressed more in the 1949 film than they are in the novel, or in the subsequent film version of the book, presumably to capitalize on the "tough guy" image which Alan Ladd had established with the mass audience in films like *This Gun for Hire* (1942). In fact the movie begins with a montage of hijackings and gangland shootouts, with Gatsby clearly visible right in the middle of the action.

Later in the film Reba, a mobster with whom Gatsby has had some dealings, shows up at one of Gatsby's parties. This surly thug embarrasses the host by drunkenly insisting on talking "business" and insolently addressing him repeatedly as Gatz. Gatsby graciously invites the intruder to join him behind a high hedge in the garden, where he summarily knocks the intruder cold and then discreetly instructs the butler to hustle the offending guest off the property.

Although this incident is not in the novel, it is decidedly in keeping with the spirit of the book, since it exemplifies Gatsby's concerted effort to keep the tainted nature of his business activities a secret from Daisy by dissociating himself in public from the likes of Reba.

This second film adaptation of *Gatsby* was directed by Elliott Nugent (*The Male Animal*), a conscientious craftsman whose films nonetheless seldom turned out to be of more than routine interest. DeWitt Bodeen tactfully mentions in the preface that at the time Nugent directed *Gatsby* he was beset with personal problems. That, as they say, is putting it mildly. Nugent, who was subject to fits of deep depression, was afraid that he would not be capable of directing a film of *Gatsby* that would do justice to the book, which he considered to be, in his own words, "Scott Fitzgerald's best novel and perhaps the best of all American novels." Then too, he was plagued with all sorts of anxieties concerning the production in general, ranging from his misgivings about the suitability of Ladd for the crucial part of Gatsby to the quality of the screenplay that had been written by Cyril Hume and Richard Maibaum.

"As the time for shooting approached, I became seriously neurotic and was filled with terror about what I had done or left undone" in terms of preparing the film to go into production, he confessed afterwards. "It seemed to me that I was betraying Fitzgerald as well as my friends at Paramount" by going through with the direction of the picture. The day before filming was scheduled to begin, Nugent became so despondent that he drove to the Roosevelt Hotel on Hollywood Boulevard, where he was determined to kill himself.

The harried man took the elevator to the tenth floor and climbed out a window onto a fire escape overlooking the alley at the back of the building, where he would be unobserved. After teetering precariously for a while on the fire escape railing, however, "abruptly I rose and went downstairs, almost without thinking or making any decision" not to commit suicide. "By the time I reached the lobby, my mood had changed, and I was scoffing at my foolish terror."[27]

During the lengthy shooting period, however, Nugent continued at times to feel edgy and unsure of himself, with the result that he frequently found it difficult to make decisions about production matters. Meanwhile Alan Ladd was nagged by persistent insecurities of his own. Because he had little faith in his acting ability, Ladd began to worry that, no matter how hard he tried, he would not be able to meet the demands of the film's key role. Moreover, he had trouble remembering his lines, and was embarrassed when he fluffed a speech in the presence of the experienced stage actor Macdonald Carey, who was consistently word perfect. According to his friend and colleague Geraldine Fitzgerald, Ladd needed a director on the picture who would have been "very warm to him, that would have supplied him with the confidence he needed. But Elliott Nugent, who directed *Gatsby*, is himself an inhibited person," and was hence too preoccupied with his own emotional problems to give Ladd much reassurance.[28]

"Somehow, in spite of all our doubts," Nugent concluded, "we got the picture finished. While it never completely satisfied me, it received good reviews and was a financial success."[29] In actual fact, the 1949 *Gatsby* is without question the most distinguished picture that Nugent ever turned out, and Ladd's portrayal of Gatsby has come to be considered one of his best performances ever, what some have called an example of perfect casting.

Richard Maibaum, co-scriptwriter and producer of the film, sensed Ladd's kinship with the role of Gatsby one evening when he was visiting Ladd at home. The star showed him his expensive wardrobe, including row after row of elegant shirts, thereby recalling Gatsby's proudly displaying his wardrobe, particularly his collection of fancy shirts, to Daisy the first time she comes to his house. "Not bad for an Okie kid, eh?" Maibaum remembers Ladd saying to him. "My God!" Maibaum thought to himself. "He's Gatsby."[30] How right he was. In summing up his assessment of the movie, film historian Lionel Godfrey has written, "Scott Fitzgerald describes Gatsby as an elegant young roughneck," and the 1949 film had Alan Ladd "to fill the role impeccably."[31]

The 1949 *Gatsby* was followed by two television adaptations of the book, a one-hour production with Robert Montgomery on "Robert Montgomery Presents," May 9, 1955, and a ninety-minute version with Robert Ryan on "Playhouse 90," June 26, 1958. Unfortunately both productions are no longer available for screening. Then, in the early 1970s, Paramount opted to produce a third film of the novel, this time in color.

Howard da Silva, who played George Wilson in the 1949 *Gatsby* and Meyer Wolfsheim in the 1974 remake starring Robert Redford, believes that Ladd's handling of the part was superior to Redford's. "As much as I admired Redford as an actor, I felt he could never play a man from the opposite side of the tracks," da Silva explained. "And Ladd could and did."[32] Perhaps Steve McQueen, who was originally supposed to play Gatsby in the 1974 production, would have been closer to Fitzgerald's "elegant young roughneck" than Redford, who replaced him for reasons Bodeen has stated above. But we shall never know.

The Great Gatsby: The Third Film

To begin with, there are several similarities between the second and third films of *Gatsby*. The third screen rendition of the book, like the second, remains faithful to the spirit of the novel, not only by retaining Fitzgerald's plot pretty much intact, but also by incorporating into the screenplay the novel's principal symbols, such as Daisy's green light, Dr. Eckelburg's eyes, and the Valley of Ashes. Furthermore, the flashback technique is once more employed to depict the wartime romance of Jay (Robert Redford) and Daisy (Mia Farrow), as it was in the earlier film. The flashback to their courtship is adroitly introduced by the camera gliding almost imperceptibly from the present, in which Jay has donned his old army uniform at Daisy's behest, to the past, where we see them on one of the dreamy evenings they spent together before Jay went overseas and Daisy subsequently threw him over for Tom.

British filmmaker Jack Clayton (*Room at the Top*) was slated to direct the movie this time around. Clayton was enthusiastic about the project because he had wanted to make the book into a movie ever since he had read it years before, and had tried unsuccessfully in the first intervening years to buy the screenrights himself. After the first screenplay which had been prepared for the new production had been rejected by the studio as unwieldy, the distinguished Academy Award winner writer-director Francis Ford Coppola

(*Godfather* I and II) took on the task of scripting the film, not with any thought of directing the picture, but as a change of pace from working on the *Godfather* films. Coppola hammered out a serviceable script within a month.

"Francis came in and did an absolute miracle job," Clayton has said, adding that he made only minor alterations in the screenplay that Coppola turned over to him. Clayton did admit to removing some passages from the script that he thought were superfluous, however, and to putting into the screenplay some material from the book that Coppola had not originally included. But anything that was added to the film, Clayton emphasized, "was *always* in the book." Yet it is precisely Clayton's additions to his screenplay that Coppola afterwards contended were responsible for extending the duration of the finished film to the point where the movie seemed, in his estimation, "interminable." One salient example will suffice to illustrate Coppola's point.

On the one hand, Coppola had included in his script the scene from the novel in which Gatsby's father, Henry Gatz, comes to town for his son's funeral, although it was left out of the earlier 1949 remake altogether. He did so because he thought it important for the viewer to see that, ironically enough, in the eyes of at least one person, little Jimmy Gatz had really grown up to be the great Gatsby; for, as far as Henry Gatz could tell, his son had become a distinguished man of business, possessed, at the time of his death, of an enormous estate complete with all the luxuries that money could buy.

On the other hand, Coppola did not believe that the film should continue on to depict the funeral itself, in spite of the fact that that scene too is in the book, because he felt that by the time such a scene were played out in detail on the screen, it would needlessly protract the running time of a film he was hoping could be kept down to a manageable length. Coppola had planned instead to have the movie conclude with a further touch of irony. As Coppola describes the final scene as he envisioned it, Gatsby's father, while looking around his son's bedroom, "sees the picture of Daisy, and he says, 'Who's the girl?'" That, Coppola maintains, should really have been "the end of the movie."

Had Mr. Gatz's remark about the photograph been used to

conclude the film, Coppola continues, it would have neatly tied in with the shot of this same photograph of Daisy which appears in the course of the movie's opening credits. In this manner the movie would have both begun and ended with the picture of Daisy, Gatsby's most cherished possession, and the symbol of his dreams and ambitions. "So what I had set up at the beginning," Coppola concludes, would have gone "all the way to the end."[33] By adding the lengthy funeral sequence to the script as a replacement for his own much more terse finale to the movie, Coppola contends that Clayton made the closing scenes of the movie which follow Gatsby's death seem less like an epilogue than an anti-climax.

Regardless of which side one takes in the matter of Clayton's adding the funeral episode to Coppola's script, it must be conceded that all of the interpolations which Clayton made in the screenplay, taken together, would eventually result in a motion picture that in the last analysis seemed at times slow paced and overlong. To that extent it seems that in the long run Coppola's complaints about Clayton's revisions of his screenplay were ultimately justified.

At any rate, once the final shooting script was completed, principal photography was set to begin on June 11, 1973, on location in Newport, Rhode Island, where one can still find along Millionaire's Road mansions expansive enough to serve for the homes of Gatsby and the Buchanans. Bruce Dern, who plays Tom Buchanan in the film, commented on the first day of shooting that Clayton was very cognizant of the fact that he was committing to film what many consider to be one of the very best American novels ever penned. "He doesn't want it to bother him," said Dern, "but it does now and then"—though certainly not to the extent that it bothered Elliott Nugent.

As a matter of fact, Clayton's temperament turned out to be precisely the opposite of Nugent's. Whereas Elliott Nugent was apt to become nervous and dejected when things went wrong during shooting, Clayton, normally gracious and polite with cast and crew, would be more liable to blow off steam impulsively in some active way—for example, smashing out a window with his fist—and then going right back to work.

Gatsby's colossal parties were going to be staged over a period of nine consecutive nights in the house and on the grounds of one of the grander estates in the millionaires' colony. As Robert Redford put it, Gatsby sees his mansion as a "monument . . . for his passion for Daisy," and so it would have to appear in the movie to be just as spectacular a showplace as the one which the film unit had in fact appropriated for the filming of the party sequences.[34]

No expense was spared to re-create the atmosphere of the period while the party scenes were being shot: antique cars lined the driveway in front of the house, and the gowns worn by the ladies were 1920 originals. To top it off, some of the extras who played Gatsby's crass menagerie of roistering party guests were actually scions of Newport's first families. One bejeweled matron, who stood from 6:00 p.m. to 6:00 a.m. while one of the party scenes was being photographed, commented afterwards that, although the extras were only "paid $1.65 an hour, . . . I would do it again if I could stand up."[35]

Except for the exterior scenes filmed at Newport, the bulk of the movie was shot in England, principally at Elstree Studios outside of London. Producer David Merrick, who is mostly known for his stage productions (*Hello Dolly*, etc.) decided to move the film unit to England to shoot the interior scenes at a British studio largely because, in the early seventies, production costs were almost double in the States what they were in Britain. So the majority of the film was shot in England for financial reasons, and not, as some industry insiders gratuitously assumed, because the film's director happened to be British.

Shooting at Elstree continued through the summer and into the fall; and Clayton photographed the last shot of the film, a closeup of Nick Carraway, at four o'clock on the afternoon of September 24, 1973. Principal photography was thus finished about a week ahead of schedule. By November 29 a preliminary assemblage of the footage had been completed; and composer Nelson Riddle recorded his background music for the film during the week of January 8, 1974. Riddle's superlative score proved to be a jazzy pastiche of popular songs from the twenties, skillfully interwoven with original music of his own; and he fully deserved the Academy Award which he received for it.

Riddle had several consultations with Clayton during the period when he was scoring the movie; and Clayton's concern about the film's incidental music is just one example of the painstaking attention to detail which he gave to every aspect of the production.

As a result, the movie is filled with the kind of subtle little touches that have become Clayton's trademark. For example, Clayton first implies Gatsby's gangland connections in the picture, not by the somewhat obvious use of a montage of Gatsby's underworld activities, as was done in the 1949 movie, but by a closeup of a revolver bulging under the jacket of one of Gatsby's retainers; this implies, rather ominously, that the man is not Gatsby's valet, as one might suppose, but his bodyguard. As one member of the film's technical crew noted, Jack Clayton thoroughly thought out every aspect of the production long before the cameras began turning. And it paid off.

Scottie Fitzgerald Smith, who watched some of the shooting in Newport, was especially impressed with the way in which Clayton had carefully chosen the location sites for the movie. In fact, she thought the settings in general were "the best thing about the third *Gatsby*. So much of what my father wrote is evocative—of music, of romantic surroundings, of the beauty with which the rich surround themselves—that the background is terribly important, it seems to me." She also judged that the screenplay as Coppola had originally conceived it, which she read in advance, "was excellent in every detail."

Nonetheless she had some serious reservations about other aspects of the film. "I was invited to fly out to Hollywood for the preview to express my opinion, which was indeed a joke; as I expressed it forcefully and nobody paid the slightest attention," she recalls. Like Coppola, she thought the film "much too long," and pointed out that it "could have been cut even at the last minute without any difficulty." Scottie Smith also found flaws in the casting. Besides being no more pleased with the casting of Robert Redford as Gatsby than Howard da Silva was, she also found it difficult to accept Mia Farrow as Daisy. Daisy is "intensely Southern," she explained; and Mia Farrow, "fine actress though she is," failed to project this aspect of Daisy's personality."[36] For the record, Manny Farber said the same thing about Betty Field's portrayal of Daisy in the 1949 film. Though in other ways she made a first-class Daisy, said Farber, her performance was "no more marked by Southern aristocracy than a cheese blintz."[37]

"Other parts were poorly cast also, in my opinion," Scottie Smith went on. "Tom, though again very well acted, did not at all fit the picture one has on reading the book of a rugged, handsome 'physical specimen.' My feeling was that the discomfort one felt on seeing the actors contrast so with one's imaginary picture of them was what doomed the movie."[38] Many of the critics shared some or all of Mrs. Smith's reasons for being disappointed with the film, though the picture was commercially successful.

Ever since the release of the Clayton *Gatsby* in 1974, film scholars have been divided on the question of whether or not it is superior to the Nugent *Gatsby* of 1949. It is true that the two movies differ in various details, such as the fact that the later version of the book carried over Gatsby's father, Henry Gatz, from the novel into the film but eliminated his father-figure, Dan Cody, from the movie's cast of characters, while the earlier movie did just the opposite. But, prescinding from such specific plot points, one still must ask what sort of overall judgment can be rendered about the relative merits of the two adaptations of one of American fiction's great novels.

First of all, Nugent's film, which was made on a relatively modest budget and runs a little more than an hour-and-a-half, tells its story in a straightforward, fast-paced fashion, with a minimum of character development. As soon as the Jazz Age prologue flashes on the screen, the story is underway; and it moves along at a brisk clip, with very little letup in the action, right straight through to the end. By contrast, Clayton's movie, a sumptuous $6.5 million production shot in color, is technically more finely wrought than the previous movie; moreover, it is also nearly an hour longer than the earlier film and therefore devotes more screen time to an in-depth examination of the psychology of character than was feasible in Nugent's shorter, sparer movie.

Hence the 1949 movie goes into overdrive before the moviegoer has a chance to get closely acquainted with the principals, with the result that one cannot identify with them to the same degree that one can in the 1974 movie. For example, in the later film the moviegoer better understands why the defeated, emotionally distraught George Wilson (Scott Wilson) is driven to commit murder in order to avenge his wife's death, simply because Clayton spends more screen time in portraying George's mental breakdown after Myrtle's death. "Most murders are crimes of passion," Scott Wilson explained on the set. George shoots the man whom he has been led to believe killed his wife because George believes that the person responsible for Myrtle's death robbed him of the one thing of value in his otherwise wretched, worthless life. Why, after all, should we necessarily assume that Myrtle means less to Wilson than Daisy means to Gatsby? "The audience should be torn by Wilson's murder of Gatsby," said Scott Wilson; but they should also be moved "to have a little sympathy for him,[39] especially when he takes his own life because, in his despair over the loss of Myrtle, he feels that he has nothing left to live for.

Because Clayton's adaptation of the novel takes its time in developing character, it is hence less tightly constructed than its immediate predecessor. Therefore, it contains some sluggish, talky stretches that occasionally cause the viewer's interest to flag, something that never happens in the Nugent film.

After all is said and done, it seems that whether or not one believes that the 1949 movie is a greater *Gatsby* than its 1974 successor largely depends on whether one prefers the freshness and spontaneity of a film that emphasizes action over character development to a slower, but denser motion picture that reflects a deeper probing of character. Ultimately an individual filmgoer's choice in this matter basically says more about his or her personal cinematic taste than perhaps it does about the relative artistic worth of the two films themselves. My own capsule comment on the two movies would be that Clayton's screen adaptation of Fitzgerald's novel is in some ways more to be admired than enjoyed, while Nugent's version of the book is the more immediately accessible of the two films.

Still, as I have indicated all along, there is much to be said for both films. If the 1949 *Gatsby* ends with the haunting image of the eyes of Dr. Eckleburg, the 1974 *Gatsby* concludes with an equally compelling image: a somber shot of Gatsby's dark deserted mansion, as it looks now that he is dead and gone. This lingering image summons up the observation that Nick Carraway makes near the end of the novel, when he sees a car pull up to Gatsby's front steps one evening not long after his murder. The auto pauses momentarily and then drives on. "Probably," Nick muses, "it was some final guest who had been away at the ends of the earth and didn't know that the party was over" (p. 181). Little did Nick or anyone else know at the time that the decade-long party that was the Jazz Age would soon be over too.

SEVEN

THE *STAG* AT EVE:

TENDER IS THE NIGHT

The stag at eve had drunk his fill.
                              —*Sir Walter Scott*

Forget your personal tragedy. We are all bitched
from the start. . . . You see, [Scott], you're not a
tragic character. Neither am I. All we are is writers
and what we should do is write.
                              —*Ernest Hemingway*

Walking along the pleasant Mediterranean coast, one may survey
the bright strip of beach where Scott Fitzgerald once frolicked
with his family and friends, accounts of which he recorded in his *Ledger*.
Some of these incidents, along with the people who principally figured
in them, were to turn up in his novel, *Tender Is the Night*, just as certain
episodes from his first years of marriage had insinuated themselves into
The Beautiful and Damned, and his courtship of Zelda had surfaced in
Gatsby.

One such real-life event that would become part of *Tender Is the
Night* was the fleeting infatuation Zelda entertained during the

summer of 1924 for a French aviator, Edouard Jozan [not Josanne, as Mizener and other Fitzgerald scholars have misspelled it, due to Fitzgerald's customarily atrocious spelling in the *Ledger* (p. 179)].

Now that all the facts are in, it does seem that Fitzgerald overreacted rather spectacularly to what in retrospect seems not to have amounted to much more than a passing fancy on Zelda's part, something of a schoolgirl crush on a he-man whom she had met on the beach. Jozan has more than once gone on record to assert in no uncertain terms that their casual flirtation never developed into anything like a full-scale love affair; much less did it result in adultery.

But the fact remains that Fitzgerald did respond to the situation in a histrionic fashion, thereby causing a lesion in his relationship with his wife that never quite healed. Indeed, his notation in the *Ledger* for August 1924, "Zelda and I close together" after "the big crisis" in July, sounds a little like wishful thinking (p. 178), since it was some time before their marriage was once more on anything like an even keel. He subsequently wrote somewhat more realistically in his *Notebooks* that he had come to realize that, by the end of the summer of 1924, "something had happened that could not be repaired" (#839); by that he meant that a fundamental sense of mutual trust had gone out of their marriage, never to return.

Furthermore, when in 1927 Fitzgerald became temporarily attracted to a young silent film star, Lois Moran, whom he first met in Hollywood while he was writing *Lipstick*, it seems that the Jozan affair was still something of a live issue. He afterwards hinted that maybe this might have been his way of subconsciously "paying back" Zelda for her earlier indiscretion. The fact of the matter is that Lois Moran's interest in Fitzgerald amounted to little more than hero worship. "I thought he was perfect," she reminisced in 1971; "a writer to me was the greatest thing in the world. I lived for books from the time I was three. To know and be with one of the great writers. . . . It was just a beautiful experience as far as I was concerned."[1] It goes without saying that Fitzgerald basked in the attentions of this young actress.

But in the last analysis, Fitzgerald was no more nor less committed to Lois Moran than his wife had been to her French flyer; still Zelda quite understandably elected to react with the same degree of outrage that her husband had displayed in the summer of 1924. So once more their mutual rapport was damaged by a crisis, which in the long run proved to be simply not worth all the fuss that was made about it. "But they both had a need of drama," commented Edouard Jozan two decades after these events took place. "Perhaps they were the victims of their own unsettled and a little unhealthy imaginations."[2]

As these and other sources of friction developed between the couple, their bitter verbal battles began to be punctuated with mutual recriminations of the kind that leave scars deeper than any physical blow could ever inflict. For instance, in the course of their quarrels, Zelda at various times challenged her husband's manhood on two counts. The first charge was that he was not adequately equipped to give her genuine sexual satisfaction. "She said it was a matter of measurements," he explained to Hemingway when he sought his friend's advice in the matter one day while they were having lunch together in Paris. "Go over to the Louvre and look at the people in the statues, and then go home and look at yourself in the mirror," Hemingway advised him reassuringly. "There's nothing wrong with you.[3]

The other question that his wife raised he could not have discussed with Hemingway (whose antipathy for Zelda was matched only by her disdain for him). This is because the point at issue involved the insinuation that her husband was a latent invert, and that his friendship with Hemingway, whom she jeeringly described as a phony he-man, "a pansy with hair on his chest,"[4] was subconsciously homosexual in bent. "The nearest I ever came to leaving you was when you told me you thought I was a fairy," Fitzgerald told his wife in a "position paper" about their marriage, which he may never actually have shown her.[5] In point of fact, Zelda's allegations concerning her husband's sexual orientation may have been a projection of her own suspicions about whether or not she was becoming too emotionally dependent on her ballet teacher, Madame Lubov Egorova, with whom she began training in the summer of 1928, while she and Scott were sojourning in Paris.

But Zelda's ballet lessons caused the tensions between husband and wife to mount for other reasons too. As noted already, Fitzgerald accused Zelda of wrongheadedly pursuing a career as a dancer at an age when she could no longer hope to become a seasoned ballerina, just to have a professional life of her own that would in some sense rival his; and he would later criticize her efforts at painting and creative writing as being spurred on by the same relentless spirit of competition.

As we know, Zelda maintained that she was only trying to carve out an identity for herself that went beyond being the wife of a famous writer. When this bone of contention was discussed in the course of a confrontation between the Fitzgeralds which took place in the presence of a psychiatrist and was recorded by a stenographer, she broached the possibility of leaving her husband. "I don't want to live with you," she explained, "because I want to live some place that I can be my own self."[6]

As things turned out, Zelda became so obsessed with becoming a ballerina that her long hours of punishing practice began to take a terrific toll on both her physical and her psychic energies. "Zelda dancing and sweating," Fitzgerald observed ruefully in his *Ledger* in September 1929 (p. 183). Inevitably, the strain of working so long and hard to become a reputable ballet dancer looms large as one of the principal reasons for Zelda Fitzgerald's mental collapse. Because the Fitzgeralds were living in Europe at the time that her mental health finally broke down in the spring of 1930, she was committed to the Prangins Clinic on Lake Geneva in Nyon, Switzerland, the first of many institutions to which she would be intermittently confined the rest of her life. Such was the background of psychological tension and turmoil in the personal lives of the Fitzgeralds which was to become the genesis of Fitzgerald's fourth novel, *Tender Is the Night*.

Tender Is the Night: The Novel

In the novel Fitzgerald fictionalizes the circumstances of his wife's mental illness by making Dick Diver, the character modeled on himself, not a writer, but a promising young psychiatrist who meets his wealthy wife-to-be, Nicole Warren, while she is a patient in a Swiss sanatarium where he is on the staff. Besides being based on the Fitzgeralds themselves, Dick and Nicole Diver are also modeled on Gerald and Sara Murphy, to whom the novel is dedicated. The Murphys were a wealthy Irish-Catholic American couple who were the hub around which revolved much of the social life of the Americans summering on the Riviera during the twenties, as are the Divers when we first meet them in the book, before tragedy takes over.

In addition, navy pilot Edouard Jozan finds a place in the novel as soldier-of-fortune Tommy Barban, whose roving eye focuses on Nicole after she and Dick are married, and who eventually lures her away from her husband for good. Then, too, Lois Moran shows up in the novel as actress Rosemary Hoyt, who for a time turns Dick's head.

Fitzgerald made a number of false starts on the novel before he found the subject he was looking for. "I began work on it very slowly indeed," turning to it whenever he wasn't composing short stories, he said in an explanatory note to the novel, which did not, however, appear in the book when it was published. "I picked it up and dropped it."[7] As a matter of fact, he found the going so tough at first that he wrote an admirer in the fall of 1929, "If I ever survive this damned thing I shall devote my life to musical comedy librettos," which is how he began his writing career at Princeton. At that point he was endeavoring without much success to make the character who would eventually evolve into Rosemary Hoyt the central figure in the novel.

In a letter written a bit earlier, Fitzgerald told Hemingway that he was so discouraged with what he had written up to that point that he hoped that the house would burn down with the manuscript, "and preferably me, in it." Hemingway responded with some typically terse advice: "You damned fool, go on and write the novel." Hemingway's point was that Fitzgerald should stop trying to turn out a masterpiece that would top *Gatsby*, because a writer only gets frustrated and bogged down when he attempts to compete with himself. All any novelist can do, Hemingway continued, is to do the best he can, going on the assumption that "if this one, when it's done, isn't a masterpiece, maybe the next one will be."[8] And so Fitzgerald kept at it.

The first indication that Fitzgerald finally had his plot well in hand, after he had scuttled several unpromising storylines for the novel, was the short story "One Trip Abroad," which the *Post* published on October 11, 1930, a few months after Zelda had been committed to Prangins. The story gives every indication of being a preliminary précis of the novel, signalled by the heroine's name being the same in both the novel and short story, as well as by the story being set in part in a Swiss convalescent home. "One Trip Abroad," writes Arthur Mizener, was "Fitzgerald's first attempt to come to terms with his life after Zelda's breakdown the previous spring."[9] It is the bud, one might say, of which the novel published four years later, is the flower.

The time span covered by the novel is from the mid-twenties, where *Gatsby* ends, to the onset of the Great Depression, which spelled the end of the "golden" twenties. "The Jazz Age is over," Fitzgerald wrote to Perkins in 1931; it had extended from the end of World War I "to the crash of the stock market in 1929—almost exactly one decade."[10] In his *Ledger* Fitzgerald summarizes his thirty-third year of life this way: "The Crash! Zelda and America" (p. 184). For Fitzgerald, then, 1929 was the year when the country as a whole went to pieces just as his own domestic life was beginning to come apart. This double crack-up is at the heart of the novel, which ends with Dick Diver experiencing his own private state of depression after his breakup with Nicole, just as the depression hits America as a whole.

As noted, Nicole belongs to the wealthy Warren clan. Like the Buchanans in *Gatsby*, the Warrens are "an American ducal family without a title."[11] Indeed, Lehan writes that it is just a short step from "the hopelessly spoiled and irresponsible" Buchanans to the Warrens of *Tender Is the Night*, a group of "parasites who have lost the capacity to love."[12] Nicole's psychological collapse was in actual fact precipitated by her incestuous relationship with her own father. The idle rich, Fitzgerald suggests, feed on each other when they are not exploiting people outside their "charmed circle," such as Dick Diver.

The Warrens' self-centered creed is epitomized in Nicole's sister, whose nickname, "Baby," aptly describes her as a selfish child at heart. Baby Warren encourages Nicole to marry Dick because she feels that if Nicole's therapist is also her husband, this will insure that he will devote himself almost exclusively to Nicole, who subconsciously sees Dick as a kind of substitute father. As Dick becomes more and more enmeshed in the Warren family's personal problems, which involve nothing less than incest and insanity, he begins to see himself as "the last hope of a decaying clan" (p. 300). But gradually he comes to realize that, to his shame, he has sold his career as a psychiatrist to the Warrens on the installment plan. In effect Dick has permitted himself to be "swallowed up like a gigolo," and has somehow allowed his professional abilities "to be locked up in the Warren safety-deposit vaults" (p. 201).

Consequently Dick gradually loses all sense of purpose; he turns more and more to alcohol to keep himself going and briefly seeks solace in the love of Rosemary Hoyt. Significantly, Rosemary's big movie hit is entitled *Daddy's Girl*, for that symbolically sums up the immature girl's relationship with Dick. Indeed, as Miller says, the difference in their ages is such as "to render their embrace a kind of reenactment of the incestuous affair between Nicole and her father."[13] Their relationship is doomed from the start; Rosemary discards Dick as a lover for pretty much the same reason that Nicole will soon shed Dick as a husband: she comes to realize that she no longer needs or wants a father figure as a mate.

And so, when Dick has depleted the last of his store of psychic reserves in helping his wife regain her sanity and is therefore of no further use to her or the family, Nicole, at Baby's urging, callously leaves him for the crass Philistine Tommy Barban (short for barbarian?). After Nicole walks out on him, Dick finds that he has sunk into a state of complete emotional exhaustion, and no longer wants anything more out of life than to fade "at last into the tender night, where he hopes nothing will ever be required of him again."[14] The stag at eve has had his fill.

Since Dick had allowed himself to be bought by the Warrens, Fitzgerald fittingly describes Dick's psychological condition at the end of the novel in financial terms: emotional bankruptcy. Fitzgerald's point is that Dick invested all of his emotional capital in Nicole, both as her husband and her doctor; and when he had spent it all on her and had nothing left to give, she and the rest of the family abandoned him. But the novelist does not mean to imply that Dick is a martyr or a saint. In his final outline of the novel's action, dated 1932, Fitzgerald goes on to call Dick a "spoiled priest" who has renounced his vocation as a healer of the spirit for an empty life of "drink and dissipation."[15] By novel's end, then, one wonders if Dick Diver, whose once promising career has definitely taken a nose dive, will ever be able to pull himself out of the lower depths; but Fitzgerald offers no clear forecast.

Still, his father's life of pastoral service as a clergyman, which Dick reflects upon more than once in the course of the novel, remains an undiminished source of inspiration for Dick, who had once consecrated himself to be a physician of the soul. In fact, it is possibly out of reverence for his father's memory that Dick makes a symbolic gesture just as he is about to depart the Riviera for good. He turns toward the shore one last time, and from the terrace on which he stands, he makes the Sign of the Cross over his loved ones down on the beach whom he is leaving behind, in much the same manner that his father would have bestowed his blessing on his flock. Despite Dick's fall from grace, then, one infers that perhaps his father will continue to be an abiding reminder of the sort of dedicated person he himself once was, and hopefully can be again.

Just before *Tender Is the Night* was published on April 12, 1934, writer James Thurber happened to meet Fitzgerald one evening in early April in a bar in downtown Manhattan. Writing nearly twenty years later about their encounter, Thurber said: "The collar of his topcoat was turned up rakishly on one side and his hat, which he kept on, was pulled down jauntily over one eye. It was an almost studied effect, but it was oddly contradicted" by the curious air of uneasiness and worry that marked Fitzgerald's behavior that night. Thurber soon discovered that Fitzgerald was not only apprehensive about the reception that would be accorded his latest novel when it appeared. He was also concerned about the success of the exhibition of his wife's paintings, which was being held throughout the month of April in a New York studio, the product of the interest in painting which Zelda had developed while she was hospitalized.

Fitzgerald's pockets were bulging with copies of the catalogue for Zelda's show, Thurber remembered; and "by midnight I must have had a dozen of these in my own pockets because he kept absently handing them to me." In the light of the bitter arguments that Fitzgerald had with his wife over her pursuing a career of her own in the arts, it is touching to think that he was just as preoccupied that evening with the success of Zelda's exhibit as he was with the imminent appearance of his new book. "All that night Zelda was in his lap," said Thurber, and anyone else whom Fitzgerald might be conversing with could just as well have been a million miles away.

Both the novel and the art show, however, got mixed reviews. "If Zelda had completely recovered in that lovely springtime, and if his novel had been well received by the critics," Thurber mused, "I think he would never have turned to destructive drinking"; and he might have gone on living and writing for a good many more years than he did.[16] But that was not to be.

Novelist John O'Hara has explained the somewhat less-than-enthusiastic response given the novel by press and public alike by saying that "the book came out at precisely the wrong time in the national history. No matter how good it was, it was about the Bad People," the rich and well-born. They were "the villains of the Depression," and hence other Americans did not want to read about them.[17] Even though O'Hara's explanation of the lukewarm reception of the book has become a critical commonplace among Fitzgerald commentators, it does not hold up under close scrutiny. For, as Bruccoli shrewdly points out, a study of the best-sellers of 1934 indicates that readers during the Great Depression were willing to read other books about the rich. The public more than likely avoided *Tender Is the Night* because it was a dark, disturbing tale of unhappiness and failure; and during the depression people were more in the market for escape fiction than for novels of grim realism.

Fitzgerald theorized that the novel might have attracted more readers had he told the story in chronological order, instead of dropping into the middle of the book a ten-chapter flashback about how the Divers came to meet and marry. He subsequently toyed with the idea of placing these ten chapters at the beginning of the novel, thereby allowing the entire plot to proceed in chronological sequence from beginning to end. This would mean, he wrote to Perkins, that the novel's real beginning, "the young psychiatrist in Switzerland," would no longer be "tucked away in the middle of the book."[18]

Some literary critics think that the sequence of events in the novel should have been reordered in the manner Fitzgerald described. But I would prefer to side with those who feel that the real reason that Fitzgerald entertained the idea of publishing a new edition of the novel, in which the story would be narrated according to the principle of strict chronology, was because he wanted to bring the book to the attention of the critics and the public a second time, and not because he was deeply committed to the idea that the story of the novel as originally published lacked narrative coherence in any essential way. One certainly cannot blame Fitzgerald for casting about for some device whereby he might give the novel a second chance at success; but, truth to tell, the present novel's time sequence is no more challenging to the reader than the somewhat similar mingling of past and present events which Fitzgerald accomplished in *The Great Gatsby*.

In both books Fitzgerald tantalizes the reader with intriguing hints about the past lives of the central characters, before he permits the facts about their earlier lives to come to light. This is a very effective way of maximizing reader interest; and hence I, for one, am glad that the standard edition of *Tender Is the Night* remains the one that was originally published.

As for Zelda Fitzgerald's reaction to *Tender*, she took a look at the completed novel just prior to publication, and was at first very angry and hurt by what she read. "What made me mad," she explained forthrightly to a doctor at the sanatarium where she was staying at the time, was that her husband had made Nicole "so awful and kept on reiterating how she had ruined [Dick's] life; and I couldn't help identifying myself with her because she had so many of my experiences." Zelda did not believe that she had behaved toward Scott in a fashion at all akin to the self-centered manner in which Nicole had manipulated Dick; and yet that seemed to her to be the implication of the story. "I don't think it's true; I don't think it's what really happened."[19]

In writing to Zelda, Fitzgerald warned his wife against projecting too much of their personal lives into the novel, and asked her not to re-read it. "It represents certain phases of life that are over now," he explained. "Forget the past—what you can of it." She replied, "You seem afraid that" reading the book a second time "will make me recapitulate the past. . . . I guess most of life is a rehashing of the tragedies and happinesses" of days gone by; and so she saw no point in avoiding another encounter with the novel.

When she did re-read *Tender* after publication, she found that her attitude toward the book had softened considerably. In one letter to Scott she dismissed the negative reviews of the novel as undiscerning and silly; and in another she added that "you have the satisfaction of having written a tragic and poetic personal drama against the background of an excellent presentation of the times we matured in."[20] She also said that she hoped that Ernest Hemingway liked the book, since she was aware of how much her husband respected Hemingway's critical judgment. But her hope was not fulfilled, for Hemingway's reaction to the novel was just as mixed as many of the reviews had been.

"I liked it and I didn't like it," he wrote to Fitzgerald. He expatiated on this remark by saying that Fitzgerald had gone ahead and made the mistake that he had cautioned him against while Fitzgerald was working on the novel: he had tried too hard to produce a masterpiece. As a result, Fitzgerald had reworked his material to the point where some passages seemed self-consciously overwritten and artificial. "It's a lot better than I say," he concluded. "But it's not as good as you can do."

Yet Hemingway also subsequently re-evaluated the novel, just as Zelda had done; and he subsequently conceded in a letter to Fitzgerald that, "the more I think back to it, the better book *Tender Is the Night* is." What's more, after Fitzgerald's death he told Perkins that his final assessment of the book was that it possessed "wonderful atmosphere and magical descriptions," and as true a tragic vision as Fitzgerald had ever put into a novel. To publisher Charles Scribner, Hemingway further noted that *Tender* was the finest thing Fitzgerald ever wrote. "Parts of it are really wonderful."[21]

It is a pity that Fitzgerald could not have read Hemingway's final thoughts about the novel at the time the book came out, since the book's reception had fallen so far below the author's expectations. Furthermore, by the mid-thirties, the high-paying slicks had lost interest in his short fiction because he had begun turning his stories out too hastily and carelessly to meet the standards of magazines like the *Post*, which had for so many years been his most dependable standby. Fitzgerald slid into the panicky, short-sighted practice of churning out short stories in a hurry when it became abundantly clear to him that the sales of his novels were never going to be sufficient to support his wife and daughter. Anne Ober, the wife of Fitzgerald's literary agent, remembers her husband showing her a story that Fitzgerald had submitted to him around this time. The typed pages were "written over in red ink, blotched, almost illegible. . . . Harold said that was the way Scott's stories had been coming in lately." And with that Ober burst into tears.[22]

"The Crack-Up"

The decline of Fitzgerald's fortunes as a writer in the thirties, mirrored in the increasing lack of critical and public acceptance of his work, left him deeply dejected, as did his wife's ongoing emotional illness. These personal and professional problems cumulatively precipitated a dark night of the soul for him at this point in his life which was marked by extreme depression and steady drinking. He was, he said, living in the black hole of Calcutta and felt mentally, emotionally, and physically exhausted. His psychological condition paralleled, he realized, "the wave of despair that swept the nation when the Boon was over,"[23] since his own personal boon was over too; for there was little doubt that his career, and his life with it, had reached its lowest ebb ever.

Looking back at the time when their troubles had first begun to multiply with a vengeance, Fitzgerald recalled for his wife that things really started to go wrong for both of them when, because of her excessive absorption in the ballet, she was "going crazy and calling it genius"; and, because of his own drinking and dissipation, he "was going to ruin and calling it anything that came to hand."[24] As he gradually tried to sort out why things had turned out so badly for both of them, he figured out that one-half of their relatives and friends, Hemingway included, were convinced that Zelda's "insanity drove me to drink"; and the other half maintained that "my drinking drove Zelda insane." But neither of these contradictory propositions was accurate, he decided because, as he observed to Zelda, "We ruined ourselves; I have never honestly thought that we ruined each other."[25]

Once he had pulled himself together and began to get over this period of profound spiritual desolation, he wrote about the experience in a trio of "confessional" articles which *Esquire* ran in the spring of 1936. The first of these essays, "The Crack-Up," gave its title to the collection of his non-fiction, already cited, which Edmund Wilson published shortly after Fitzgerald died. The "Crack-Up" essays as a group, Turnbull comments, are patently "the work of a lapsed Catholic, for whom confession was a rhythm of the soul." Reflecting the spiritual values that his Catholic education had afforded him, these essays embody a public examination of conscience which testifies to the fact that, as noted, the Catholic faith had a firmer hold on Fitzgerald than he was aware of. "He was fundamentally a moralist and a very religious person," Nora Flynn, a close friend of Fitzgerald's during the thirties, used to say. "He kept his soul."[26]

Tender Is the Night: Fitzgerald's Scenario

One of the things that Fitzgerald did in the hope of giving his failing bank account a transfusion was to offer the movie rights of *Tender Is the Night* to Hollywood. Toward this end he prepared a ten-thousand-word screen treatment of the novel with the help of a young protégé of his, Charles Warren, later a successful TV producer (*Gunsmoke*). But Warren did not succeed in finding financial backing for the scenario when Fitzgerald dispatched him to Hollywood to promote the property around the studio circuit. One need only examine the treatment to see why.

Suffice it to say that Fitzgerald took the same approach to the film adaptation of *Tender* that he adopted in creating scenarios for *This Side of Paradise* and "Babylon Revisited," already discussed. He overburdened the action-packed plot line of the scenario with a plethora of melodramatic incidents; and once again Fitzgerald managed to serve up a happy ending which his original story did not have, this time by having Dick and Nicole reconciled after he saves her life on the operating table. In the nick of time Dick removes a brain tumor which Nicole had developed after she was thrown from a horse in a riding incident. This is just the kind of contrived finale that Fitzgerald would have given the horse laugh if it had been dreamed up by some Hollywood hack and tacked onto his tale. The closing lines of the treatment indicate how far the scenario had wandered from the tragic import of its literary source: "Both Dick and Nicole are happily content to look towards a future that promises brighter than it ever has before."[27]

Admittedly, because Fitzgerald was desperate for money when he undertook to fashion a movie scenario from the novel, he had tried to come up with the sort of sure-fire plot that he thought the Hollywood moguls would be most interested in buying. But the fact remains that the compelling psychological study which he had originally fashioned for his novel has been so oversimplified in the scenario based upon it that the latter reads like cookbook Freud and bargain basement Fitzgerald. Therefore it does not begin to do justice to his own book.

Tender Is the Night: Malcolm Lowry's Scenario

Fitzgerald was not the only novelist to try his hand at adapting *Tender Is the Night* to the screen. British novelist Malcolm Lowry (*Under the Volcano*), aided by his wife Margerie (not Marjorie, as her name is often misspelled), also took a crack at this challenging endeavor. The possibility of writing a film adaptation of *Tender* was brought to Lowry's attention in July 1949, by MGM producer Frank Taylor, who had been editor in chief at Reynal Hitchcock when that firm had published *Under the Volcano* two years before. He sent to Lowry, who was living in Canada at this point in his life, a treatment derived from Fitzgerald's novel, which he had done himself in collaboration with MGM production chief Dore Schary. Taylor explained that plans to produce the film had been shelved because he and Schary were not satisfied with their scenario; and he asked Lowry if he could devise something better.

Lowry became so taken with the task of making a viable screen adaptation of Fitzgerald's novel that he, along with his wife, worked on the project all summer long and straight through to the spring of the following year. In the end, the brief treatment which Taylor had asked for had grown into a gargantuan screenplay of more than four hundred pages. This Lowry mailed to Taylor on April 12, 1950, accompanied by a set of explanatory notes which run to nearly one hundred pages by themselves, and are intended to provide a running commentary on the script.

In the covering letter which he sent with the script, Lowry conceded that the screenplay might be considered unusually long, since it was about three times the length of the average movie script. Nevertheless, he insisted that enough material from the novel had been left out of the screenplay to form the plot of a Puccini opera. Besides, he was quite willing to shorten the screenplay according to studio specifications, since the script as it stood was designed to be no more than "an adjustable blueprint" for the proposed film. If the script were to be condensed, however, Lowry wanted to avoid, if at all possible, employing the disembodied voice of a narrator on the sound track to bridge the gaps left in the narrative by the excised plot material. When a narrator is used in a film in this artificial manner, he contended, it is "as if the cinema manager were to get up and give a speech"; in short, a narrator "is indefensible in a film unless he or she is personally part of the plot,"[28] as, say, Nick Carraway was in *The Great Gatsby.*

As might be expected, Taylor was not able to stir up much enthusiasm at Metro for Lowry's enormous screenplay; but in January 1951, he advised Lowry that he had left MGM for Fox, and had brought the *Tender* script with him. Still he had no better luck in exciting enthusiasm at Fox than he had had at MGM. Then, in November 1954, Taylor advised Lowry that he had submitted the script to independent producer David O. Selznick, who had recently purchased the screen rights to the novel. Selznick, however, had already engaged a more experienced screenwriter, Ivan Moffat, to do the script for his production; and neither he nor Moffat was interested in reading the Lowry adaptation.

Fitzgerald scholar Benjamin Dunlap has written that the wholesale rejection of the Lowry script all but restores one's faith in Hollywood's commercial wisdom, since Lowry's mammoth screenplay, labor of love though it might have been, was simply too lengthy and too complex to serve as the basis of a motion picture of normal length. Practically speaking, it was easier for Selznick to commission a new adaptation of the novel by a different screenwriter than to have Lowry undertake the daunting task of distilling his sprawling screenplay into a script of workable dimensions. So, when a movie version of *Tender Is the Night* finally went before the cameras in 1961, it was Moffat's screenplay, not Lowry's that was filmed.

One must say in favor of the Lowry script that at least it did not reduce the plot line of the novel to superficial melodrama, as Fitzgerald's own scenario tended to do. On the other hand, the ending which Lowry supplied for his film version of the book is not any more acceptable than the one that Fitzgerald himself had devised for his own adaptation of the novel. In the book the last we hear of Dick Diver, after he leaves France and returns to the United States, is that he has become a small town general practitioner somewhere in New York State; after that, he drops out of sight completely. As said before, Fitzgerald concluded the novel in a way that leaves Dick's eventual fate in doubt, and thus permits the reader to speculate about whether or not Dick will ever again become a mender of hearts and minds, or will instead remain emotionally and spiritually bankrupt.

For Lowry the novel's dénouement was a real letdown, since for him the book concluded, not with a bang but a whimper. In contrast, Lowry believed that "Dick deserves better of his creator than a half-written exit," and hence in his screenplay he accorded the story a more "spectacular ending." So Lowry has Dick drown in a shipwreck at sea on his way back to America, thereby implicitly making "final atonement" for his misspent life.[29] I am compelled to concur with Dunlap that, despite the fact that the name Diver assumes new irony in Lowry's ending for the story, Dick's "obscurely drawn-out purgatory in the American hinterlands is a far more terrible and appropriate" kind of expiation for his sins than that proposed by Lowry.[30]

Malcolm Lowry did not live to see the film that was finally made of *Tender Is the Night* when it was released in 1962, for he died in 1957 at the age of forty-eight, his career, like that of Fitzgerald, cut short in mid-life. There was a lapse of some seven years between the time that Selznick bought the screen rights for *Tender* in 1954 and the point at which the movie actually went into production.

Tender Is the Night: The Film

Selznick, for whom Fitzgerald worked briefly on *Gone with the Wind*, had been enamored with the idea of filming *Tender Is the Night* from the time of its publication. More than once over the years he had tried without success to secure financial backing for a movie version of *Tender*; and at one stage he had hoped that George Cukor, who had directed *Gatsby* on the stage, would direct the picture. Furthermore, Selznick's wife, actress Jennifer Jones, had her heart set on playing Nicole. Once the new screenplay was finished, Selznick's plan was to put the film into production (with his wife playing the female lead) in 1958—as soon as his movie version of *A Farewell to Arms* went into release. But after the failure of *A Farewell to Arms*, Selznick found it difficult to obtain financing for *Tender* or any other movie he wished to produce. For this and other reasons he reluctantly decided the following year to sell the screenplay on which he had worked with Ivan Moffat, along with the services of Ms. Jones as star, to Twentieth Century-Fox, the studio where Frank Taylor had futilely tried to get Lowry's screenplay accepted for production. The picture was finally placed on the production schedule for 1961. "It is one of the great regrets of my career that I did not make *Tender Is the Night*," Selznick recalled afterwards. According to the agreement he made with Fox, he continued, "I was supposed to have approvals of casting, and they were obliged not to change the script without my approval; but they ignored my advice, and, in my opinion, ruined the film."[31]

Selznick's severe judgment of the film may, to some extent, have been triggered by his keen disappointment at not having been able to produce personally a movie he had been involved with for such a long time. Nevertheless, throughout the production period he did make every effort to influence the making of the picture in whatever way he could.

For example, he attempted to veto the choice of Jason Robards,

Jr., to play Dick Diver. Selznick considered Robards to be physically unprepossessing and therefore to lack the kind of imposing screen presence necessary to play the central figure around whom the entire film revolves. But the thinking at Fox was: since Robards had recently played the lead on Broadway in Budd Schulberg's stage version of his own novel *The Disenchanted*, a part which, as we know, was based on Scott Fitzgerald, then logically Robards would be equally effective in enacting in the present film a role that Fitzgerald had partially modeled on himself. Selznick's opinion was ignored by the front office in this and in some of the other matters about which he gave advice; and, as a matter of fact, Robards went on to give a creditable performance as Dick Diver.

Throughout his career Selznick had sought to dominate the individual taste and talent of everyone associated with any movie he was producing by bombarding them during shooting with a barrage of memos, a practice that earned him the unflattering nickname of *"the great dictater."* Selznick became more of a martinet as he grew older; and the fact that he was not officially producing *Tender* did not stop him from compulsively churning out a staggering succession of communiques for the movie's veteran director, Henry King (*The Sun Also Rises*).

King, a feisty moviemaker who had directed his first film in 1915, was, at seventy-five, Fox's senior director. Predictably, he resented Selznick's incessant interference with his work and fired off a memo of his own to Selznick that said as much. Selznick privately confided to an associate that he did not want to alienate an experienced director like King because "he is wonderful with Jennifer, and gets a better result from her than any other director she has ever worked with." (It was King who drew from Ms. Jones her Academy Award-winning performance in *The Song of Bernadette* in 1943.) Nevertheless Selznick added that he was still determined to make King "leave the script as close to the form in which we delivered it as I can manage." Selznick's objections notwithstanding, King favored making some cuts in the screenplay in order to keep the film's ultimate running time down to no more than two-and-a-half hours as the outside limit, and a number of these excisions were approved by the studio.

Referring to the way that his advice about casting and script alterations largely went unheeded during the making of *Tender*,

Selznick stated in a memo—which he wrote but did not send—to Fox's studio head, Spyros Skouros, "All of this is water under the dam. It is literally true that I worked harder and longer on this film than I did on *Gone with the Wind*—the difference being that it took five times as much time and effort to have only a fraction of my ideas listened to than it did to actually do them, down to the last detail, in *Gone with the Wind*. . . . To me, it is heartbreaking."[32]

Henry King, of course, saw things differently. When I went over Selznick's mountain of memos about the picture with him at his home in North Hollywood before he died in 1982, King had this to say about Selznick: "When David Selznick sold the screen rights of *Tender Is the Night* to Fox, it is true that he got a provision in his legal arrangement with the studio whereby he had a say in how the picture was made—something I didn't know about when I agreed to make the movie." But when King decided that the movie was going to be overlength unless some judicious deletions were made in the screenplay, he believed that they were going to have to be made, over Selznick's protests if need be, in order to keep the story from slowing down to a sluggish pace that would prove boring for the audience. In actual fact, King would have liked to have made some additional cuts in the film when the shooting was over:

"When the movie was finished, I wanted to edit out an eight-minute segment from the honeymoon scene, which would have tightened the overall construction of the movie considerably. I wanted to end the sequence in which Nicole and Dick are on their honeymoon just as the train goes into a tunnel, and let the audience fill in the rest of the details for themselves. But Selznick insisted that the rest of this long, drawn-out sequence, in which Nicole and Dick travel about Europe on their honeymoon, be included in the final print of the film just as it was, even though I found that it slowed down the progress of the story noticeably. He was working on the assumption that the more of Jennifer there was in the film, the better it would be. As much as I like and respect Jennifer, that was not true in this case. More was less.

"The studio let Selznick have his way, however, because they said he had caused so much trouble during shooting that they just wanted to get the picture out into the theaters as soon as possible, and be done with his meddling. If the front office had only let me tighten the honeymoon sequence, it would have improved the whole movie; and the picture would have done better at the box office in the bargain."

As things turned out, the film was at least a moderate success. King was, however, vindicated—just as Coppola had been in the case of the running time of the third *Gatsby*—for endeavoring to trim the running time of *Tender* even more than he had. The critics agreed that the picture, two-and-a-half hours long, still could have, and should have, been shorter.

In assessing the film, which was to be King's last, British film historian Roy Pickard has rightly rated *Tender Is the Night* a faithful, literate screenplay that captures the essence of Fitzgerald's novel. For one thing, the film does not skirt the issue of incest, as did both Fitzgerald's and Lowry's proposed screen adaptations of the novel, but delicately indicates the source of Nicole's psychological trauma in the course of an interview between Dick Diver and Baby Warren (Joan Fontaine).

For another, the film sticks closely to the sequence of events as they are found in the standard text of the novel, and does not attempt to tell the story chronologically, which, as said above, was an alternate way of narrating the action that Fitzgerald seriously considered after the book first appeared in print. Following the order of events as they are unfolded in the original novel has the advantage of generating dramatic tension by making the moviegoer suspect that the Divers's marriage is really not as idyllic as it seems on the surface. In this manner the moviegoer, like the reader of the novel, becomes increasingly involved with the central characters as the startling events of the past are gradually revealed in flashback.

Pickard also notes that some of the actors, notably Jennifer Jones, were too old for their roles, a point raised by many reviewers as well. King was aware that Ms. Jones had reached forty by the time she undertook the role of Nicole, but he agreed with Selznick that "the main thing" which the part of Nicole calls for "is a good, experienced actress."[33] That, Jennifer Jones certainly was.

King and Selznick were also in accord about the appropriateness of retaining as much of the novel's dialogue in the film as possible. Yet writer-director Joseph Mankiewicz, Fitzgerald's old boss at MGM, took occasion to criticize this aspect of the film's screenplay in more than one interview he has given in recent years. In recalling that Selznick had approached him early on about working on the script for *Tender Is the Night*, he explained that he had turned Selznick down because, in the light of his earlier experience with Fitzgerald, "I couldn't see myself slaving over the dialogue. Some novelists cannot write dialogue and Scott Fitzgerald is one of them."[34]

On the contrary, the passages of Fitzgerald's dialogue that were incorporated into the screenplay of *Tender* played very well when spoken from the screen. Of course, literary dialogue, as always, must be carefully pared down when used in a movie, because, as said above, motion pictures are principally a visual art. But the fact remains that the substance of Fitzgerald's lines in each case is still there, as in the interchange between Dick and Rosemary Hoyt (Jill St. John) late in the picture when he informs her that he is going into a process of deterioration. He concludes, as he does in the novel, with the grim observation that this change in his character began a long time ago; but "the manner remains intact for some time after the decay has started" (p. 283).

In short, Fitzgerald aficionados who are inclined to dismiss condescendingly Henry King's film of *Tender Is the Night* as a routine piece of Hollywood merchandise turned out on the studio conveyor belt should be aware that his movie is far truer to the spirit and the thematic intent of Fitzgerald's novel than was Fitzgerald's own screen treatment, or Lowry's screenplay, for that matter. There is, for example, no riding accident to explain away the novel's darker explanation of Nicole's madness, as there is in the Fitzgerald treatment; nor is there a sea disaster to avert the even bleaker, more prolonged fate that the novel held in store for Dick, as there is in the Lowry script. The plot of the King movie, with its myriad complications and final resolution, is by and large worked out just as Fitzgerald conceived it, and is therefore in accord with the spirit of the novel.

Pickard points out that "the atmosphere of the sad, lost midsummer world of the twenties was magnificently conjured up by King," who shot the exterior scenes on the French Riviera and in Zurich, Switzerland. Clive Denton, in his book on King and some other Hollywood veterans, adds that *Tender Is the Night* has enough true and delicate moments to be "certainly worthy of concluding a career which had some honor in it."[35]

As for David Selznick, *Tender Is the Night* was also the last movie he was ever involved with. Officious to the end, he characteristically composed one last memo before his death three years later, in which he dictated the details of his own funeral.

EIGHT

DECLINE AND FALL:

THE LAST TYCOON

I, more than any single person in Hollywood, have
my finger on the pulse of America.

—*Irving Thalberg*

Never any luck with movies. . . . Stick to your last,
boy.

—*F. Scott Fitzgerald*

"Hollywood's like Egypt, full of crumbled pyramids. It will keep crumbling until finally the winds blow the last studio prop across the sand," David O. Selznick once exclaimed. "Hollywood might have become the center of a new human expression if it hadn't been grabbed by a little group of bookkeepers and turned into a junk industry."[1] These are bitter words to come from the man responsible for producing memorable movies like *Gone with the Wind*. Nevertheless, Selznick had his share of disappointments as well as triumphs, as his numerous abortive attempts to mount a production of *Tender Is the Night* attest.

Fitzgerald, too, had no illusions about Tinsel Town by the time he quit working for the studios near the end of his life. After three excursions to Hollywood throughout the course of his career, he finally characterized the film colony, in a remark already cited, as a hideous dump that debases the human spirit. Yet the time he spent there was not wasted. If what he wrote while he was in the employ of a studio often did not reach the screen, still the income paid his bills and allowed him to go on writing fiction. Indeed, his experiences in Hollywood often provided fodder for his fiction, both short and long. Thus, even though his screenplay for *Red-Headed Woman* was not used, he garnered enough material while he was in Hollywood working on the script in the fall of 1931 to write the excellent short story "Crazy Sunday." What's more, when he went back to Hollywood in the late thirties, Fitzgerald managed to put together a sequence of no less than seventeen short stories for *Esquire*, later published posthumously as a book, in which he parodied his life in Hollywood as a screenwriter.

The Pat Hobby Stories

The central character of this series of stories, Pat Hobby, is a broken down, aging has-been who hangs around the studios looking for whatever work he can find as a scriptwriter, and babbling to anyone who will listen about the good old days when he was on the payroll. "Pat wasn't the author himself," Fitzgerald scholar Malcolm Cowley has aptly pointed out for the benefit of those readers of the stories who have erroneously assumed that he was; but in Pat's "comic degradation he was what the author sometimes feared that he might become."[2]

Pat Hobby, after all, is a seedy, down-at-the-heels rummy "with permanently bloodshot eyes,"[3] who at times is even reduced to filching food furtively from the tables on a studio set where a banquet scene is about to be shot, or to borrowing a winter overcoat from a rack in the costume department. In contrast to his fictional creation, Pat Hobby, Fitzgerald rarely allowed his drinking to interfere with his work (the *Winter Carnival* fiasco, treated above, was a notable exception). As a result, Fitzgerald, unlike Pat, normally received top dollar from the studios for his professional services.

Yet for all of Pat Hobby's clumsy knavery, he remains a likeable rascal, probably because the reader realizes that, in his straightened circumstances, Pat invents all manner of devious ploys to try to get back in the good graces of the studio brass, not in order to get ahead, but just to survive. Hence Fitzgerald speaks for us all when he describes him to Arnold Gingrich, the editor of *Esquire*, as "Pat Hobby, the scenario hack, to whom I am rather attached."[4] Although the Pat Hobby stories comprise a delightful and diverting series of vignettes about Hollywood, these brief tales are too slight to be placed among Fitzgerald's finest short fiction. "Crazy Sunday," in contrast, is right out of Fitzgerald's top drawer.

"Crazy Sunday"

"Crazy Sunday," unlike "Absolution," was never intended to be a prologue to a novel; yet in some ways its link to Fitzgerald's Hollywood novel, *The Last Tycoon*, is just as close as the connection between "Absolution" and *The Great Gatsby*. In both "Crazy Sunday" and *The Last Tycoon* one of the central characters who figures in the plot is based on Irving Thalberg, the young production chief at MGM for whom Fitzgerald worked while he was collaborating on the script of *Red-Headed Woman* in 1931. Fitzgerald first met Thalberg, as mentioned, on his first trip to Hollywood in 1927 and was so impressed with him that he readily accepted Thalberg's offer four years later to work for him.

During the course of this second Hollywood stay, Fitzgerald was doubly delighted to be singled out to receive a personal invitation from Thalberg and his wife, the Oscar-winning actress Norma Shearer (*The Divorcee*), to an exclusive Sunday afternoon cocktail party at the Thalbergs's Malibu beach house, since the invitation seemed to be a mark of special favor from his employer. Fitzgerald's fellow scriptwriter Dwight Taylor, who attended the affair with him, remembered that Fitzgerald was determined to stay totally sober at all costs, so that he could make as favorable an impression as possible on the big boss. Nevertheless, the nervous strain of trying to be on one's very best behavior while surrounded by the cream of Hollywood's elite finally became too much for Fitzgerald; and he downed some martinis for moral support.

From then on the situation rapidly deteriorated, as Fitzgerald drew everyone's attention to himself by singing an apparently endless barroom ballad that was utterly inappropriate for the occasion. The other guests, whose ranks included several superstars, watched Fitzgerald showing off, said Taylor, with the sullen demeanor of a crowd "gathered at the scene of an accident." Taylor's eyes instinctively sought out the host and hostess, in order to get a reading of their reaction to Fitzgerald's sophomoric behavior. Thalberg's frail, diminutive build allowed him to shrink inconspicuously into the background, where he stood in a doorway with "a slight, not unkind smile on his lips." Norma Shearer, too, was wearing a smile, "but there was no longer any conviction in it." When a couple of the film stars present started to hiss Fitzgerald's impromptu performance, Taylor did the only thing there was left to do. "Come on," he whispered to Fitzgerald; "we're going home."[5]

Gore Vidal's subsequent comment on the incident was that movie actors, who are exhibitionists by trade, invariably resent being upstaged by movie writers, particularly by drunk movie writers. Putting the matter in more universal terms in the story, Fitzgerald brilliantly observes that the reaction of the two actors to the hero's admittedly foolish display fundamentally mirrored the age-old rejection of the outsider by the insider, the thumbs-down of the tribe for someone who must be reminded that he does not belong.

The following day Fitzgerald received a gracious telegram from Norma Shearer which read, "I thought you were one of the most agreeable persons at our tea." But that was not the end of the story; in one sense, it was only the beginning. For Fitzgerald made this unpleasant episode the center of his touching short story "Crazy Sunday," in which the fictional counterparts of Irving Thalberg and his wife Norma Shearer are called Miles Calman and Stella Walker, and the character Fitzgerald based on himself is named Joel Coles.

The closest parallel between "Crazy Sunday" and *The Last Tycoon* is that in both the short story and the novel Fitzgerald had destined the character inspired by Irving Thalberg to die in a plane crash. When this catastrophe takes place in the story, Joel Coles, reflecting on the loss of a filmmaker whom he much admired, pays tribute to Calman in terms that could just as easily be applied to the Thalberg character in *The Last Tycoon* after his demise: "What a hell of a hole he leaves in this damn wilderness—already!"[7]

Furthermore, Fitzgerald could have used these same words to eulogize Irving Thalberg himself a few years later, since by the time

Fitzgerald returned to Hollywood in 1937, Thalberg, Metro's "boy wonder," would have already died at age thirty-seven of exhaustion and ill health. Almost everyone agreed at the time of his death in the fall of 1936 that Thalberg's canny showmanship and high artistic standards would be very much missed in the industry. For he had somehow managed to squeeze a lifetime of impressive moviemaking into his meteoric career. George Cukor, who worked at Metro in the Thalberg years, told me more than four decades after Thalberg died that he still regarded him as "the most brilliant, the most creative producer that I ever worked with. That includes *everyone!*"[8] Little wonder that Fitzgerald's own personal esteem for Thalberg was such that he was moved to build an entire movie around Thalberg's legendary career as a moviemaker.

The Last Tycoon: The Novel

When the editor of *Scribner's Magazine* inquired in the fall of 1932 about an article Fitzgerald had initially intended to write about Hollywood after he finished "Crazy Sunday," Fitzgerald responded that he had abandoned the project, because "I seem to have put all the stuff I had on Hollywood into 'Crazy Sunday.'"[9] It may have been true that at that date Fitzgerald had temporarily exhausted whatever inspiration he could draw from his experiences in the movie colony as a source of material for his writing. But as time went on he realized that he still had a good deal more to say about Hollywood and its denizens, not only when he created the character of Rosemary in *Tender Is the Night* but especially when he got around to planning a new novel in the midst of his third and final stay in the movie capital in the late thirties.

Into *The Last Tycoon* Fitzgerald poured all of his experience of living and working in Hollywood off and on for more than a decade. He reached back to the very first conversation that he had ever had with Thalberg, back in 1927, and from it gleaned the substance of some remarks that Monroe Stahr, the hero of the novel, who is modeled after Thalberg, makes in the book about the nature of authority.

When one is in charge of a large enterprise, Thalberg had said to Fitzgerald, one's subordinates "mustn't ever dream that you're in doubt about any decision," since they all need to have someone to look up to. An executive must exude self-confidence for the sake of reassuring others, regardless of any personal misgivings he might have about a particular course of action he has chosen to pursue. When Fitzgerald set down in his notes for the novel these and other reflections of Thalberg about the pressures involved in the exercise of authority, the novelist added, "I was very much impressed by the shrewdness of what he said—something more than shrewdness—by the largeness of what he thought and how he reached it at the age of twenty-six, which he was then."[10] (Thalberg was actually twenty-eight at the time.)

In outlining his plan for the novel for Kenneth Littauer, fiction editor at *Collier's*, who, he hoped, would consider serializing the book when it was finished, Fitzgerald explained in more detail why Thalberg had so captured his imagination. He was, he said, fascinated by Thalberg's "peculiar charm, his extraordinary good looks, his bountiful success, the tragic end of his great adventure." He went on to say that the events which he had imagined as taking place in the novel were all things that very well might have happened to Thalberg in real life; but he also wanted to emphasize that no single incident in the story would be "actually true," though it might well be founded on something that had really happened."[11] For example, Monroe Stahr, like Irving Thalberg, marries a movie star; but Stahr outlives his wife in the book, whereas Thalberg's wife survived him.

Fitzgerald also wanted to be certain that Thalberg's widow, Norma Shearer, understood that the plot of his novel, though based on fact, was primarily the product of his own creative imagination. In drafting the inscription which he planned to write in the copy of the book which he intended to give to her, he noted that, while her late husband had inspired the best part of Stahr's character, there was something of the author himself in Stahr as well. (It was Fitzgerald, and not Thalberg, who had the romantic relationship with an English girl which served as the basis for Stahr's courtship of Kathleen Moore in the book.)

Besides drawing on his own observations of Thalberg in order to create the character of Monroe Stahr, Fitzgerald also questioned screenwriters Budd Schulberg and Maurice Rapf about Thalberg, both of whom Fitzgerald had originally met in connection with his work on *Winter Carnival*. Schulberg and Rapf were the sons of studio executives and consequently had had the opportunity to meet Thalberg on several occasions when they were growing up in Hollywood. He was a colleague of both of their fathers; moreover, during the thirties Rapf had for a time been employed by Thalberg at MGM.

"I met Scott again in mid-1940, about a year-and-a-half after the *Winter Carnival* episode," Maurice Rapf told me recently. "Both Scott and I were at that time working at Fox. His office was on the floor below mine, and one day I went down to see him, just to reestablish contact with him. He told me he was working on a novel about Hollywood, and he asked me to come down at lunchtime for the next few days to tell him what I knew about the film industry in general and about Thalberg in particular. He was terribly nice, but he pumped the hell out of me during the five meetings we had together. I told him, for example, about the visits to my home of a Communist party organizer" who wanted to unionize the screenwriters.

Rapf continued, "My father disagreed with my views" about the writers in the film industry forming a union, "and he therefore sicked Thalberg on me. Irving was very much against unionizing the writers," because he saw it as a challenge to his authority. "So he called me in and angrily told me what he thought of the idea. I was amazed at his manner, because this was not the soft-spoken Thalberg one usually pictured him to be. This incident was the most specific thing that Fitzgerald used in *The Last Tycoon* based on our conversations about Thalberg." In the book Fitzgerald dramatized the incident that Rapf had recounted for him by portraying a very bitter confrontation between Monroe Stahr and Brimmer, the union organizer. Stahr becomes so upset in the course of the heated argument, which they are having over drinks, that he overimbibes and abruptly brings their meeting to a halt by drunkenly challenging his antagonist to a fistfight.

Needless to say, Maurice Rapf was not pleased with Thalberg's attitude toward screenwriters. He especially deplored Thalberg's practice, which was adhered to by other producers, of assigning a series of writers to work on the same script in teams, one pair after another. Irving Thalberg, Jr., agrees to some extent with Rapf's view: "Many of the writers my father employed were distinguished artists in their own right," including such prestigious playwrights as Robert E. Sherwood, George S. Kaufman, and Sydney Howard. "Making these men work on an assembly line," he concludes, "didn't respect their individuality"—a point which Fitzgerald, despite his admiration for Thalberg, felt obliged to make in *The Last Tycoon* about Thalberg's fictional counterpart.

Like Maurice Rapf, Budd Schulberg remembers Fitzgerald making mental notes about what he said about Thalberg and the film colony whenever he reminisced with Fitzgerald about his youth in

Hollywood. In fact, Cecilia Brady, one of the subordinate characters in the novel, has much in common with both Schulberg and Rapf, to the extent that Cecilia is also the offspring of a studio bigwig, and likewise knows Hollywood from the inside. The character of Cecilia's father, Pat Brady, is based on Metro executive Louis B. Mayer, Thalberg's arch rival for supreme authority at MGM.

Schulberg reports that after L. B. Mayer received the news of Thalberg's death, he remarked, "God saw fit to take Irving away," implying, according to Schulberg, that, by so doing, God had in effect also seen fit to "leave me in peace to run my studio." When screenwriter Ben Hecht heard this anecdote, he commented sardonically, "It doesn't surprise me. L. B. and God have always had a close working relationship."[12]

As for other parallels between fiction and fact in the novel, Fitzgerald based the love affair of Stahr and Kathleen Moore, as we have seen, on his own amorous relationship with British journalist Sheilah Graham, a Hollywood columnist. Fitzgerald saw Sheilah Graham, who reminded him of Zelda, for the first time at a party given by writer Robert Benchley on Bastille Day, July 14, 1937, soon after he arrived in Hollywood for his final stint as a screenwriter. A week later, on July 22, Fitzgerald met Ms. Graham at the Screenwriters Ball, the same occasion on which Monroe Stahr becomes acquainted with Kathleen Moore in the novel. Finally, after the paths of Fitzgerald and Ms. Graham had crossed at some other Hollywood functions, they became romantically involved and remained so for the balance of Fitzgerald's life.

There has been a great deal of speculation about whether or not Zelda Fitzgerald ever came to suspect the nature of his relationship with Ms. Graham. Some Fitzgerald scholars believe Zelda hinted that she was aware that the love affair of Stahr and Kathleen was founded on a similar involvement between her husband and Sheilah Graham because of the negative comments that Zelda made about Kathleen after she read the book. To Zelda, Kathleen Moore seemed to be the kind of manipulative female who knows how to capitalize coyly on the advances of the iceman. Then, perhaps punning on Sheilah Graham's first name, Zelda goes on to say that Kathleen is the vulgar, sweaty type of female "who smells of the rubber-shields in her dress,"[13] a reference to an appurtenance that some women choose to wear in certain of their dresses in order to protect the material from underarm perspiration.

Granted that Zelda Fitzgerald takes a much more critical view of Kathleen than anything we know about Kathleen from the novel would seem to warrant, it nevertheless seems to be stretching a point to assume, merely on the basis of the coincidental similarity of the words *Sheilah* and *shields*, that Zelda Fitzgerald was cognizant of her husband's association with Ms. Graham. It is more likely that, given Zelda's ongoing emotional problems, both family and friends would have been at pains to see to it that this situation was not brought to her attention, and there is no other way she could have known about it, since Zelda never visited Hollywood during the period when Fitzgerald knew Ms. Graham. At any rate, the love story of Stahr and Kathleen is so central to the novel that Fitzgerald had considered entitling the book *The Love of the Last Tycoon: A Western.*

According to Ms. Graham, by 1939 Fitzgerald had accumulated a huge collection of notes for his novel; and he finally began to put pen to paper in the fall of that year. The bulk of the manuscript was actually composed in 1940, the last year of his life, with time out for freelance scriptwriting in order to pay his living expenses and debts.

Fitzgerald's notes show how he wanted to portray Stahr's love for "the great thing he has built out here . . . an empire of his own—an empire he has made" (p. 135). Then, as the plot unfolds, Fitzgerald gradually reveals that both Stahr and his kingdom are doomed. As the film industry continues to expand into an ever larger, more complex corporate enterprise, it becomes increasingly clear that there will soon be no place in Hollywood for a princely figure like Stahr, whose paternalistic rule is founded on the loyal allegiance of all his subordinates to himself personally. This is why Fitzgerald dubbed Stahr the last of the Hollywood tycoons. "Stahr, in short, is the self-made man whose destruction is brought about by the business organization that his talents and imagination have created," Piper writes. "His studio has become so large and complex that he can no longer control its destiny. Instead he is caught between the devisive forces that are fighting for domination."[14]

Those hostile forces include Stahr's ambitious rival for control of the studio, Pat Brady, who all along has coveted Stahr's power and influence, as well as union agitators like Brimmer. When Stahr's negotiations with Brimmer, as we have seen, degenerate into a free-for-all, the husky Brimmer flattens the slightly built Stahr. Brimmer's reaction to the scuffle is one of surprise; he finds it hard to believe that this frail, little man, who, unknown to Brimmer, is deathly ill with heart disease, has for so long carried the burden of governing a major motion picture studio.

Stahr's disastrous bout with Brimmer spells the beginning of the end of his reign at the studio, for the opportunistic Brady will take advantage of Stahr's failure to handle Brimmer properly and use it as the means of convincing the studio's board of directors that Stahr is no longer capable of heading their organization. As if that were not enough, Kathleen has already rejected Stahr's marriage proposal and married someone else. Stahr simply cannot accept her behavior because, as a business executive accustomed to being surrounded by "yes men," he finds it almost impossible to take no for an answer in any sector of his life.

As a matter of fact, when the dazed Stahr regains consciousness after his brief battle with Brimmer, for an instant he thinks it is Kathleen's new mate, and not Brimmer, whom he has been sparring with. By momentarily confusing Kathleen's husband with Brimmer, Stahr implicitly suggests how his personal and professional life have both gone to pieces almost simultaneously. Thus, with supreme irony, Fitzgerald has set his final novel in the very heart of movieland, a place committed to the merchandizing of glamor and illusion, and then proceeded to tell a stark tale drenched in the atmosphere of failure, one which must inevitably end, like *The Great Gatsby*, with its defeated hero's disillusionment and death. "Show me a hero, and I'll write you a tragedy," Fitzgerald jotted down in one of his notes for *The Last Tycoon*; and so he did.[15]

At the point where Stahr is about to be ousted as studio chief and has lost Kathleen to another, the narrative breaks off, for Fitzgerald did not live to complete *The Last Tycoon*. Fitzgerald was writing the sixth chapter of the book when he died at the end of 1940, but he had projected three more. Indeed, his notes for the novel, a significant sampling of which were selected and edited by Edmund Wilson for the posthumous publication of *The Last Tycoon* in 1941, indicate that Fitzgerald had plotted the story right to the end.

According to Fitzgerald's plan for the final chapters, Brady arranges to have Stahr murdered in order to get him out of the way all the sooner. In retaliation Stahr hires a hit man of his own to do in Brady, but changes his mind in the midst of a flight to the East Coast on business, because he realizes that stooping to such tactics would only degrade him to Brady's level of ruthlessness and corruption. But the aircraft on which Stahr is flying east collides with a mountain en route. And so Stahr, whose days were already numbered because of his weak heart, was slated by Fitzgerald to die, like Miles Calman in "Crazy Sunday," in an air disaster.

According to his notes, Fitzgerald seems to have considered more than one possible epilogue for the novel. But he apparently opted for the one that portrays Stahr's state funeral, at which several of his former adversaries, awash in crocodile tears, lugubriously mourn his passing; for this is the only epilogue mentioned in the plot outline contained in Fitzgerald's notes for the novel. Furthermore, Sheilah Graham has said that Fitzgerald had given her to understand that "the final scene of all was to have been Stahr's funeral."[16]

When *The Last Tycoon* was published as an unfinished novel in 1941, James Thurber's review of the book was typical of the response that the book evoked. "It is the last work of a first-rate novelist," he wrote; and as such "it rounds out his all-too-brief career." Although Fitzgerald did not live to give the existing chapters a final polishing or to write the last chapters, Thurber noted that the book nonetheless "is filled with a great many excellent things as it stands."[17]

Bruccoli states that *The Last Tycoon* as Fitzgerald left it is generally thought to be two-thirds finished simply because Fitzgerald was writing the sixth of his projected nine chapters when he died. But, Bruccoli points out, Fitzgerald had allocated a number of complicated episodes to the novel's concluding chapters; and therefore, at the time he stopped writing, "a great deal of the plot was left undeveloped." Hence, Bruccoli concludes, the finished novel "might well have been almost twice as long as projected."[18]

With all due respect to one of the foremost living Fitzgerald scholars, I would contend that the novel was far closer to completion than Bruccoli would allow. For a start, Bruccoli assumes that, had Fitzgerald lived, he would have actually included in the completed novel just about every incident in his outline that still remained to be written. On the contrary, I submit that often Fitzgerald initially mapped out many more episodes for a projected novel than he eventually made use of. We are already familiar with his plans to depict Gatsby's criminal activities in far greater detail than the scattered references he makes to them in the final version of *The Great Gatsby*. Similarly, Fitzgerald decided against using a subplot that appears in the synopsis he prepared for *Tender Is the Night*. In this subplot, Nicole, who suffers from a mad mania to revenge herself on the male population for what her father has done to her, feels compelled to murder members of the opposite sex. There is absolutely no hint of this material in the final version of *Tender Is the Night*, and Mizener makes a point of noting "the book's failure to follow" the outline in this and other ways. [19]

One is not being hasty, then, in proposing that Fitzgerald would have ultimately judged some of the additional material he had initially lined up for the closing chapters of *The Last Tycoon* to be superfluous and allowed it to fall by the wayside, just as he had suppressed some of the episodes which were originally intended to be incorporated into his previous novels. And a good thing too, since such items as Brady's conspiracy to do away with Stahr and Stahr's counterplan to have Brady slain represent precisely the same sort of lurid melodramatics that Fitzgerald had wisely left out of *Gatsby* and *Tender*. (Fitzgerald may have been unduly partial to melodramatic plot complications in his film scenarios, for the reasons given earlier, but not in his serious fiction.)

In summary, there seems to be little doubt that Fitzgerald's better judgment would have prompted him to drop some of the more sensational episodes, which he had earlier conceived as possibilities for *The Last Tycoon*. In fact, after Ernest Hemingway read the published novel, he wrote to Maxwell Perkins that he was confident that Perkins would agree with him that "Scott would never have finished it with that gigantic, preposterous outline" of how the plot was to be worked out.[20] One finds it easy to share these sentiments, especially when they are expressed both *by* and *to* someone who knew Fitzgerald and his work so intimately.

Some Fitzgerald scholars have criticized Wilson's foreword to the published edition of the novel for giving the impression that the first six chapters of the novel were being presented to the public in a more polished form than was actually the case. This does not appear to be a fair complaint to make against Wilson, since he is careful to point out in his prefatory remarks that the text of the six chapters does not represent the final draft of the manuscript and, consequently, is "by no means a finished version" of the material. Nevertheless Wilson also emphasizes, quite correctly, that the published version of the novel reflects a "considerable rewriting" on the part of the author, and that "even in its imperfect state" the story has considerable power and the character of Monroe Stahr emerges with a great deal of "intensity and reality."[21]

Ernest Hemingway agreed. "I read all of Scott's book," he wrote to Maxwell Perkins after it was published. "I thought the part about Stahr was all very good. You can recognize Irving Thalberg, his charm and skill, and grasp of business and the sentence of death over him." Piper writes in a similar vein that, "even in its fragmentary condition," Fitzgerald's revised draft of *The Last Tycoon* is an "accomplished piece of writing," adding that the best scenes in the book reflect a controlled craftsmanship and a precision of language "unlike anything he had written before."[22] Therefore it does not seem that Wilson is guilty of overstatement when he maintains that, in spite of the unfinished quality of the manuscript, *The Last Tycoon* is in some ways Fitzgerald's most mature piece of writing, the product of twenty-years experience as a professional writer.

For myself, the existing six chapters of *The Last Tycoon* read more like a nearly completed novella than an unfinished novel. For one can read *The Last Tycoon* without adverting in any way to the outline of the uncompleted chapters appended to the end of the book and still come away from the book with a sense that Monroe Stahr's tragic end is inevitable. At the point where the narrative stops we already know that Stahr is soon to die of a heart ailment, symbolic of his being heartsick, bereft as he is of all the things that for him made life worthwhile. In the words of Sheilah Graham, things are going "badly for Stahr in business and love."[23] Since that is the case, one does not need to know that Fitzgerald planned a plane crash to round off his plot, because Stahr's life is already over. Therefore one can experience the air of tragic finality that permeates the last pages of the novel's text just as it stands, without any reference to what might have come later.

By the same token, the distinguished British playwright-screenwriter Harold Pinter, who wrote the screenplay for the movie version of *The Last Tycoon,* did not attempt to carry the story line of his script much beyond the point where Fitzgerald's manuscript halts, as we shall soon see.

The Last Tycoon: The Film

There was a ninety-minute TV adaptation of *The Last Tycoon* presented on CBS's acclaimed *Playhouse 90* on March 14, 1957, with Jack Palance in the title role. But like the teleplays of *The Great Gatsby* referred to above, the production is not available for screening. There was no serious attempt to bring *The Last Tycoon* to the big screen until producer Lester Cowan announced on November 1, 1965, that he was soon going to put *Tycoon* into production. This is, of course, the same Lester Cowan who did not carry through his plans to bring to the screen Fitzgerald's own film adaptation of "Babylon Revisited," which he had himself commissioned. Cowan's efforts to launch a production of *The Last Tycoon* did not come to fruition either. In 1973 he therefore sold the screen rights of Fitzgerald's unfinished novel to Oscar-winning producer Sam Spiegel (*The Bridge on the River Kwai*), who in turn hired Pinter to write the screenplay. *The Last Tycoon* was ready to go before the cameras by October 1975.

The basic intent of the movie adaptation of *The Last Tycoon* is to depict on the screen the first six chapters of the book which, as I have indicated, virtually constitute a complete novella. This the film does faithfully; indeed, the script includes more passages of dialogue brought over verbatim from the book than perhaps any other movie made from a Fitzgerald story. In the following passage of dialogue from the novel, brackets have been inserted to indicate which lines were omitted in the film script, so that one can readily see how deftly Pinter extracted the essence of the dialogue. This particular scene is the one in which Stahr (Robert De Niro) and Kathleen (Ingrid Boulting) formally introduce themselves to each other in front of her home, prior to their getting to know one another better at the Screenwriters Ball:

> "I suppose the girls are all after you to put them on the screen."
> "They've given up," he said. . . .
> ["I'm thinking that it would turn you into a cynic," she said.]
> "You didn't want to put me in the pictures?"
> "No."
> "That's good. I'm no actress. [Once in London a man came up to me in the Carlton and asked me to make a test, but I thought a while and finally I didn't go. . . ."]
> "I feel as if I had my foot in the door—like a collector."
> She laughed too (pp. 65-66).

When it came time to construct a scenario for the film, the director of the movie, Academy Award winner Elia Kazan (*On the Waterfront*) agreed with his creative associates, Pinter and Spiegel, that the screenplay should bypass nearly all of the additional material on which Fitzgerald had planned to draw in order to fill out the balance of the plot. Kazan strongly believed that Fitzgerald himself would have ultimately discarded a number of the episodes he had outlined for the final three chapters of his book.

"Since I write novels myself," Kazan, the author of *The Arrangement* and other novels, remarks, "I know that you make structural plans that you do not follow." For example, Kazan is personally convinced that Fitzgerald would have eventually decided against developing in detail the considerable amount of the material he had projected in his plot synopsis about the rise of the labor unions as a potent force in running the film industry. Based on his knowledge of Fitzgerald and his work, Kazan feels that "he just didn't give a damn about union struggles" as such.[24] Elsewhere Kazan has gone on to explain that Stahr's brawl with Brimmer (Jack Nicholson) had little to do with Stahr's antagonism toward the labor movement and a great deal to do with what was going on inside Stahr at the point that he was faced with the necessity of coping with the labor agitator. "It was all the pain in Stahr's gut over Kathleen," says Kazan, and not his hostility toward a representative of the union movement, that drove Stahr to erupt into physical violence and drunkenly attack Brimmer physically. "Normally he would have horse-traded with Brimmer," Kazan concludes.[25] Kazan's contention is borne out by the fact that, as already mentioned, when Stahr comes to after Brimmer knocks him cold, his remarks indicate that he was subconsciously taking out on Brimmer his grief and frustration over the loss of Kathleen.

Kazan likewise believes that, as I have also indicated above, Fitzgerald in all probability would have scotched his original plan to have Brady (Robert Mitchum) and Stahr both hire professional killers to murder one another. "Fitzgerald's main interest in *The Last Tycoon*," Kazan says in summary, was not "in gangsters or labor hoods," but in depicting the tragic decline and fall of his central character. So Kazan feels that in the last analysis he was right in maintaining that the only way to make a movie of the Fitzgerald novel was to "stick to what he actually wrote."[26]

Logically that meant no plane wreck. And so the ending of the movie grows directly out of the plot as it has been developed in the existing chapters of the book. At the point where Fitzgerald left off, we know Stahr is a mortally ill man whose career and love life are both in eclipse. At the final fade-out, therefore, Kazan simply has Stahr walk into the black abyss of a deserted soundstage, as if he were being swallowed up in the shadows of the Valley of Death itself. Before disappearing from sight Stahr can be heard murmuring touchingly, "I don't want to lose you." He refers, of course, to his beloved studio as well as to his beloved Kathleen.

Kazan finished principal photography on the film on Friday, January 30, 1976; and I spoke with him on the following Monday in his office at Paramount, where we discussed the relationship of director and writer. After Kazan had signed on to direct the film, it seems he went to England to confer with Pinter about his adaptation of Fitzgerald's novel for the screen; and in the course of their consultations Kazan made some suggestions to Pinter which the writer incorporated into the script. But once Kazan had the final shooting script in hand, he promised Pinter that he would not venture to alter the screenplay in any way on his own; and he kept his promise.

Budd Schulberg, who won an Oscar for writing the screenplay of *On the Waterfront* for Kazan, has said that Elia Kazan is one of the very few directors who treats a film script with the same respect that he would give a work written for the stage. When this remark was brought to Kazan's attention, he replied, "When you are working with a fine playwright in the theater, you use what he gives you and you don't juggle his material. You're his servant. Nor should you do it when you are filming a screenplay by an author you esteem," such as Harold Pinter.

Kazan's estimation of Fitzgerald is also high. He read *The Last Tycoon* several times before going onto the studio floor to direct the picture. He found it, line for line, a beautifully composed work of art.

Asked why he invited Kazan to direct *The Last Tycoon*, Sam Spiegel responded, "Kazan can get more out of an actor than any director I've ever worked with. ... I don't know a director who is as skillful at releasing an actor of his inhibitions."[27] A case in point is the way Kazan helped Oscar-winning actor Robert De Niro (*Godfather* II) work into the role of Monroe Stahr. Prior to making *The Last Tycoon*, De Niro had specialized in playing street-smart young hoodlums. He had never before essayed the role of anyone like Monroe Stahr, a wealthy, sophisticated, very powerful business executive. Consequently, Kazan helped De Niro prepare for his part by having some extra rehearsals with him. The purpose of these rehearsals, Kazan explained afterward, was to impress De Niro with the fact that when Stahr is functioning in his capacity as production chief, he never makes an idle remark. "Whatever he says is an instruction which someone has to do something about." In this way, said Kazan, he made De Niro grasp "what it means to be an executive."[28]

Kazan's special attention to De Niro paid off handsomely, since even Pauline Kael, who did not much care for the film as a whole, praised De Niro for his authentic interpretation of the role of a studio boss. "Everything seems right," she wrote; "the quiet, flat, uninflected" voice, "the formal manner . . . the controlled exercise of power." In fine, she thought that, in playing a part based on "the boy wonder" Irving Thalberg, "De Niro catches the seriousness of a young genius who acts much older than he is."[29] An even more significant comment about De Niro's performance was made to me by Irving Thalberg, Jr., who said that when he saw *The Last Tycoon* he thought that "De Niro acted the part of my father as I remember him."

The Last Tycoon, Kazan's last film to date, did not receive uniformly positive reviews, with the majority of the critics complaining in particular that newcomer Ingrid Boulting's performance as Kathleen was so vapid that, without even trying, De Niro all but wiped her right off the screen. Nevertheless, most reviewers thought that there was much to admire in the movie. One of the scenes, which was singled out as very effective, comes straight from the book. Stahr explains to George Boxley (Donald Pleasence), a pompous, supercilious English writer, how to hook an audience in a key sequence by teasing them with a series of provocative images. Displaying a masterful talent for pantomime, Stahr impersonates a *femme fatale* who is stealthily burning a pair of black gloves in a fireplace just as the phone rings. Stahr pretends to pick up an imaginary phone and then speaks the single line of dialogue required for his playlet: "I've never owned a pair of black gloves in my life."

"As played by Robert De Niro," cinema scholar Lloyd Michaels comments, Stahr's charade is a striking *tour de force* which serves to define his "capacity for inventing plot and for understanding movies" and thus goes a long way in demonstrating why Stahr has been such a successful producer."[30] Fascinated by the slice of cinematic illusion that Stahr has dished up for him, Boxley inquires what the lady in the scene was really up to. "I don't know," Stahr answers. "I was just making pictures."

Making motion pictures, of course, is what Stahr has devoted his life to. Consequently, when he repeats these words to himself at the end of the movie, just before he evaporates into the darkness of the empty sound stage, Monroe Stahr is, perhaps without knowing it, pronouncing his own epitaph. No wonder Kazan believes that "the line where he says, 'I was just making pictures'—I think that's the best line in the picture."[31]

By not venturing in the screen version to go much beyond the chapters of *The Last Tycoon* which Fitzgerald had actually set down on paper, Kazan and company have created a faithful adaptation of Fizgerald's Hollywood novel as we have it, in a way that perhaps would have made the novelist feel that the time he spent laboring on the studio treadmill had finally been rewarded.

Looking back at the film adaptations of Fitzgerald's novels, one finds that not all of them were as faithful to their respective literary sources as was *The Last Tycoon*. As we have seen, the movie of *The Beautiful and Damned* undercut the theme that so often surfaces in Fitzgerald's fiction—whereby he examines the unhappiness caused by those who do not live up to their convictions—by rewarding Anthony Patch for virtually having no meaningful convictions at all. On the credit side there are, for example, the two sound versions of *Gatsby*, which remained faithful to Fitzgerald's personal vision by showing how Gatsby was destroyed because his moral values rose no higher than the attainment of the American success myth, as embodied for him in his spurious goddess, Daisy Buchanan. By the same token, the film of *Tender Is the Night* showed how Dick Diver ruined his life by failing to live up to the tenets of his high calling as a healer of the spirit.

In most of the films of Fitzgerald's novels, then, enough of the spirit of the author's original work survives to allow the films to be called fundamentally faithful to their sources. To that extent Fitzgerald himself may even have liked some of the movies himself. What he would have thought of the biographical films that have sought to dramatize portions of his actual life story, which we shall examine in the epilogue, is something else again.

EPILOGUE

I don't know whether Zelda and I are real or whether we are characters in one of my novels.

—*F. Scott Fitzgerald*

Ironically, the movies, which so fascinated and frustrated Fitzgerald, have turned him and Zelda into huge mythic monsters, forever sweeping 'round to *Wiener* waltzes en route to the last reel, where they sputter out like a pair of Roman candles on a rainy Fourth of July—disenchanted, beloved infidels.

—*Gore Vidal*

Fitzgerald's Last Years

Ernest Hemingway wrote to Maxwell Perkins in late 1941 that he was pleased that Fitzgerald had been able to make use of his experiences in Hollywood in *The Last Tycoon*. Then he ended on a more somber note, "You said that Hollywood had not hurt Scott. I guess perhaps it had not because he was long past being hurt before he went there."

Hemingway was referring to Fitzgerald's final years, when he was pretty much neglected by both the critical establishment and the reading public alike, and went to Hollywood to try his hand at screenwriting one last time. Fitzgerald's last years have been examined in this book up to this point primarily in terms of the fortunes of his professional life during that period. Let us now briefly recap those same years in terms of his personal life at the time, before proceeding to an analysis of the films that have been made about the closing years of his life; for it is his personal, rather than his professional life, that is largely the focus of these biographical films.

To begin with, Ernest Hemingway, who felt that, with the exception of Maxwell Perkins, he knew Fitzgerald, "possibly, the best of any of them,"[1] had much to say in his correspondence about this part of Fitzgerald's life. References to Fitzgerald in Hemingway's letters show that he was growing increasingly more concerned about Fitzgerald's drinking during those days because, as he put it, Fitzgerald's behavior when he was drunk was becoming ever more nasty and unpleasant as the years went by. (The same would be true of Hemingway later on, but that is another story.)

Fitzgerald's daughter Scottie Smith remembers that her father "was a totally different person when drunk; not just gay or tiddly, but *mean*." According to fellow novelist Louis Bromfield, when Fitzgerald was drinking "he usually became very disagreeable and rude and quarrelsome, as if all his resentments were released at once."[2] This phenomenon, which was to be depicted in more than one of the films based on Fitzgerald's life, was specially frustrating, Hemingway said, because Fitzgerald could be so generous and engaging at other times. In his letters to Fitzgerald himself, Hemingway often scolded him about his drinking habits; but sometimes he took to encouraging his friend in order to raise his morale. Hemingway pointed out, for example, that, even though drinking to excess had undoubtedly hurt Fitzgerald's productivity, he was no more of a drinking man than James Joyce and some other writers were. "But, Scott," he added, "good writers always come back. Always."

Hemingway grew particularly concerned about Fitzgerald's morale after the publication of the "Crack-Up" articles in *Esquire* only a year or so before he made his last expedition to Hollywood. "My God, did you read Scott's account of his crack-up," Hemingway exclaimed in a letter to novelist John Dos Passos. He went on to say that he had been recently writing to their mutual friend to cheer him up, but he had clearly failed to do so, because Fitzgerald had obviously persuaded himself that he was "officially cracked up." To Perkins, Hemingway lamented that he felt simply awful about the *Esquire* pieces because Fitzgerald had "a marvelous talent; and the thing is to use it" for serious writing, and not to employ it just to "whine in public." Hemingway, who was a convert to Catholicism, then added, "Maybe the Church could help him. You can't tell. ... I wish we could help him."

Looking back on his relationship with Fitzgerald later on, Hemingway told Perkins, "I loved Scott very much, but ... he was almost like a guided missile with no one guiding him." Indeed, Hemingway's conviction that he managed his life much better than Fitzgerald ever managed his led him, he confessed, to have "a very stupid little boy feeling of superiority about Scott—like a tough little boy sneering at a delicate but talented little boy."[3]

The supreme example of this condescending sort of "big brother" attitude towards Fitzgerald was Hemingway's reference to Fitzgerald in his short story "The Snows of Kilimanjaro," which originally appeared in the August 1936 number of *Esquire*, only a few months after the last of the three "Crack-Up" articles had appeared in the same magazine. The hero of the story recalls "poor old Scott Fitzgerald" and his "romantic awe" of the rich, "and how he had started a story once that began, 'The very rich are different from you and me.' And how someone had said to Scott, 'Yes, they have more money.' But that was not humorous to Scott."[4] Hemingway's snide reference to Fitzgerald and to his superb short story, "The Rich Boy," were not "humorous to Scott" either.

Hemingway's remark is unfair on several counts, not the least of which is that it is abundantly clear from the manner in which Fitzgerald skewered the wealthy aristocratic class in *Gatsby* and *Tender Is the Night* that he was not naively dazzled by the rich. But even more to the point, it was Hemingway himself, and not Fitzgerald, who had boasted to a friend that hobnobbing with the rich enabled him to understand them better; to which Hemingway's friend retorted, "The only difference between the rich and other people is that the rich have more money."[5]

Fitzgerald let Hemingway know that he was deeply offended by this gratuitous public insult; he did so by sending him a letter in which he demanded that Hemingway lay off him in print. He continued by saying that if he chose to intone a dirge about his personal misfortunes in *Esquire*, "it doesn't mean I want my friends praying aloud over my corpse."[6] Hemingway explained to Perkins that the lines about

Fitzgerald in "Snows" were frankly intended to shock his old friend out of the unhealthy mood of self-pity into which he had drifted. But to Fitzgerald himself he replied dyspeptically that he figured that, since Fitzgerald had elected to expose his personal problems in a national magazine, it was now open season on "poor Scott." At any rate, Hemingway replaced Fitzgerald's name with a different one when the story was subsequently reprinted in a collection of Hemingway's short fiction.

Perhaps Fitzgerald had this incident in mind when he wrote in his *Notebooks*: "I talk with the authority of failure—Ernest with the authority of success. We could never sit across the table again" (#1915). This observation seems to imply that, as far as Fitzgerald was concerned, their relationship was at an end. Yet, only a month later, when a journalist named Mok proclaimed in *The New York Post* that Fitzgerald was all washed up as a writer, Fitzgerald wired none other than Ernest Hemingway for help in mounting a protest to the *Post* about the reporter, whom he aptly referred to elsewhere as Muck. Moreover, even though Fitzgerald subsequently decided that, on second thought, it was more prudent in the long run to let the matter die, it is significant that Hemingway willingly offered his assistance.

At the risk of oversimplifying a very complicated friendship, I would characterize Hemingway's relationship with Fitzgerald by expanding on Hemingway's "little boy" analogy. It appears that Fitzgerald and Hemingway shared a love-hate relationship like that of two boyhood playmates who may be irritably scrapping in the schoolyard one moment, and loyally sticking up for one another the next. Regardless of their myriad disagreements, they both mutually regretted that they did not see each other more often. Fitzgerald expressed as much to Hemingway the summer following the "Snows" episode after they had had a get-together. For his part, Hemingway wrote to Fitzgerald, "I'm damned fond of you, and I'd like to have a chance to talk sometimes. We had good times talking."[7]

A few years after Fitzgerald's death, Hemingway mentioned to Perkins that he intended to set down in writing his recollections of the years that he had known Fitzgerald, before he got too punchy to remember the facts. Fifteen years later he included three sketches about Fitzgerald in *A Moveable Feast*, already cited. "If the reader prefers, this book may be regarded as fiction," Hemingway noted in the preface to these memoirs. "But there is always the chance that such a book of fiction may throw some light on what has been written as fact."[8]

Both fictional and factual works have been derived from Fitzgerald's life, and at times even Fitzgerald commentators get confused about which is which. The bibliography in James Miller's critical study of Fitzgerald lists two fictional accounts of Fitzgerald's final years. One is Budd Schulberg's novel *The Disenchanted*, referred to above; but the other is Sheilah Graham's autobiography, *Beloved Infidel*, which is an account of the time she spent as Fitzgerald's companion, and is not fiction at all. Ms. Graham, in turn, has herself compounded the confusion by lumping together Schulberg's novel and Mizener's non-fictional life of Fitzgerald, *The Far Side of Paradise*, cited earlier, and mistakenly labeling them *both* as biographies of Fitzgerald.

In recent years Fitzgerald's life has become a frequent source for plays and movies. The only noteworthy instance of Fitzgerald's life being used as source material for a dramatic work of any kind during his lifetime, however, was a picture called *The Wedding Night*.

The Wedding Night

The Wedding Night was released in 1935, in the midst of Fitzgerald's "Crack-up" period. It is unfortunate that at this low point in his life Hollywood would make a fiction film which presented a thinly disguised portrait of himself, and of his wife too, as emblems of the foolish, flashy twenties, who seemed very much out of place in the bleak, bankrupt thirties, where they appeared to be anachronisms left over from the previous decade. In brief, the film seems bent on turning the Fitzgeralds into the "mythic monsters" Gore Vidal refers to above. That Fitzgerald was aware of the implicit link between the film and his personal life is clear from the presence among his papers at Princeton of a copy of the one-hundred-page scenario composed by Edwin Knopf which bears the film's original title, *Broken Soil*, and which Knopf apparently sent to him.

Knopf, a friend of Fitzgerald's, was later instrumental, as said before, in getting Fitzgerald hired in 1937 by MGM, where he was in the story department. In the scenario the main characters are called Scott and Zelda Fitzpatrick; but when screenwriter Edith Fitzgerald (no relation to Scott) came to write the final shooting script for the film, their names were changed to Tony and Dora Barrett, so that the connection between them and their real-life counterparts would not be quite so blatant.

Curiously enough, the movie was directed by King Vidor, who also knew the Fitzgeralds, and hence must have been conscious of the fact that Scott and Zelda Fitzgerald were the prototypes of Tony and Dora Barrett; and he has suggested as much in a letter to literary scholar Alan Margolies. Vidor may have felt that turnabout is fair play, since Fitzgerald had employed a row between Vidor and his actress wife Eleanor Boardman as the source of the marital tiff between Miles and Stella Calman in "Crazy Sunday," although, as noted, the Calmans were primarily based on the Thalbergs.

In *The Wedding Night* Tony Barrett (Gary Cooper) is a failed novelist who retires, along with his wife Dora (Helen Vinson), to a ramshackle lodge in Connecticut, away from their hectic social life back in the city, so that he can get down to writing a serious work of fiction, just as the Fitzgeralds had at various times moved to Connecticut and to Maryland for the same reason. At the beginning of the film, Dora is portrayed as a flibbertigibbet who resents her husband's decision to make them both sequester themselves in the country just so he can get on with his writing; and for a time she goes back to town without him. Nonetheless, she is quite impressed, when she rejoins him, to see what he has been able to accomplish while he was cooped up in the old house without her.

Fitzgerald's struggles to finish *Tender Is the Night*, his first major work in nearly a decade, could not have been far from Knopf's mind when he pictured the hero of his screen story trying to turn out his first substantial fictional work in some time. In addition, there are some other, less obvious parallels between the hero of the film on the one hand and Fitzgerald and his work on the other, such as when Tony recalls at one point in the film, "When I was a boy, it was hard work making the pennies sound like quarters in the collection plate." This remark is very reminiscent of young Rudolph Miller's admission in Fitzgerald's short story "Absolution," treated earlier, that he was always very embarrassed that he could not contribute more handsomely to the collection basket during Sunday Mass.

One negative critical reaction to the film when it was released was that the movie fails to show in a very credible fashion the Fitzgerald character's painful endeavors to turn out a first-class piece of fiction. But then, as cinema critic Vincent Canby notes, the movies have never found a satisfactory way to depict the process of artistic creation. Once the novelist being portrayed in a film finally gets down to work in earnest, says Canby, he is generally shown to experience little difficulty in pouring out reams of immortal prose, "which, from the evidence portrayed on the screen, appears to come straight from God, pre-paragraphed."[9] Certainly *The Wedding Night* is no exception to Canby's rule in this regard.

An experienced writer like Fitzgerald may have found this aspect of the film's plot laughable when he saw the picture, but he may well have been flattered by Cooper's charming depiction of the character based on him as a fundamentally likeable and decent human being. Rarely does one find an actor bringing a character to life on the screen, wrote critic Otis Ferguson, "with the warmth and feeling . . . that one gets from Mr. Cooper before his part is played out."[10]

After the publication of Mizener's best-selling biography of Fitzgerald in 1951, David 0. Selznick became interested in making a biographical film about Fitzgerald, as opposed to a fictionalized version of his life, as was done in *The Wedding Night*. For several months, he wrote to one of his staff, "I tried to persuade Scott Fitzgerald's daughter to let me" create a scenario based on the lives of her parents. "She listened attentively, knowing of my long personal friendship and professional association with Fitzgerald." But she was still bitter about some books and articles which she believed had sensationalized her parents' lives; and hence, said Selznick, she was against "any biographical material portraying them" on the screen.[11] So Selznick gave up on his idea to do a biographical film about the Fitzgeralds and turned his attention to the screen version of *Tender Is the Night*, with the results that we are already aware of.

Beloved Infidel

Then, in 1958, along came Sheilah Graham's autobiography, *Beloved Infidel*, to which Fox acquired the screen rights. The 1959 movie, like the film of *Tender Is the Night* a couple of years later, was directed by Henry King and handsomely photographed in widescreen and color. The film follows the book closely in depicting, for example, the first important meeting of Scott (Gregory Peck) and Sheilah (Deborah Kerr) at the Screenwriters Ball. (Fitzgerald himself had already dramatized this incident in *The Last Tycoon* as the occasion when Monroe Stahr and Kathleen Moore got acquainted.)

The major source of tension which inevitably develops between Scott and Sheilah in the film, as in the book, is his fractious behavior when drunk. The worst incident of this kind that is portrayed in the movie occurs when Scott learns that no major commercial magazine is willing to subsidize the writing of *The Last Tycoon* in return for the pre-publication serial rights of the novel. Ms. Graham has said that this "rejection by magazines which in the past had been proud to print almost anything he wrote overwhelmed Scott," and accounted for one of his worst benders ever.[12]

As this scene develops in the film, Scott's drinking spree occasions a harrowing quarrel between himself and Sheilah, and she summarily breaks off their relationship, vowing never to see him again. But when he at long last makes good his promise to swear off liquor and work conscientiously on *The Last Tycoon*, they are reconciled. Then, in the film as in life, Scott Fitzgerald dies of a heart attack in Sheilah Graham's apartment on the afternoon of Saturday, December 21, 1940. It is just after lunch, and Scott has settled down to read *The Princeton Alumni Magazine*. Suddenly he stands up, grabs for the mantelpiece as if to steady himself, and slumps to the floor in an unconscious state. A few minutes later he is officially declared dead; and the film quickly draws to a close.

Gregory Peck earned plaudits for his basically sympathetic, dignified performance as Scott Fitzgerald, projecting a picture of Fitzgerald as a distinguished writer down on his luck. But, as film historian Tony Thomas points out, it was nevertheless difficult to accept the robust Peck in the role of a sickly man who died at age forty-four of a weak heart. If Peck was to some degree miscast as Fitzgerald, Sheilah Graham thought the refined Deborah Kerr was completely wrong for the part of a girl from the London slums who had to struggle hard against a deprived background and lack of an adequate formal education in order finally to make something of herself as a Hollywood columnist.

Furthermore, Peck had this to say about what he saw as a more fundamental weakness in the movie: "The schizophrenic quality of the script spoiled it. They didn't know whether they wanted it to be the last episode in the life of an American writer, which I would have liked, or a Cinderella yarn about Little Nell from Cockney London" making the big time as a successful journalist in the film colony.[13] Perhaps it was precisely the lack of focus in the screenplay of which Peck speaks that moved Henry King to describe the movie to me as an ill-conceived project. "In retrospect," he added, "it seems that it was a mistake to make the movie at all." Beyond that statement, he declined to discuss the film any further, since the movie was a disappointing venture for all concerned.

F. Scott Fitzgerald in Hollywood

Sheilah Graham was more favorably impressed by *F. Scott Fitzgerald in Hollywood*, a two-hour telefilm, directed by Anthony Page, scripted by James Costigan (who had also written the script for *F. Scott Fitzgerald and "The Last of the Belles"*), and first broadcast on May 6, 1976. This telefilm covers some of the same ground as the movie of *Beloved Infidel*; as a matter of fact, the key scenes from that film, which have already been described, turn up one way or another in *Fitzgerald in Hollywood*. In the teleplay, however, the material from *Beloved Infidel* is intercut with flashbacks from the first trip to Hollywood that Scott (Jason Miller) made with Zelda (Tuesday Weld) in 1927.

Sheilah Graham thought that the casting of the key roles in the teleplay was much more felicitous than in the case of *Beloved Infidel*. "Tuesday Weld as Zelda is superb," she commented afterwards; and while Jason Miller does not look much like Scott, "he evolved into the character so well that, before the end, he was completely the man he was portraying. Julia Foster, the young British actress who played me, was great."[14]

Another plus for the telefilm is the deft way in which Anthony Page uses the juxtaposition of scenes from Fitzgerald's first and last visits to Hollywood as the source of several ironic contrasts. First of all, there is the distinct difference between Scott and Zelda's splendiferous arrival in Hollywood in 1927, accompanied by all the hoopla the studio can dream up in order to welcome appropriately the celebrated chronicler of the Jazz Age, as opposed to his unheralded arrival a decade later as a forgotten author sneaking into town alone and unnoticed. He is pictured entering the city for his last sojourn there wearing an overcoat and scarf even though it is the middle of summer—a visual symbol of the chill he feels deep in his bones, emanating from the cold reception he has received this time around. Then there is the contrast between Fitzgerald's efforts to work seriously at the craft of screenwriting on his third visit to Hollywood and the flashback to 1927, which shows him at poolside, casually doodling with the scenario of *Lipstick*.

But perhaps the most effective visual contrast between Fitzgerald's first and third excursions to Hollywood is embodied in the closeup of Fitzgerald with which Page begins his telefilm and the one with which he ends it. In the opening closeup, Scott is pictured being made up for a screen test in 1927 on the outside chance that he may have what it takes to be a screen star. He later comments how appalled he was when he saw the test because, with all that makeup on his face, he "looked like a corpse." In the final closeup, Scott is shown lying in his coffin, his face once more painted with cosmetics, but this time by a mortician. Now he really is a corpse; and his friend and colleague Dorothy Parker (Dolores Sutton), who turns out to be one of the very few mourners at his wake, looks down at him and blurts out—as Ms. Parker did in real life—what Fitzgerald had one of the few mourners at Gatsby's funeral say about Jay: "The poor son-of-a-bitch." With that, the movie ends.

For the record, despite the fact that Fitzgerald's screen test has never been located, Lois Moran, who arranged for the test, assured Arthur Mizener that it was made. Also Zelda wrote to Scottie from Hollywood at the time that "daddy was offered a job to be a leading man in a picture with Lois Moran," but he turned it down.[15] Given Zelda's suspicions about his association with Ms. Moran, it seems unlikely that Fitzgerald would have ever co-starred with her in a film under any circumstances.

Although Lois Moran is not referred to by name in *F. Scott Fitzgerald in Hollywood*, there is an important allusion to her in one of the flashbacks to 1927. It occurs in a scene in which Zelda and Scott argue in their hotel suite about his manifest interest in a young actress. Scott angrily responds to his wife that this young movie star has at least made something of herself, while Zelda never sticks at any one artistic pursuit long enough to master it. Hurt by this spiteful jab, Zelda reminds her husband that she designs her own clothes; then, scooping up some of the garments from her wardrobe, she carries them into the bathroom, hurls them into the bathtub, and sets them on fire. As the flames leap upward, Zelda retreats back into the bedroom, away from the blaze, and calls plaintively for Scott to help her put out the fire.

Fitzgerald mentions this dramatic incident in his *Notebooks*, where he cryptically refers to it with the phrase, "burning clothes" (#1449). Bruccoli describes the episode by saying that, when Fitzgerald told his wife that he admired Lois Moran because she had done something with her talents, Zelda burnt her clothes to express "her resentment."[16] This was in effect her way of negating an accomplishment of her own which her husband apparently did not appreciate.

This real-life encounter between the Fitzgeralds makes a stunning scene in *F. Scott Fitzgerald in Hollywood* and, along with some of the other compelling scenes in the telefilm already described, gives a strong indication why *Fitzgerald in Hollywood* is a better account of Fitzgerald's Hollywood years than *Beloved Infidel*. Another element that places Page's telefilm above King's feature film is that there is no confusion about who the central figure is in *Fitzgerald in Hollywood* as there is in *Infidel*. Scott Fitzgerald is squarely at the center of the telefilm from the opening image to the final fade-out.

Zelig

It is true that nothing came of the plans to star Fitzgerald in a film opposite Lois Moran, nor of the suggestion a few years earlier that he play the lead in the movie version of *This Side of Paradise*, which was never produced. Fitzgerald did, however, appear in person in a feature film that was made more than four decades after his death by writer-director-actor Woody Allen. The picture, entitled *Zelig* (1983), is a pseudo-documentary which ingeniously mingles a great deal of newsreel material from the twenties with the dramatic scenes shot expressly for the film. A montage sequence at the beginning of the movie includes authentic newsreel footage of Fitzgerald busily writing at a table. These shots are worked into the film's story line by a narrator who comments, voice-over on the sound track, that Mr. Fitzgerald is hard at work on an article about the film's hero, Leonard Zelig (Woody Allen), an eccentric young man whose bizarre behavior captured the nation's interest during the madcap twenties and made him an instant celebrity. The commentator goes on to explain that it was Fitzgerald who initially brought this curious individual nationwide attention by writing an important article about him, which perceptively analyzed Zelig's strange personality. At the conclusion of the movie, the narrator "quotes" from Fitzgerald's fictitious essay about Zelig and goes on to explain how Zelig's fickle following inevitably deserted him, leaving him to sink back into the obscurity from which he had come.

Toward the end of Fitzgerald's life, when he was not yet acknowledged to be a major American writer, it appeared that he too had been forgotten by the public. He lamented to Arnold Gingrich at the time, "I'm getting awfully tired of being Scott Fitzgerald . . . as there doesn't seem to be so much money in it."[17] Reflecting on Fitzgerald's remark afterward, Gingrich said that, even though simply being F. Scott Fitzgerald did not seem to be very profitable financially for the man himself in his last days, it would not be long before movies and plays about Fitzgerald would be making a great deal of money for other people.

The Biographical Plays

Besides the biographical films already discussed, there have also been some plays that have drawn upon the Fitzgerald legend. Budd Schulberg and Harvey Breit dramatized Schulberg's novel *The Disenchanted* for presentation on the Broadway stage during the 1958-59 season with Jason Robards, Jr., in the role of the character modeled on Fitzgerald. "I hope your play is a miserable failure," Rosalind Sayre Smith, Zelda Fitzgerald's sister, wrote to Schulberg on the eve of the New York opening. Schulberg adds that "there followed the humanly understandable but professionally unrealistic plea" on the part of Fitzgerald's sister-in-law "to let sleeping bones rest." His immediate reaction to her contention that Fitzgerald was not worth all the attention he was getting in the media was that "it is futile to deny Fitzgerald's claim on our attention" as an important literary figure.[18]

Another writer who, like Fitzgerald, looms large in twentieth-century American literature has also tried his hand at writing a play about Fitzgerald. In his 1980 drama, *Clothes for a Summer Hotel*, Tennessee Williams pictures Scott Fitzgerald (Kenneth Haigh) visiting Zelda (Geraldine Page) in an asylum and discussing with her several episodes from their past, such as the Jozan affair. Each episode is duly reenacted on the stage as a flashback. In contrast to the stage version of *The Disenchanted, Clothes for a Summer Hotel* did not find a wide audience. By dramatizing the story of "heroic real-life legends,"

Williams later explained, he had made the mistake of locking himself into a plot that could "hold no surprises for well-read critics and audiences."[19]

Having seen the original Broadway production, I must counter that the more fundamental problem with Williams's drama is that the playwright did not really create a sharply defined plot. That is to say, *Clothes for a Summer Hotel* lacks a strong story line, with the result that Williams seems to be utilizing the lives of the Fitzgeralds merely as the point of departure for presenting his own private reflections on personal failure and death. Consequently, the drama remains rather abstract and, as a result, never comes to life.

More recently, in the fall of 1984, William Luce's play *Zelda*, based on the life of Zelda Fitzgerald, was produced in New York, with Olga Bellin in the title role. It seems, then, that Mrs. Fitzgerald, as well as Mr. Fitzgerald, continues to spark the imaginations of creative writers.

Television Productions

Meanwhile, although there are no adaptations of Fitzgerald's fiction coming out of Hollywood at the moment, television continues to turn to his work as a source for telefilms. BBC-TV joined with Showtime, an American cable network, to co-produce a five-part, six-hour version of *Tender Is the Night*, filmed on location in Switzerland, Paris, and the French Riviera. The miniseries, in which Dick and Nicole Diver are played by Peter Strauss and Mary Steenburgen, premiered in 1985. The teleplay is the work of Dennis Potter, who is in charge of drama at BBC-TV. Peter Chernin, Showtime's senior vice-president for original programming, says that the TV *Tender* is clearly better than King's two-and-a-half-hour theatrical motion picture version if for no other reason than that the miniseries format afforded "the time to tell the whole story."[20]

That is not necessarily so. Even though a television adaptation of a novel may run considerably longer than a feature film derived from the same literary source, TV scriptwriters have discovered that they still have to eliminate several sections of a novel in order to bring the finished telefilm down to the stipulated running time determined in advance by network executives. In short, not even a television miniseries allows for filming the complete scope of a novel.

On the contrary, TV producer Stan Margulies (*The Thorn Birds*), who has overseen the transplanting of many a king-sized novel to the television screen, concedes that one of the built-in problems of working in television is that "you are locked into an inexorable time frame." If one of the installments of a miniseries is overlength, some footage will inevitably have to be deleted in order to shorten the segment to the desired running time. "The scenes that come out are inevitably the scenes devoted to character rather than plot," says Margulies; "and I hate to lose those scenes." Margulies also admits that feature films are made with more polish than telefilms of whatever length. The makers of a theatrical feature have the luxury of reshooting a scene until it is satisfactory. "In television," he says, "there are always scenes that you would like to redo, but you simply don't have the time or money."[21] In summary, a carefully crafted feature film version of a novel, such as King's movie of *Tender Is the Night*, is not automatically overshadowed by a TV miniseries of the same work, for the very reasons advanced by one of television's own top producers.

Maybe television is best suited to dramatizing short fiction, which can be comfortably presented in a one-hour time slot, without the need to extend the plot line to the degree that is called for by a feature-length film. The mini-feature that Joan Silver made of "Bernice Bobs Her Hair" is a case in point, since its running time of under an hour discouraged motion picture distributors from trying to book it theatrically, but it was quickly snapped up by a TV network for presentation on the small screen. What's more, Fitzgerald's short fiction continues to be a welcome challenge to those who would adapt it for television. On April 22, 1985, PBS presented its adaptation of "Myra Meets His Family," which was filmed as *The Husband Hunter* in 1920. The televersion, called *Under the Biltmore Clock,* turned out to be what TV critic Stanley Marcus tagged a superb dramatization of Fitzgerald's crafty Jazz Age tale. Like *Bernice,* the TV adaptation of "Myra" provided a delightful hour of entertainment.

In looking back on the adaptations of Fitzgerald's fiction discussed in this book, one must concede that even the best of them is not flawless. Still, although some Fitzgerald commentators claim that his subtle, evocative prose simply resists being transferred successfully to another medium of artistic expression, Scottie Smith does not think so. "I have read many times," she told me, "that it is impossible to translate my father's writings into films. I do not agree with this, as there are always portions of the movies which have certainly done the writer justice."

As a fitting example of the memorable moments enshrined in the film adaptations of Fitzgerald's fiction I would nominate the scene in the 1949 *Gatsby* in which Gatsby sheds his carefully cultivated facade of a gentleman long enough to lambaste the thug who has had the affrontery to crash one of his swanky parties. I would also nominate the painfully touching scene in the 1974 *Gatsby* when the pathetic George Wilson goes completely to pieces over the loss of his worthless wife because his dogged devotion to her was the only thing that gave any meaning to his miserable existence. And what about Monroe Stahr's exuberant demonstration on how to captivate an audience with visual storytelling, which makes evident his lifelong dedication to the movies. These and other segments of the Fitzgerald films, which have been analyzed in this study, should go a long way in helping to disprove what Scottie Smith calls "the myth that my father's stories are not translatable to the screen."[22]

Envoi

When Fitzgerald died on December 21, 1940, not many literary or cinema critics would have predicted that his work would endure, both on page and screen, to the extent that it has. His wake, which was held at Pierce Brothers Mortuary in a less fashionable section of Los Angeles, was, as mentioned, sparsely attended, giving the impression that he was all but forgotten already. His body was shipped for burial to Maryland, which was where his father's family had originated. The funeral was held on Friday, December 27, at the Pumphrey Funeral Home in Bethesda; unfortunately Zelda was not well enough to attend.

Fitzgerald had wanted to be buried in the Fitzgerald family plot in St. Mary's Catholic Cemetery in Rockville, Maryland; but because he had not been a practicing Catholic for some time, Baltimore's Catholic prelate, Archbishop Michael Curley, officially declined to permit it. The burial consequently took place in Union Cemetery, following an Episcopalian burial service conducted by Rev. Raymond Black. The interment was held in the rain; and perhaps some of the mourners recalled what someone murmured during the downpour that accompanied Jay Gatsby's funeral in the novel: "Blessed are the dead that the rain falls on" (p. 176).

It took some time for that benediction to bear fruit for Fitzgerald, at least where the blessing of a Catholic burial is concerned. His desire to be laid to rest next to his father in hallowed ground, according to the rites of the Roman Catholic Church, was finally granted on November 8, 1975. On that date his remains and those of his wife (who perished in 1948—victim of a fire at the asylum where she resided) were transferred to St. Mary's Cemetery, with the pastor of St. Mary's Church, Father William Silk, presiding at the ceremony. It was Fitzgerald's daughter Scottie who had petitioned William Cardinal Baum, Archbishop of Washington, to allow the interment of both her father and her non-Catholic mother at St. Mary's, which by then was officially within the jurisdiction of the archdiocese of Washington. In granting her request, Cardinal Baum issued the following proclamation:

"F. Scott Fitzgerald came out of the Maryland Catholic tradition. He was a man touched by the faith of the Catholic Church. There can be perceived in his work a Catholic consciousness. . . . He found in this faith an understanding of the human heart caught in the struggle between grace and death. His characters are involved in this great drama, seeking God and seeking love. As an artist he was able with lucidity and poetic imagination to portray this struggle. He also experienced in his own life the mystery of suffering and, we hope, the power of God's grace."[23]

Apparently Cardinal Baum was willing to accept, as implicit evidence of Fitzgerald's enduring acceptance of the faith of his fathers, the manner in which his Catholic beliefs are reflected in his work, a phenomenon which has been noted more than once in the present study. In any case, Mizener is quite wrong in assuming that Fitzgerald was originally denied burial in consecrated ground because his books had been banned by the Church. Mizener's gratuitous assertion, which has no foundation whatever in fact, has nevertheless been parroted by other commentators on Fitzgerald's life and work, including Sara Mayfield, Nancy Milford, and Kenneth Eble.

As a matter of fact, Fitzgerald's fiction, with its interlocking Catholic themes of sin, repentance, and redemption, have for many years found a place in the literature courses of Catholic schools and universities, as well as in other institutions of learning throughout America; all of which means that Fitzgerald ultimately succeeded in his endeavor to write his fiction, not just "for the youth of his own generation," but for "the critics of the next," and "the schoolmasters of ever afterward."[24]

Yet, with his penchant for pessimism, Fitzgerald frequently worried during his lifetime that his writing ability would one day give out on him. "He thought of his talent as something that could be lost, like his watch, or mislaid, like his hat, or slowly depleted, like his bank account," wrote James Thurber a decade after Fitzgerald's death. But it stayed with him right to the end, "perhaps surer and more mature than it had ever been. This is a happy thing to remember."

Nor should one find cause for unhappiness in the thought that some of Fitzgerald's works were going out of print at the time of his death, Thurber continues. Even the work of the most popular writers does not always stay in print continuously, says Thurber, "in a country of fickle and restless tastes that goes in for the Book of the Month Club, the Man of the Year, and the Song of the Week. The good and simple truth is," Thurber concludes, "that Fitzgerald never disappeared into a lonely literary limbo,"[25] as he always feared he might.

Zelda Fitzgerald was made fully aware of the widespread interest in her late husband's life and work a year or so before her own untimely death when Henry Piper went to see her in order to discuss the biography he proposed to write about Fitzgerald. Piper remembers how amazed and touched Zelda was by this renewed interest in her husband. "Oh, how flattered Scott would be," she said, "to think that people still remember him."[26] As Hemingway reminded Fitzgerald during his "crack-up" period in the thirties, "Scott, good writers always come back. Always."[27]

Scott Fitzgerald was a good writer. He came back.

NOTES

Prologue

1. Scottie Fitzgerald Smith, Introduction to *The Romantic Egoists: Scott and Zelda Fitzgerald*, ed. Matthew J. Bruccoli, Scottie Fitzgerald Smith, and Joan Kerr (New York: Scribner's, 1974), ix, x. This volume of Fitzgerald memorabilia reproduces many pages from their scrapbooks.

2. Morris Beja, *Film and Literature* (New York: Longman, 1979), 27.

3. David Lodge, "Graham Greene," in *The Tablet* (London), September 28, 1974, 937.

4. Pauline Kael, "The Darned," in *Reeling* (New York: Warner, 1976), 630-31.

5. Sheilah Graham, *College for One* (New York: Viking, 1967), 167.

6. Michiko Kakutani, "Books into Movies," *New York Times Book Review*, July 10, 1983, 39.

7. Arthur Hoomberg, "Proust Is Filmed at Last," *New York Times*, July 24, 1983, 2:15.

8. Fitzgerald to Mr. and Mrs. Philip McQuillan, December 28, 1920, *The Letters*, ed. Andrew Turnbull (New York: Dell, 1966), 484. Subsequently referred to as *Letters*, to distinguish it from the other volumes of Fitzgerald's correspondence.

9. Graham, *College*, 156.

10. Henry Dan Piper, *F. Scott Fitzgerald: A Critical Portrait* (Carbondale: Southern Illinois University Press, 1968), 260.

11. "Fitzgerald on Film," *Newsweek*, July 17, 1961, 83-84.

1   Crazy Mondays

1. Fitzgerald to Alice Richardson, July 29, 1940, *Letters*, 628.

2. F. Scott Fitzgerald, *The Ledger: A Facsimile*, limited ed. (Washington, D.C.: NCR/Microcard Editions, 1972), 161. Subsequent page references to the *Ledger* will appear in parentheses after each citation from it. In cases where Fitzgerald's handwriting was not sufficiently clear in this facsimile, the author has checked his reading of the passage in question with the copy of the *Ledger* at the Princeton Library. The reader will note in the quotations from the *Ledger* that Fitzgerald usually referred to himself in the third person.

3. Fitzgerald to Perkins, October 27, 1924, *Dear Scott/Dear Max: The Fitzgerald-Perkins Correspondence*, ed. John Kuehl and Jackson R. Bryer (New York: Scribner's, 1971), 80.

4. Graham, *College*, 168.

5. Maurice Zolotow, *Billy Wilder in Hollywood* (New York: Putnam's, 1977), 72.

6. F. Scott Fitzgerald, "Pasting It Together," in *The Crack-Up*, ed. Edmund Wilson (New York: New Directions, 1956), 78. In this anthology of Fitzgerald's non-fiction, Wilson reversed the titles of this essay and the one that follows it in the book from the way that the titles appeared when the two pieces were originally published in *Esquire*. Following Fitzgerald's lead rather than Wilson's, the present essay shall be referred to in this book as "Pasting It Together," and the one after it as "Handle with Care," rather than the other way round.

7. Dwight Taylor, "Scott Fitzgerald in Hollywood," *Harper's Magazine*, March 1959, 68.

8. Fitzgerald to his daughter Scottie, July 7, 1938, *Letters to His Daughter*, ed. Andrew Turnbull (New York: Scribner's, 1965), 52-53. Hereafter, *Daughter.*

9. Review of film, *Grit, Film Daily*, January 6, 1924, 381.

10. Fitzgerald to Bishop, April 1925, *Letters*, 381.

11. Budd Schulberg, *The Disenchanted* (New York: Random House, 1950), 47.

12. Fitzgerald to Scottie, July 1937, *Daughter*, 25.

13. F. Scott Fitzgerald, *The Notebooks*, ed. Matthew J. Bruccoli (New York: Harcourt, Brace, Jovanovich, 1978), #962. Subsequent references to the numbered items in the *Notebooks* will appear in parentheses after each citation from them.

14. F. Scott Fitzgerald, "Lipstick," in *Fitzgerald/Hemingway Annual*, 10 (1978), 6.

15. Matthew J. Bruccoli, *Some Sort of Epic Grandeur: The Life of F. Scott Fitzgerald* (New York: Harcourt, Brace, Jovanovich, 1981), 259.

16. Fitzgerald to Scottie, July 1937, *Daughter*, 25.

17. Laurence Stallings, "The Youth in the Abyss," *Esquire*, October 1951, 47.

18. Fitzgerald to Ober, January 10, 1935, *As Ever, Scott Fitz—: Letters between F. Scott Fitzgerald and His Literary Agent Harold Ober, 1919-40*, ed. Matthew J. Bruccoli and Jennifer McCabe Atkinson (New York: Lippincott, 1972), 216.

19. Arthur Mizener, *The Far Side of Paradise: A Biography of F. Scott Fitzgerald*, rev. ed. (New York: Avon, 1974), 294.

20. Anthony Powell, "Hollywood Canteen: A Memoir of Scott

Fitzgerald in 1937," *Fitzgerald/Hemingway Annual,* 3 (1971), 75-76.

21. *See* Graham Greene, "Film Lunch," in *The Collected Essays* (Baltimore: Penguin, 1981), 317-19, for a satirical account of the production of the film, *A Yank at Oxford.*

22. F. Scott Fitzgerald, *Three Comrades: A Screenplay* (Carbondale: Southern Illinois University Press, 1978), 44.

23. Stallings, "Youth in Abyss," 110.

24. Fitzgerald to Mankiewicz, January 20, 1938, *Letters,* 586-87.

25. Andrew Sarris, "Mankiewicz of the Movies," *Show,* March 1970, 29.

26. Fitzgerald, *Comrades,* 270-72.

27. Sheilah Graham and Gerold Frank, *Beloved Infidel: The Education of a Woman* (New York: Bantam, 1974), 161.

2   Revisiting Babylon

1. Fitzgerald to Ober, March 4, 1938, *As Ever,* 357.

2. Alan Margolies, *The Impact of Theater and Film on F. Scott Fitzgerald,* unpublished dissertation (New York: New York University, 1969), 193.

3. Aaron Latham, *Crazy Sundays: F. Scott Fitzgerald in Hollywood* (New York: Pocket Books, 1972), 169.

4. F. Scott Fitzgerald, "*Infidelity*: A Screenplay," *Esquire,* December 1973, 292.

5. Tom Dardis, *Some Time in the Sun* (New York: Scribner's, 1976), 53.

6. Latham, *Crazy Sundays,* 66. Latham cites these lines, but does not apply them to Fitzgerald's scenario for *The Women,* as I do here.

7. Fitzgerald to Leland Hayward, December 6, 1939, *Correspondence,* ed. Matthew J. Bruccoli and Margaret M. Duggan (New York: Random House, 1980), 565.

8. Fitzgerald to Perkins, February 25, 1939, *Dear Scott/Dear Max,* 255.

9. Fitzgerald to Ober, January 18, 1939, *As Ever,* 381.

10. Piper, *Critical Portrait,* 249.

11. F. Scott Fitzgerald, "The Feather Fan," *Fitzgerald/Hemingway Annual,* 9 (1977), 8.

12. Fitzgerald to Ober, May 29, 1939, *As Ever,* 388.

13. Budd Schulberg, *The Four Seasons of Success* (Garden City, N.Y.: Doubleday, 1972), 95. Republished as *Writers in America: The Four Seasons of Success* (New York: Stein and Day, 1983), but with no essential changes.

14. Andrew Turnbull, *Scott Fitzgerald* (New York: Scribner's, 1962), 296.

15. Schulberg, *Seasons,* 130.

16. David Niven, *Bring on the Empty Horses* (New York: Dell, 1976), 100-101.

3   Echoes of the Jazz Age

1. Fitzgerald, *Ledger,* Introduction by Matthew Bruccoli, i.

2. F. Scott Fitzgerald, "Echoes of the Jazz Age," in *Crack-Up,* 15.

3. Margaret Reid, "Flappers Are Just Girls with a Splendid Talent for Life," in *F. Scott Fitzgerald in His Own Time: A Miscellany,* ed. Matthew J. Bruccoli and Jackson R. Bryer (New York: Popular Library, 1971), 277.

4. *Romantic Egoists,* 74. Fitzgerald did not indicate the original source of the clippings that he pasted in his scrapbooks; therefore, the sources of these clippings are not identified in the pages of the scrapbooks which are reproduced in facsimile in *Romantic Egoists.*

5. Fitzgerald to Ober, July 17, 1920, *As Ever,* 16.

6. Robert Garland, "The Off-Shore Pirate," in *Romantic Egoists,* 74.

7. Matthew J. Bruccoli, Introduction to "The Pusher-in-the-Face," by F. Scott Fitzgerald, in *The Price Was High: The Last Uncollected Stories,* ed. Matthew J. Bruccoli (New York: Harcourt, Brace, Jovanovich, 1979), 98.

8. Calvin Skaggs, "Interview with Joan Micklin Silver," in *The American Short Story,* ed. Calvin Skaggs, vol. 1 (New York: Dell, 1977), 213.

9. Fitzgerald to his sister Annabel, c. 1915, *Correspondence*, 16.

10. Joan Micklin Silver, *"Bernice Bobs Her Hair:* A Screenplay," in Skaggs, ed., *American Short Story,* 1:201.

11. Joan M. Allen, *Candles and Carnival Lights: The Catholic Sensibility of F. Scott Fitzgerald* (New York: New York University Press, 1978), 147.

12. F. Scott Fitzgerald, "Bernice Bobs Her Hair," in *The Stories,* ed. Malcolm Cowley (New York: Scribner's, 1951), 49; cf. Silver, "Bernice," in Skaggs, ed., *American Short Story,* 1:193.

13. Scottie Fitzgerald Smith to the author, August 9, 1983; September 13, 1983.

4   Paradise Lost

1. Zelda Fitzgerald, "Show Mr. and Mrs. Fitzgerald to Number—," in Wilson, ed., *Crack-Up,* 47. When this article originally appeared in a magazine, it was credited both to Scott and Zelda Fitzgerald because periodical editors often insisted on attaching his name to her byline. But the *Ledger* (143) identifies this essay as the work of Zelda Fitzgerald.

2. Hollis Alpert, "Scott, Zelda, and the Last of the Southern Belles," *Saturday Review,* November 20, 1973, 52.

3. F. Scott Fitzgerald, "The Last of the Belles," in *Stories,* 240.

4. *Ibid.,* 244.

5. *Ibid.,* 253.

6. Alpert, "Southern Belles," 52.

7. Scottie Fitzgerald Smith to the author, September 13, 1983.

8. Alpert, "Southern Belles," 54.

9. Fitzgerald to Rosalind Smith, July 19, 1934, *Correspondence,* 373-74. This particular letter may not have been mailed.

10. Fitzgerald, "Echoes," in Wilson, ed., *Crack-Up,* 21-22.

11. F. Scott Fitzgerald, "Babylon Revisited," in *Babylon Revisited and Other Stories* (New York: Scribner's, 1960), 229.

12. Fitzgerald to Scottie, January 25, 1940, *Daughter,* 103.

13. Fitzgerald to William Dozier, May 15, 1940, *Correspondence,* 596.

14. Fitzgerald to Perkins, August 15, 1940, *Dear Scott/Dear Max*, 264.

15. Fitzgerald to Zelda, September 21, 1940, *Letters*, 144.

16. Latham, *Crazy Sundays,* 253.

17. Mizener, *Far Side of Paradise*, 316.

18. Schulberg, *Seasons*, 129.

19. Piper, *Critical Portrait*, 258.

20. Robert Gessner, *The Moving Image* (New York: Dutton, 1970), 248.

21. Fitzgerald, "Babylon," in *Babylon Revisited,* 220.

22. "Richard Brooks," *Movie*, Spring 1965, 5.

23. Aljean Harmetz, "Hollywood Survival: Fifty Years of Success and Oblivion," *New York Times*, February 5, 1984, 2:1.

24. Foster Hirsch, *Elizabeth Taylor* (New York: Pyramid, 1973), 51.

25. Fitzgerald, "Babylon," in *Babylon Revisited*, 230.

26. James Powers, "Dialogue on Film: Richard Brooks," *American Film*, October 1977, 48.

27. "Richard Brooks," *Movie,* Spring 1965, 5.

28. Bosley Crowther, "The Screen in Review," *New York Times*, November 19, 1954, 20.

5   The Lost Generation

1. Fitzgerald to Ruth Sturtevant, September 22, 1919, *Letters*, 474.

2. Allen, *Candles and Carnival Lights*, 37.

3. Fitzgerald to Shane Leslie, late January 1919, *Letters*, 400.

4. Scott Donaldson, *Fool for Love: F. Scott Fitzgerald* (New York: Congdon and Weed, 1983), 18.

5. Fitzgerald to Scottie, July 12, 1940, in *Daughter*, 137.

6. Bruccoli, *Epic Grandeur*, 89.

7. Mizener, *Far Side of Paradise*, 73, 355.

8. Fitzgerald to Scottie, November 4, 1937, *Daughter*, 32.

9. Fitzgerald, "Echoes," in Wilson, ed., *Crack-Up,* 87.

10. F. Scott Fitzgerald, *This Side of Paradise* (New York: Scribner's, 1960), 282. Subsequent page references to the novel will appear in parentheses after each citation from it.

11. Mizener, *Far Side of Paradise*, 125.

12. Kenneth Eble, *F. Scott Fitzgerald* (New Haven: Twayne, 1963), 50.

13. Mizener, *Far Side of Paradise*, 122.

14. Fitzgerald to Wilson, August 15, 1919, *Letters*, 349.

15. Mizener, *Far Side of Paradise*, 145.

16. Allen, *Candles and Carnival Lights,* 92.

17. Charles G. Shaw, "F. Scott Fitzgerald," Bruccoli and Bryer, eds., *In His Own Time*, 283.

18. Eble, *Fitzgerald*, 58.

19. Bruccoli, *Epic Grandeur*, 95; cf. Mizener, *Far Side of Paradise*, 86; Turnbull, *Scott Fitzgerald*, 37.

20. Mizener, *Far Side of Paradise*, 86.

21. Latham, *Crazy Sundays*, 40.

22. *Ibid.*, 41.

23. F. Scott Fitzgerald, *The Beautiful and Damned* (New York: Scribner's, 1950), 421. Subsequent page references to the novel will appear in parentheses after each citation from it.

24. Fitzgerald to Charles Scribner II, August 12, 1920, *Letters*, 163.

25. F. Scott Fitzgerald, "Early Success," in Wilson, ed., *Crack-Up*, 87.

26. Fitzgerald to Scottie, June 14, 1940, *Correspondence*, 600.

27. Sara Mayfield, *Exiles from Paradise: Zelda and Scott Fitzgerald* (New York: Dell, 1974), 53.

28. Allen, *Candles and Carnival Lights*, 62.

29. Bruccoli, *Epic Grandeur*, 145.

30. Fitzgerald to Perkins, August 25, 1921, *Dear Scott/Dear Max,* 41.

31. Fitzgerald to Zelda, February 1920, *Correspondence,* 50.

32. Mayfield, *Exiles* 81.

33. Zelda to Fitzgerald, Fall 1930, *Correspondence*, 247.

34. Donaldson, *Fool for Love,* 69.

35. Zelda Sayre (Fitzgerald), *"The Beautiful and Damned*: Friend Husband's Latest," in Bruccoli and Bryer, eds., *In His Own Time,* 333.

36. Fitzgerald to Ober, May 18, 1923, *As Ever,* 54.

37. Fitzgerald to Oscar Kalman, December 10, 1922, *Correspondence,* 119.

38. Review of film, *The Beautiful and Damned,* "Another Flapper Story," *New York Times,* December 11, 1922, 22.

39. Richard Griffith and Arthur Mayer, *The Movies,* rev. ed. (New York: Simon and Schuster, 1970), 191.

40. Thomas Boyd, "Hugh Walpole Was the Man Who Started Me Writing Novels," in Bruccoli and Bryer, eds., *In His Own Time,* 250.

41. Charles Jackson, *The Lost Weekend* (New York: Farrar and Rinehart, 1944), 149.

6 Knight without Armor

1. Fitzgerald to Perkins, June 20, 1922, *Dear Scott/Dear Max,* 61.

2. Fitzgerald to John Jamieson, April 15, 1934, *Letters,* 529.

3. Dardis, *Time in the Sun,* 64.

4. Charles E. Shain, *F. Scott Fitzgerald* (Minneapolis: University of Minnesota Pamphlets, 1961), 18.

5. Fitzgerald, "Pasting It Together," in Wilson, ed., *Crack-Up,* 57.

6. F. Scott Fitzgerald, "How to Live on $36,000 a Year," in *Afternoon of an Author: A Selection of Uncollected Stories and Essays,* ed. Arthur Mizener (New York: Scribner's, 1957), 93.

7. André Le Vot, *F. Scott Fitzgerald: A Biography,* trans. William Byron (Garden City, N.Y.: Doubleday, 1983), 130.

8. Matthew J. Bruccoli, "Gerlach and Gatsby," in *Fitzgerald/Hemingway Annual,* 7 (1975), 33, 34.

9. F. Scott Fitzgerald, *The Great Gatsby* (New York: Scribner's, 1925), 74. Subsequent page references to the novel will appear in parentheses after each citation from it.

10. Fitzgerald to Trinkaus, March 4, 1938, *Correspondence*, 490.

11. Marius Bewley, "Scott Fitzgerald's Criticism of America," in *F. Scott Fitzgerald: A Collection of Critical Essays*, ed. Arthur Mizener (Englewood Cliffs, N.J.: Prentice-Hall, 1963), 125.

12. Mizener, *Far Side of Paradise*, 195.

13. Fitzgerald to Ober, February 17, 1926, *As Ever*, 86.

14. Alexander Woollcott, "The Stage," in Bruccoli, Smith, and Kerr, eds., *Romantic Egoists*, 136.

15. John M. Kenny, Jr., *"The Great Gatsby,"* in Bruccoli and Bryer, eds., *In His Own Time*, 358.

16. Ernest Hemingway to Fitzgerald, late April 1926, Hemingway, *Selected Letters: 1917-61,* ed. Carlos Baker (New York: Scribner's, 1981), 200.

17. John S. Cohen, Jr., *"The Great Gatsby* Enters the Cinema Mill,"* in Bruccoli, Smith, and Kerr, eds., *Romantic Egoists*, 139.

18. Eileen Creelman, "Three in Cast Dominate *Great Gatsby* on Screen," in Bruccoli, Smith, and Kerr, eds., *Romantic Egotists*, 139.

19. William M. Drew, "Lois Wilson," *American Classic Screen*, January-February 1984, 19.

20. John O'Hara, "Remarks on the Silent *Gatsby*," in *Fitzgerald/Hemingway Annual*, 6 (1974), 27.

21. James E. Miller, *F. Scott Fitzgerald: His Art and His Technique* (New York: New York University Press, 1967), 123.

22. Mayfield, *Exiles,* 86.

23. Perkins to Fitzgerald, November 20, 1924, *Dear Scott/Dear Max*, 82-83.

24. Le Vot, *Fitzgerald,* 155.

25. Edwin Fussell, "Fitzgerald's Brave New World," in Mizener, ed., *Critical Essays*, 44.

26. Manny Farber, "East Egg on the Face: *Gatsby,* 1949," in Gerald Peary and Roger Shatzkin, eds., *The Classic American Novel and the Movies* (New York: Ungar, 1977), 260.

27. Elliott Nugent, *Events Leading up to the Comedy: An Autobiography* (New York: Trident Press, 1965), 213-14.

28. Ralph Haven Wolfe, "Ladd," *Journal of Popular Film*, 7 (#4), 1980, 459.

29. Nugent, *Autobiography*, 215.

30. Irene Kahn Atkins, "In Search of the Greatest *Gatsby*," *Literature/Film Quarterly*, 3 (Summer 1974), 217.

31. Lionel Godfrey, "It Wasn't Like That in the Book," *Films and Filming*, April 1967, 14.

32. Wolfe, "Ladd," 459.

33. Robert K. Johnson, *Francis Ford Coppola* (Boston: Twayne, 1977), 170-74, *passim*.

34. Bruce Bahrenburg, *Filming "The Great Gatsby"* (New York: Berkeley Medallion Books, 1974), 18, 191.

35. "Wanted: Aristocrats, $1.65 Per Hour," *Time*, July 23, 1973, 87.

36. Scottie Fitzgerald Smith to the author, September 13, 1983; August 9, 1983.

37. Farber, "East Egg," in Peary and Shatzkin, eds., *Classic American Novel*, 258.

38. Scottie Fitzgerald Smith to the author, August 9, 1983.

39. Bahrenburg, *Filming Gatsby*, 183.

7   The Stag at Eve

1. Joan Govan Reiter, *F. Scott Fitzgerald: Hollywood As Literary Material*, unpublished dissertation (Evanston, Ill.: Northwestern University, 1972), 66.

2. Nancy Milford, *Zelda* (New York: Avon, 1971), 145.

3. Ernest Hemingway, *A Moveable Feast* (New York: Bantam, 1970), 188.

4. Mayfield, *Exiles*, 141.

5. "Written with Zelda Gone to the Clinic," Summer 1930, in *Correspondence*, 239.

6. Bruccoli, *Epic Grandeur*, 351.

7. *Ibid.*, 368.

8. From Fitzgerald to Betty Markell, September 16, 1929; from Fitzgerald to Hemingway, September 9, 1929, *Letters*, 513, 333. From Hemingway to Fitzgerald, September 13, 1929; September 4, 1929, in Hemingway, *Selected Letters*, 307, 305.

9. Mizener, Introduction to "One Trip Abroad," in *Afternoon of an Author*, 142.

10. Fitzgerald to Perkins, May 15, 1931, in *Dear Scott/Dear Max*, 171.

11. F. Scott Fitzgerald, *Tender Is the Night* (New York: Scribner's, 1934), 157. Subsequent page references to the novel will appear in parentheses after each citation from it.

12. Richard Lehan, *F. Scott Fitzgerald and the Craft of Fiction* (Carbondale: Southern Illinois University Press, 1966), 171.

13. Miller, *Art and Technique*, 142.

14. Shain, *Fitzgerald*, 40.

15. Mizener, *Far Side of Paradise*, 338.

16. James Thurber, "Scott in Thorns," in *Credos and Curios* (New York: Harper and Row, 1962), 157-60.

17. Bruccoli, *Epic Grandeur*, 367.

18. Fitzgerald to Perkins, December 24, 1938, *Dear Scott/Dear Max*, 251.

19. Milford, *Zelda*, 342.

20. Fitzgerald to Zelda, April 26, 1934, *Correspondence*, 356; Milford, *Zelda*, 352.

21. Hemingway to Fitzgerald, May 28, 1934; Hemingway to Perkins, November 15, 1941; Hemingway to Charles Scribner, December 12, 1941, in Hemingway, *Selected Letters*, 407, 527, 533.

22. Matthew J. Bruccoli, Introduction to *As Ever*, xx.

23. Fitzgerald, "Handle with Care," in Wilson, ed., *Crack-Up*, 84.

24. Fitzgerald to Zelda, Summer 1930, *Correspondence*, 241.

25. Milford, *Zelda*, 269; Fitzgerald to Zelda, Summer 1930, *Correspondence*, 241.

26. Turnbull, *Scott Fitzgerald*, 270.

27. F. Scott Fitzgerald and Charles Warren, "Movie Treatment for *Tender Is the Night*," in Bruccoli, *Epic Grandeur*, 523.

28. Malcolm Lowry and Margerie Bonner Lowry, *Notes on a Screenplay for F. Scott Fitzgerald's "Tender Is the Night,"* ed. Matthew J. Bruccoli (Bloomfield Hills, Mich.: Bruccoli-Clark, 1976), 4, 52.

29. Ibid., 15, 26.

30. Benjamin B. Dunlap, "Notes on a Screenplay for F. Scott Fitzgerald's *Tender Is the Night*," *Fitzgerald/Hemingway Annual*, 8 (1976), 285.

31. David O. Selznick, *Memo from: David O. Selznick,* ed. Rudy Behlmer (New York: Avon, 1973), 489.

32. *Ibid.*, 524, 538.

33. "Fitzgerald on Film," *Newsweek*, July 17, 1961, 84.

34. David Shipman, "A Conversation with Joseph L. Mankiewicz," *Films and Filming* (November 1982), 14.

35. Roy Pickard, "The Tough Race: The Films of Henry King," September 1971, 41; Clive Denton, "Henry King," *The Hollywood Professionals*, vol. 6 (New York: Barnes, 1974), 45.

8 Decline and Fall

1. Ben Hecht, "Enter the Movies," in *Film: An Anthology* ed. Daniel Talbot (Berkeley: University of California Press, 1966), 258.

2. Malcolm Cowley, editor's note, *Stories*, 384.

3. F. Scott Fitzgerald, "Pat Hobby's Christmas Wish," in *The Pat Hobby Stories* (New York: Scribner's, 1970), 3.

4. Arnold Gingrich, Introduction to *Pat Hobby Stories*, xi.

5. Dwight Taylor, "Scott Fitzgerald in Hollywood," in *Harper's Magazine,* March 1959, 69-70.

6. Norma Shearer to Fitzgerald, December 1931, in *Correspondence*, 282.

7. F. Scott Fitzgerald, "Crazy Sunday," in *Babylon Revisited and Other Stories*, 248.

8. George Cukor to the author, August 13, 1980.

9. Fitzgerald to Alfred Dashiell, October 1932, in *Correspondence*, 299.

10. F. Scott Fitzgerald, *The Last Tycoon* (New York: Scribner's, 1941), 135. Subsequent page references to the novel itself and to the selection of Fitzgerald's notes about its composition, which appear in an appendix at the end of the text, will be found in parentheses after each citation from the book.

11. Bruccoli, *Epic Grandeur*, 462. Most of this letter is reproduced in the notes at the end of *The Last Tycoon*, but not the portion just cited.

12. Budd Schulberg, "Gentle Genius at Large in Jungletown," *Life*, February 28, 1969, 6.

13. Mizener, *Far Side of Paradise*, 384.

14. Piper, *Critical Portrait*, 271.

15. Latham, *Crazy Sundays*, 57. Latham cites this note, which is not one of the ones Wilson included in the appendix of the novel mentioned in footnote 10.

16. Matthew J. Bruccoli, *The Last of the Novelists: F. Scott Fitzgerald and "The Last Tycoon"* (Carbondale: Southern Illinois University Press, 1977), 117.

17. Bob Thomas, *Thalberg: Life and Legend* (Garden City, N.Y.: Doubleday, 1970), 12-13.

18. Bruccoli, *Epic Grandeur*, 474.

19. Mizener, *Far Side of Paradise*, 332.

20. Hemingway to Perkins, November 15, 1941, in Hemingway, *Selected Letters*, 527.

21. Edmund Wilson, Foreword to *The Last Tycoon*, ix-x.

22. Hemingway to Perkins, November 15, 1941, in Hemingway, *Selected Letters*, 527; Piper, *Critical Portrait*, 284.

23. Bruccoli, *The Last of the Novelists*, 117.

24. Charles Silver and Mary Corliss, "Hollywood Under Water: Elia Kazan on *The Last Tycoon*," *Film Comment*, January-February, 1977, 41.

25. Aden Whitman, "Elia Kazan: 'The Movie We Made is Realistic Hollywood,'" *New York Times*, November 14, 1976, 2:15.

26. *Ibid.*, 2:1.

27. Stephen Farber, "Hollywood Takes on *The Last Tycoon*," *New York Times*, March 21, 1976, 2:15.

28. James Powers, "Dialogue on Film: Elia Kazan," *American Film*, March 1976, 38.

29. Pauline Kael, *When the Lights Go Down* (New York: Holt, Rinehart, and Winston, 1980), 217.

30. I. Lloyd Michaels, "Auterism, Creativity, and Entrophy in

The Last Tycoon," *Literature/Film Quarterly*, 10 (Spring 1982), 114.

    31. Silver and Corliss, "Hollywood under Water," 44.

Epilogue

    1. Hemingway to Perkins, November 15, 1941; July 23, 1945, in Hemingway, *Selected Letters*, 528; 594.

    2. Donaldson, *Fool for Love*, 158; Mizener, *Far Side of Paradise* 103.

    3. Hemingway to Fitzgerald, May 28, 1934; Hemingway to Dos Passos, January 13, 1936; Hemingway to Perkins, February 7, 1936; Hemingway to Mizener, July 6, 1949; Hemingway to Perkins, March 25, 1939, in Hemingway, *Selected Letters*, 408, 433, 437, 657, 483.

    4. Ernest Hemingway, "The Snows of Kilimanjaro," *Esquire*, August 1936, 200.

    5. Bruccoli, *Epic Grandeur*, 412.

    6. Fitzgerald to Hemingway, August 1936, *Letters*, 338.

    7. Hemingway to Fitzgerald, May 28, 1934, in Hemingway, *Selected Letters*, 408.

    8. Hemingway, *A Moveable Feast*, ix.

    9. Vincent Canby, "Film View," *New York Times*, April 22, 1984, 2:17.

    10. Otis Ferguson, *The Film Criticism*, ed. Robert Wilson (Philadelphia: Temple University Press, 1971), 70.

    11. *Memo from: David O. Selznick*, 511, 513.

    12. Graham and Frank, *Beloved Infidel*, 223.

    13. Tony Thomas, *Gregory Peck* (New York: Pyramid, 1977), 96.

    14. Sheilah Graham, *The Real F. Scott Fitzgerald: Thirty-Five Years Later* (New York: Grosset and Dunlap, 1976), 234-35.

    15. Bruccoli, *Epic Grandeur*, 258-59.

    16. Milford, *Zelda*, 163.

    17. Gingrich, Introduction to *Pat Hobby*, xvii.

    18. Schulberg, *Seasons*, 91-92.

    19. "Tennessee Williams Replies," *New York Times*, August 3, 1980, 2:4.

20. Steve Knoll, "Getting on the Mini-Series Bandwagon," *New York Times*, June 3, 1984, 2:28.

21. Stephen Farber, "Making Book on TV," *Film Comment*, November-December 1982, 45.

22. Scottie Fitzgerald Smith to the author, August 9, 1983; September 21, 1984.

23. Allen, *Candles and Carnival Lights*, 144-45.

24. F. Scott Fitzgerald, "The Author's Apology," Bruccoli and Bryer, eds., *In His Own Time*, 164.

25. Thurber, *Credos*, 162-63.

26. Milford, *Zelda*, 449.

27. Hemingway to Fitzgerald, May 28, 1934, in Hemingway, *Selected Letters*, 408.

SELECTED BIBLIOGRAPHY

I. Works by F. Scott Fitzgerald

The Apprenticeship Fiction of F. Scott Fitzgerald: 1909-17. Edited by John Kuehl. New Brunswick, N.J.: Rutgers University Press, 1961.

Afternoon of an Author: A Selection of Uncollected Stories and Essays. Edited by Arthur Mizener. New York: Scribner's, 1957.

As Ever, Scott Fitz—: Letters between F. Scott Fitzgerald and His Literary Agent Harold Ober: 1919-40. Edited by Matthew J. Bruccoli and Jennifer McCabe Atkinson. New York: Lippincott, 1972.

Babylon Revisited and Other Stories. New York: Scribner's, 1960.

The Beautiful and Damned. New York: Scribner's, 1950.

Correspondence. Edited by Matthew J. Bruccoli and Margaret M. Duggan. New York: Random House, 1980.

The Crack-Up. Edited by Edmund Wilson. New York: New Directions, 1956.

Dear Scott/Dear Max: The Fitzgerald-Perkins Correspondence. Edited by John Kuehl and Jackson R. Bryer. New York: Scribner's, 1971.

Flappers and Philosophers. New York: Scribner's, 1959.

The Great Gatsby. New York: Scribner's, 1925.

In His Own Time: A Miscellany. Edited by Matthew J. Bruccoli and Jackson R. Bryer. New York: Popular Library, 1971.

"*Infidelity*: A Screenplay," *Esquire*, 80 (December, 1973), 193-200, 290-304.

The Last Tycoon. New York: Scribner's, 1941.

The Ledger: A Facsimile. Limited edition. Washington, D.C.: NCR/Microcard Editions, 1972.

The Letters. Edited by Andrew Turnbull. New York: Dell, 1966.

Letters to His Daughter. Edited by Andrew Turnbull. New York: Scribner's, 1965.

The Notebooks. Edited by Matthew J. Bruccoli. New York: Harcourt, Brace, Jovanovich, 1978.

The Pat Hobby Stories. New York: Scribner's, 1970.

The Price Was High: The Last Uncollected Stories. Edited by Matthew J. Bruccoli. New York: Harcourt, Brace, Jovanovich, 1979.

Six Tales of the Jazz Age and Other Stories. New York: Scribner's, 1960.

The Stories. Edited by Malcolm Cowley. New York: Scribner's, 1951.

Tender Is the Night. New York: Scribner's, 1934.

This Side of Paradise. New York: Scribner's, 1960.

Three Comrades: A Screenplay. Carbondale: Southern Illinois University Press, 1978.

The Vegetable. New York: Scribner's, 1976.

II. Works about F. Scott Fitzgerald

(Note: Only the more significant and substantial research materials are included here; thus books and articles alluded to in the text that are only tangential to Fitzgerald's life and work are not listed below.)

A. Books

Allen, Joan M. *Candles and Carnival Lights: The Catholic Sensibility of F. Scott Fitzgerald.* New York: New York University Press, 1978.

Bahrenburg, Bruce. *Filming "The Great Gatsby."* New York: Berkley, 1974.

Bruccoli, Matthew J. *The Last of the Novelists: F. Scott Fitzgerald and "The Last Tycoon."* Carbondale: Southern Illinois University Press, 1977.

———. *Some Sort of Epic Grandeur: The Life of F. Scott Fitzgerald.* New York: Harcourt, Brace, Jovanovich, 1981.

Bruccoli, Matthew J., Scottie Fitzgerald Smith, and Joan P. Kerr, eds. *The Romantic Egoists: Scott and Zelda Fitzgerald.* New York: Scribner's, 1974.

Bryer, Jackson R., ed. *The Short Stories of F. Scott Fitzgerald: New Approaches in Criticism.* Madison: The University of Wisconsin Press, 1982.

Dardis, Tom. *Some Time in the Sun.* New York: Scribner's, 1976.

Donaldson, Scott. *Fool for Love: F. Scott Fitzgerald.* New York: Congdon and Weed, 1983.

Donaldson, Scott, ed. *Critical Essays on F. Scott Fitzgerald's "The Great Gatsby."* Boston: G. K. Hall, 1984.

Eble, Kenneth E. *F. Scott Fitzgerald.* New Haven: Twayne, 1963.

Graham, Sheilah. *College of One.* New York: Viking, 1967.

———. *The Real F. Scott Fitzgerald: Thirty-five Years Later.* New York: Grosset and Dunlap, 1976.

Graham, Sheila, and Gerold Frank. *Beloved Infidel: The Education of a Woman.* New York: Bantam, 1974.

Hemingway, Ernest. *A Moveable Feast.* New York: Scribner's, 1970.

———. *Selected Letters: 1917-61.* Edited by Carlos Baker. New York: Scribner's, 1981.

Johnson, Robert K. *Francis Ford Coppola.* Boston: Twayne, 1977.

Kazin, Alfred, ed. *F. Scott Fitzgerald: The Man and His Work.* New York: Collier Books, 1966.

Koblas, John J. *F. Scott Fitzgerald in Minnesota: His Homes and Haunts.* St. Paul: Minnesota Historical Society Press, 1978.

Latham, Aaron. *Crazy Sundays: F. Scott Fitzgerald in Hollywood.* New York: Pocket Books, 1972.

Lehan, Richard D. *F. Scott Fitzgerald and the Craft of Fiction.* Carbondale: Southern Illinois University Press, 1966.

Le Vot, André. *F. Scott Fitzgerald: A Biography.* Translated by William Byron. Garden City, N.Y.: Doubleday, 1983.

Lowry, Malcolm, and Margerie Bonner Lowry. *Notes on a Screenplay for F. Scott Fitzgerald's "Tender Is the Night."* Edited by Matthew J. Bruccoli. Bloomfield Hills, Mich.: Bruccoli-Clark, 1976.

Mayfield, Sara. *Exiles from Paradise: Zelda and Scott Fitzgerald.* New York: Dell, 1974.

Mellow, James R. *Invented Lives: F. Scott and Zelda Fitzgerald.* Boston: Houghton Mifflin, 1984.

Milford, Nancy. *Zelda.* New York: Avon, 1971.

Miller, James E. *F. Scott Fitzgerald: His Art and His Technique.* New York: New York University Press, 1967.

Mizener, Arthur. *The Far Side of Paradise: A Biography of F. Scott Fitzgerald.* Rev. ed. New York: Avon, 1974.

Mizener, Arthur, ed. *F. Scott Fitzgerald: A Collection of Critical Essays.* Englewood Cliffs, N.J.: Prentice-Hall, 1963.

Murray, Edward. *The Cinematic Imagination: Writers and the Motion Pictures.* New York: Ungar, 1972.

Nugent, Elliott. *Events Leading Up to the Comedy: An Autobiography.* New York: Trident, 1965.

Peary, Gerald, and Roger Shatzkin, eds. *The Classic American Novel and the Movies.* New York: Ungar, 1977.

Piper, Henry Dan. *F. Scott Fitzgerald: A Critical Portrait.* Carbondale: Southern Illinois University Press, 1968.

Schulberg, Budd. *The Disenchanted*. New York: Random House, 1950.

———. *The Four Seasons of Success*. Garden City, N.Y.: Doubleday, 1972.

Selznick, David O. *Memo From: David O. Selznick*. Edited by Rudy Behlmer. New York: Avon, 1973.

Skaggs, Calvin, ed. *The American Short Story*. Vol. 1. New York: Dell, 1982.

Sklar, Robert. *F. Scott Fitzgerald: The Last Laocoon*. New York: Oxford University Press, 1969.

Thomas, Bob. *Thalberg: Life and Legend*. Garden City, N.Y.: Doubleday, 1969.

Thurber, James. *Credos and Curios*. New York: Harper and Row, 1963.

Turnbull, Andrew. *Scott Fitzgerald*. New York: Scribner's, 1962.

Williams, Tennessee. *Clothes for a Summer Hotel: A Ghost Play*. New York: New Directions, 1983.

B. Articles

Alpert, Hollis. "Scott, Zelda, and the Last of the Southern Belles." *Saturday Review*, November 20, 1973, 52-54.

Atkins, Irene Kahn. "In Search of the Greatest *Gatsby*." *Literature/Film Quarterly*, 3 (Summer 1974), 216-27.

Fitzgerald/Hemingway Annual. 11 vols. 1969-79.

Fitzgerald Newsletter. 11 vols. 1958-68.

"Fitzgerald on Film." *Newsweek*, July 17, 1961, 83-84.

Michaels, I. Lloyd. "Auteurism, Creativity, and Entropy in *The Last Tycoon*." *Literature/Film Quarterly*, 10 (Spring 1982), 110-19.

Pickard, Roy. "The Tough Race: The Films of Henry King." *Films and Filming*, September 1971, 38-44.

Sarris, Andrew. "Mankiewicz of the Movies." *Show*, March 1970, 27-30; 78.

Shain, Charles E. *F. Scott Fitzgerald*. Minneapolis: University of Minnesota Pamphlets, 1961.

Silver, Charles, and Mary Corliss. "Hollywood Under Water: Elia Kazan on *The Last Tycoon*." *Film Comment*, January-February 1977, 40-44.

Taylor, Dwight. "Scott Fitzgerald in Hollywood." *Harper's Magazine*, March 1959, 67-71.

Vidal, Gore. "Scott's Case." *The New York Review of Books,* May 1, 1980, 12-20.

III. Unpublished Material

Cukor, George. Letter to Gene Phillips, August 13, 1980.

Frost, Frank. *The Films of Richard Brooks*. Unpublished dissertation. Los Angeles: University of Southern California, 1976.

Margolies, Alan. *The Impact of Theater and Film on F. Scott Fitzgerald*. Unpublished dissertation. New York: New York University, 1969.

Reiter, Joan Govan. *F. Scott Fitzgerald: Hollywood as Literary Material* Unpublished dissertation. Evanston, Ill.: Northwestern University, 1972.

Smith, Scottie Fitzgerald. Letters to Gene Phillips. August 9, 1983; September 13, 1983; September 21, 1984.

FILMOGRAPHY

1. *The Chorus Girl's Romance* (Metro, 1920)
   Director: William C. Dowlan
   Screenwriter: Percy Heath (based on "Head and Shoulders")
   Cast: Viola Dana (Marcia Meadows), Gareth Hughes (Horace Tarbox), Phil Ainsworth (Steve Reynolds), William Quinn (P. P. Anderson), Jere Sundin (Betty Darrell), Sidney De Grey (Fred Ward), Lawrence Grant (Jose Brasswine), Tom Gallery (Charlie Moon), Edward Jobson (Dr. Tarbox)
   Running Time: 5 reels

2. *The Husband Hunter* (Fox, 1920)

Director: Howard M. Mitchell

Screenwriter: Joseph F. Poland (based on "Myra Meets His Family")

Cast: Eileen Percy (Myra Hastings), Emory Johnson (Kent Whitney), Jane Miller (Lilah Elkins), Harry Dunkinson (Arthur Elkins), Evans Kirk (Bob Harkness), Edward McWade (Charles Mack), John Stepling (Kelly)

Running Time: 5 reels

3. *The Offshore Pirate* (Metro, 1921)

Director: Dallas M. Fitzgerald

Producer: Bayard Veiller

Screenwriter: Waldemar Young (based on the short story)

Cast: Viola Dana (Ardita Farnam), Jack Mulhall (Toby Moreland), Edward Jobson (Uncle John Farnam), Edward Cecil (Ivan Nevkova)

Running Time: 6 reels

4. *The Beautiful and Damned* (Warners, 1922)

Director: William A. Seiter

Screenwriter: Olga Printzlau (based on the novel)

Cast: Kenneth Harlan (Anthony Patch), Marie Prevost (Gloria), Tully Marshall (Adam Patch), Harry Myers (Dick), Louise Fazenda (Muriel), Cleo Ridgely (Dot), Emmett King (Mr. Gilbert), Walter Long (Hull), Clarence Burton (Bloeckman), Parker McConnell (Maury), Charles McHugh (Shuttlesworth), Kathleen Key (Rachel), George Kuwa (Tanner).

Running Time: 7 reels

5. *Grit* (Film Guild/W. W. Hodkinson Corp., 1924)

Director:	Frank Tuttle
Screenwriter:	James Ashmore Creelman (based on an original screen story by F. Scott Fitzgerald)

Cast: Glenn Hunter ("Kid" Hart), Helenka Adamowska (Annie Hart), Roland Young (Houdini Hart), Osgood Perkins (Boris Giovanni Smith), Townsend Martin (Flashy Joe), Clara Bow (Orchid McGonigle), Dore Davidson (Pop Finkel), Martin Broder (Bennie Finkel), Joseph Depew (Tony O'Cohen).

Running Time: 6 reels

6. *The Great Gatsby* (Famous Players-Lasky-Paramount, 1926)

Director:	Herbert Brenon
Producers:	Adolph Zukor and Jesse L. Lasky
Cinematographer:	Leo Tolver
Screenwriters:	Becky Gardiner and Elizabeth Meehan (based on the F. Scott Fitzgerald novel and the Owen Davis play)

Cast: Warner Baxter (Jay Gatsby), Lois Wilson (Daisy Buchanan), Hale Hamilton (Tom Buchanan), Neil Hamilton (Nick Carraway), Carmelita Geraghty (Jordan Baker), Georgia Hale (Myrtle Wilson), William Powell (George Wilson), George Nash (Charles Wolf), Eric Blore (Lord Digby), "Gunboat" Smith (Bert), Claire Whitney (Catherine)

Running Time: 8 reels

7. *Pusher-in-the-Face* (Paramount, 1929)

Director: Robert Florey
Producer: Daniel Frohman
Screenwriter: Unknown (based on the story)

Cast: Lester Allen (Charles David Stewart), Estelle Taylor (Edna), Raymond Hitchcock (Cafe owner), Carroll McComas (One who is pushed), Lillian Walker (Other waitress)

Running Time: 20 minutes

8. *The Great Gatsby* (Paramount, 1949)

Director: Elliott Nugent
Producer: Richard Maibaum
Cinematographer: John F. Seitz
Screenwriters: Cyril Hume and Richard Maibaum (based on the F. Scott Fitzgerald novel and the Owen Davis play)
Editor: Ellsworth Hoagland

Cast: Alan Ladd (Jay Gatsby), Betty Field (Daisy Buchanan), Barry Sullivan (Tom Buchanan), Macdonald Carey (Nick Carraway), Ruth Hussey (Jordan Baker), Shelley Winters (Myrtle Wilson), Howard da Silva (George Wilson), Elisha Cook Jr. (Klipspringer), Ed Begley (Myron Lupus), Henry Hull (Dan Cody), Carole Mathews (Ella Cody) Nicholas Joy (Owl Man), Tito Vuolo (Mavromichaelis)

Running Time: 92 minutes
16mm Rental: Swank

9. *The Last Time I Saw Paris* (MGM, 1954)

Director:	Richard Brooks
Producer:	Jack Cummings
Cinematographer:	Joseph Ruttenberg (color)
Screenwriters:	Julius J. and Philip G. Epstein (based on "Babylon Revisited")

Cast: Elizabeth Taylor (Helen Ellswirth), Van Johnson (Charles Wills), Walter Pidgeon (James Ellswirth), Donna Reed (Marion Ellswirth), Eva Gabor (Lorraine Quarl), Kurt Kaszner (Maurice), George Dolenz (Claude Matine), Roger Moore (Paul), Sandra Descher (Vicki), Celia Lovsky (Mama), Peter Leeds (Barney), John Doucette (Campbell), Odetta (Singer)

Running Time:	116 minutes
16mm Rental:	MGM/United Artists

10. *Tender Is The Night* (Twentieth Century-Fox, 1962)

Director:	Henry King
Producer:	Henry T. Weinstein
Cinematographer:	Leon Shamroy (color/CinemaScope)
Screenwriter:	Ivan Moffat (based on the novel)
Editor:	William Reynolds

Cast: Jason Robards, Jr. (Dick Diver), Jennifer Jones (Nicole Diver), Joan Fontaine (Baby Warren), Tom Ewell (Abe North), Jill St. John (Rosemary Hoyt), Cesare Danova (Tommy Barban), Paul Lukas (Dr. Dohmler), Sanford Meisner (Dr. Gregorovius), Charles Fredericks (McKisco), Bea Benaderet (Mrs. McKisco), Carole

Mathews (Mrs. Hoyt), Mac McWhorter (Collis Clay),
Albert Carrier (Louis), Richard de Combray (Francisco),
Alan Napier (Pardo), Michael Crisalli (Lanier Diver),
Leslie Farrell (Topsy Diver), Arlette Clark (Governess),
Maurice Dallimore (Sir Charles Golding), Carol Veazie
(Mrs. Dunphrey), Earl Grant (Piano Player)

Running Time:	146 minutes
16mm Rental:	Films Inc.

11. *The Great Gatsby* (Paramount, 1974)

Director:	Jack Clayton
Producer:	David Merrick
Cinematographer:	Douglas Slocombe (color)
Screenwriter:	Francis Ford Coppola (based on the novel)
Editor:	Tom Priestley

Cast: Robert Redford (Jay Gatsby), Mia Farrow (Daisy
Buchanan), Bruce Dern (Tom Buchanan), Sam Waterston
(Nick Carraway), Lois Chiles (Jordan Baker), Karen Black
(Myrtle Wilson), Scott Wilson (George Wilson), Edward
Hermann (Klipspringer), Howard da Silva (Meyer
Wolfsheim), Roberts Blossom (Mr. Gatz), Elliot Sullivan
(Wilson's friend), John Devlin (Gatsby's bodyguard),
Janet and Louise Arters (Twins)

Running Time:	145 minutes
16mm Rental:	Films Inc.

12. *The Last Tycoon* (Paramount, 1976)

Director:	Elia Kazan
Producer:	Sam Spiegel
Cinematographer:	Victor Kemper (color)
Screenwriter:	Harold Pinter (based on the novel)
Editor:	Richard Marks

Cast: Robert De Niro (Monroe Stahr), Ingrid Boulting (Kathleen), Theresa Russell (Cecilia), Robert Mitchum (Pat Brady), Jack Nicholson (Brimmer), Peter Strauss (Wylie), Donald Pleasence (Boxley), Dana Andrews (Ridingwood), Ray Milland (Fleishacker), Jeanne Moreau (Didi), Tony Curtis (Rodriguez), Tige Andrews (Popolos), Morgan Farley (Marcus), Angelica Huston (Edna), Diane Shalet (Stahr's secretary), John Carradine (Guide), Jeff Corey (Doctor), Seymour Cassell (Seal Trainer)

Running Time: 122 minutes

16mm Rental: Films Inc.

13. *Bernice Bobs Her Hair* (Learning in Focus, Inc., 1976)

Director: Joan Micklin Silver

Producer: Paul R. Gurian

Cinematographer: Ken Van Sickle (color)

Screenwriter: Joan Micklin Silver (based on the short story)

Editor: Ralph Rosenblum

Cast: Shelley Duvall (Bernice), Veronica Cartwright (Marjorie), Bud Cort (Warren), Patrick Reynolds (Draycott), Dennis Christopher (Charley), Claudette Warlick (Annie), Leslie Thorsen (Genevieve), Mark Newkirk (Reece), Lane Binkley (Roberta), Polly Holliday (Mrs. Harvey), Gary Springer (Otis), Mark LaMura (Carpenter), Stuart Germain, Murray Mosten (Barbers)

Running Time: 45 minutes

16mm Rental: Coronet/Perspective

NAME INDEX

TITLE INDEX